Nightmare Success

BRENT CASSITY

Published by
Hybrid Global Publishing
301 E 57th Street
4th Floor
New York, NY 10022

Manufactured in the United States of America.

Cassity, Brent
Nightmare Success: Loyalty, Betrayal, Life Behind Bars, Adapting, and Finally Breaking Free: A Memoir
    ISBN: 978-1-951943-95-0
    eBook: 978-1-951943-97-4

Cover design by: Jonathan Pleska
Copyediting by: Dea Gunning
Interior design by: Suba Murugan
Author photo by: David Evans

Disclaimer:
While this is a work of nonfiction, some names of people have been changed.

Brentcassity.com

ACKNOWLEDGEMENTS

This book has been a therapeutic journey for me to keep stepping towards the goals I have for the second part of my life. No one ever accomplishes anything worthwhile on their own and I have so many people to whom I am thankful.

I want to thank my wife Julie who has been my rock since I was a teenager. There is no one more loving, resilient, beautiful, and courageous. I am lucky enough to live everyday with the Homecoming Queen. My daughters Courtney, Carly, and Connor have delivered their own profiles in courage steadfastly remaining strong continuing to make a difference in all things they do in their lives. I could not be a prouder Dad. Big Dad fist pump to the Cassity Girls!

My friend Eddie Logan, at lunch one day, encouraged me to just start writing every day, and I did. Thank you, Eddie! I want to thank Shep Hyken. He has stayed in touch through it all. I so respect what he has accomplished in his life. Shep read my first page, and told me to keep writing, and I did.

I want to thank my new friend and editor Joy Stocke. You grabbed on to my story and believed in what I was trying to communicate. I will always be grateful for your patience and wisdom. None of this could have happened without the guidance and support of Karen Strauss of Hybrid Global Publishing.

David Evans has been my creative "go to" guy. He helped when I couldn't afford his help. Thank you, David!

Jose Ponce deserves a big high five for helping me make this book come to life. He has been in my corner when I needed it the most. Everyone needs a Jose in their lives.

TABLE OF CONTENTS

INTRO: NIGHTMARE SUCCESS

As I stand at the gate of Leavenworth prison and voluntarily surrender my freedom for the next five years of my life, a million thoughts flood through my mind. But, I can't push one thought away: How did the thing I most feared… the *one* thing I told myself would never happen…happen to me?

I have coined the phrase Nightmare Success. You probably think those two words don't belong together. Let me take you on a journey to demonstrate how these words have always existed together. Often, we don't recognize them, but If we look into ourselves and develop enough grit to step through our fears and nightmares, we will set ourselves free to succeed in whatever we aspire to be.

Outside the barbed wire monstrosity of Leavenworth Prison's gate, January winds blow across the Kansas prairie through our bones. Suddenly, we hear a loud buzzing noise. A voice through a speaker shouts, "Step inside!"

We enter and the gate slams shut. A man in a blue uniform steps out and tells us to follow him into an old gray stone, castle-like building. Our minds switch to terror. We know in our now-shivering bones that our usual coping methods won't work here. What, we wonder, is going to happen next?

In a cinderblock room with shockingly white fluorescent lights, our new wardrobe is stacked in colors of gray, khaki, and white. "Strip," says the guard, his voice cold with authority. We don't have time to be embarrassed. We remove our jeans, the leather belt we got for a birthday present, our warm wool sweater, our socks and boots. We, who were once admired and successful, stand completely naked in front of a stranger.

Our clothes go into a heaping pile with those of other prisoners who have come before us. We are told to bend over to show the guard we had sense enough not to enter prison with contraband. We put on the institution's bland white t-shirt, khaki elastic waist pants, and strange-looking blue tennis shoes with no laces.

Finally, the guard leads us to a rundown building that looks like an old school house. This will be our home for the next five years. The old-timers stop to look at the new guys, sizing us up. If it hasn't hit us before, it hits us now. This isn't a story we've read in the news, or the latest movie we've seen on Netflix. We are in prison. We, in fact, are the prisoners.

The guard walks ahead. His keys jangle from his chain. Our cell is down a dark, dimly lit hallway. The only light comes from a tiny window laced with wire mesh. Our new home is a dingy, stained, white cinderblock, 8'x10', with a beat-up gray, six-shelf locker, a chipped gray-painted bunk bed, and an uncomfortable beige, plastic chair.

How has our world shrunk to this space? But, the truth is we now have all the time in the world to think about what put us in this prison cell. We have time to ask ourselves, how did we get to such a place in our lives where everything feels totally out of control? What really put us here?

Our life experiences build an invisible prison in our minds, creating daily obstacles that don't allow us to be free. So, let's ask the question again. How did we get here? Is it a job that has held us hostage from our potential? A bad marriage? Past failures or loss of hope? A health crisis? A specific tragedy? A death of a loved one?

The guard walks past our cell. If we could just grab one of his keys, what key would we grab? What key would set us free?

If we can identify that key, we can step toward our freedom and our potential, regardless of our fears because we will survive, adapt, and thrive, no matter where we might find ourselves. I've made the journey and am here to tell you that if you open your eyes, and if you face your fears, every step, no matter how painful, will bring you to yourself.

Why am I telling you my story? I am confident that paying attention to our mindset is the real game changer. Henry Ford said it best, "Whether you think you can, or you can't...you are right!"

So, walk beside me through these pages. As I share my experiences, and the lessons I've learned, I will help you find the key that unlocks you from your own prison cell. The key that sets you free to reach your full potential to achieve all you aspire to be, and to fully integrate every aspect of your life.

One more important thing: Do me a favor and find a pen and a sheet of paper. Do you have it? Now, write down the one thing that keeps you from getting what you want in life. Tuck that piece of paper away until we get to the end of the book.

CHAPTER 1:

The Wonder Years

I was born at St. John's Hospital in Springfield Missouri. My Mom, Rhonda Leigh Roller, was 20 years old. My Dad, James Douglas Cassity, was 21. They were high school sweethearts at Buffalo High in Buffalo Missouri--population maybe 4,000--and everyone knew they were destined to be together. Dad was the basketball star and valedictorian, and Mom was the beautiful girl on the Buffalo Gal squad. They had one thing in common, they wanted to get out of their little town and conquer the world. Dad was a year ahead of Mom in school, but as soon as she graduated, they planned to marry.

Dad was born outside of Buffalo in an area the Cassity clan had named Red Top. His ticket off the family farm was to focus on basketball, and he got a golden ticket, a full ride athletic scholarship to Missouri State. As the papers wrote, '...young Doug, "Cat-like" Cassity led the Buffalo Bison's to the 1964 State Championship', it earned him the recognition he needed to jump in his Ford convertible and put the dreaded farm life in his rear-view mirror forever.

Mom entered her senior year cheering Dad on. Once he arrived on campus, his basketball coach told him that girls were only a distraction, so he promptly ended things with Mom.

She was having none of that. She was determined to get out of Buffalo, ASAP. And if Doug wasn't going to step up to the plate, she was a beautiful 18-year-old girl who had several interested suitors. Her brother JR had a good friend, Jerry, who was always hanging around the Roller house. Jerry presented Mom with his big plan. He would join the Air force, marry her, and they would be stationed in West Germany.

Word of this spread quickly to Doug. One day, he rolled up to Rhonda's house in his convertible, and they drove out to one of their favorite country roads where he asked her to leave right then and there; to elope. But, they were underage and needed a parent's consent. Now they had to tell their parents. Mom's parents, Jeanne and Ralph Roller, were not big fans of Doug Cassity. They much preferred JR's friend, Jerry.

Dad's parents believed it was moving too fast, too, but all sides caved and threw a small wedding at Ralph and Jeanne's house. And so, the kids with big dreams from a small town, settled in Springfield, Missouri, in the kind of neighborhood where we could ride bikes all over town, and safely stay out until dark. Behind our neighborhood were dirt paths with a creek running through it; our own private world. My neighborhood friends and I were always building forts and rafts by borrowing lumber from the new construction sites. We never could figure out how to make our homemade rafts float. Playing in the neighborhood, I started to figure out I was a pretty good athlete. I was getting picked by the older kids to be on the neighborhood football, basketball, or baseball teams. Sports became a big part of my life. I was always so proud of my Dad winning a State High School Basketball Championship and playing on a scholarship in college. I wanted to do all of that too.

After getting his law degree, my Dad's career blossomed. We moved from smaller houses to bigger houses nearly every year, and they were always in the same school district. Mom found she had a flair for design. She would put her special touch on a house, sell it, make a profit, and we'd move again. As the years went by, my Mom became recognized nationally, making the cover of *Traditional Home Magazine* along with several other design magazines.

Dad was making a splash in high-profile cases against companies like Blue Cross Blue Shield. As his reputation grew, he began acquiring businesses, and putting together partnerships for several apartment complexes, a cattle ranch, a hotel in Branson just down the street from the popular Silver Dollar City theme park, a medical malpractice company for doctors, and the well-known regional bank named Empire. The only business he owned that made a difference in my world was when he opened Wet Willy's Water Slide, the coolest, most popular destination in town. My Dad got some good advertisement by sponsoring our Boys Club Basketball team with our light North Carolina blue uniforms, with the popular Wet Willy logo emblazoned on the front of our jerseys. We were styling with the best uniforms, and the best teams at the Springfield Boy's Club league.

I was always observing the sales and business world. My grandparents on my Mom's side, Ralph and Jean, had a shoe store on the Buffalo town square called R&J Shoes. I loved the shoe store. Grandma Jean was an incredible saleswoman, and people would come from miles around in Dallas County to be fitted up for her shoes. I helped her after school and she showed me where the shoes were in the back. "Brent Douglas," she'd say. "I need a Connie Shoe in a 6, 6 1/2, and 7." At day's end, she would pay my brother and helper, Tyler, and me a few dollars for an ice cream cone.

I thought that the idea of selling could work in my neighborhood. I would drag Tyler into my scheme, and we would take my parents shoes and clothes and set up an outdoor store at the end of the driveway. We even made some signs directing the neighbors to our sale of my parent's stuff. The neighbors would call mom and say, "Your boys are at it again, trying to sell your stuff."

Grandma Jean would never miss an opportunity to get the adults together to play cards, and whatever game they played involved money and gambling. She also loved the sport of bad-mouthing her husband, Ralph. She had one saying for him that slowly rolled off her tongue..." You dirty rotten low life son of a bitch."

If my grandpa really wanted to get her ramped up another octave, he would drop the F-bomb, which she hated. I was very close with Grandpa Ralph. I always thought of my grandpa as a real old-fashioned cowboy. When he was dressed for going out, he wore the starched white shirt, pressed wrangler jeans with the crease down the middle, with his cowboy hat always kicked to the side. I am not sure if it was because I was the first grandchild, but we had a special connection all the way up to the end of his 85 years.

These family gatherings, coupled with some neighbors who would drop by were loud and rowdy events. Often a fight could break out on the family room floor. This was a very common occurrence on the holidays once the drinking got revved up.

Grandma Jean's mom, my Great-grandmother Katherine, known as GG, was Chinese. GG met my great-grandfather, Clarence Newton, when he visited China as a Christian missionary. He was 51 and GG was 17. Well-educated, GG had taught English in her small Chinese village, and when she decided to leave China, GG never saw her family again. Clarence promised her that he was going to take her to Manhattan, and they ended up not too far from the other Manhattan, this one in Kansas, not New York, in a town called Chetopa.

Grandma Jean loved gambling, fishing, and business. She was always self-conscious about being part Chinese. People thought she looked more Native American or Mexican. She never wanted to get too much sun in fear that she would be discriminated against in some form or fashion in a small town.

Tyler and I also spent part of our summers down at the Cassity farm with my Grandma Ruth, who lived to have her family and grandkids around her, and my Grandpa Bill Cassity, who worked the farm. Grandma Ruth, by everybody's account was a "saint," and the best country cook. You could say she was a farm-to-table cook harvesting and putting up produce from her garden, and slaughtering and eating cows and chickens from the farm. In the summer, that meant feeding a crew of young guys who bailed hay in the hot fields. We would join them for a country breakfast. Grandpa Bill took the farm to table one step further, eating the squirrels he caught, fried in bacon grease that Grandma kept in a plastic milk jug.

Grandma Ruth was not a stickler about too many things except attending Sunday church. The little Red Top Missionary Baptist Church, along with the small cemetery of mostly Cassity relatives, was literally right next door. There was no hiding not going to church. Only a white fence divided the gravel church parking lot and the Cassity's front yard. Grandma was the piano player.

As a young boy, I was always so proud that Grandma was the one sitting playing the piano for everyone. The preacher would get up for his sermon with the Bible in one hand, and his other arm flaying with all kinds of gestures. "The Lord is thy Shepherd," he would say, and sometimes shout and yell his sermon at the obliging congregation.. It seemed to me he was mad at everyone.

Time moved like molasses with those Sunday summer church services. I could not wait to get out of there and get those Sunday clothes off and eat some more of Grandma's home cooking.

People say that opposites attract. My Grandpa Bill could not have been more opposite than Grandma Ruth. She was a hard worker, always busy with something. Grandpa Bill fancied himself as a gentleman farmer. He was a tall, tanned, good-looking man. I always thought he looked like he had just walked out of a western movie. He often drove around in his truck watching the farm hands work or admiring his herd of cattle. He treated Grandma like she was part of the hired help barking orders at her from "his" chair parked in front of "his" TV. No one sat in his chair, and no one turned the channel from his daily shows.

The only exercise I remember my Grandpa Bill doing was hunting. He would sometimes take Tyler, our cousin Scott, and me out hunting with him, telling us to run and scurry the squirrels up the trees, so he could shoot them. All I can say is that we were lucky grandkids. Grandpa Bill had good aim!

CHAPTER 2:

The Severe Winds of Change

I had taken a big growth spurt before I entered the 7th grade, and was now 6'1" tall. I had waited my whole life to walk up the long hallway to the big junior high that was attached to our elementary school. To me, the kids were like kings and queens, and now I would be the tallest kid in the grade. I loved looking at the big cabinet outside the boys' locker room that had all the Hickory Hills school records for basketball and football. My goal was to make those records mine.

Coach Greeves had played division one football at Kansas State. He was a cool, soft-spoken coach with a big beard, and he knew how to motivate young athletes. I was the running back on the team with some speed. He would always tell me, "Cassity you have talent, but if you want to be a D-1 athlete, you are going to have to work harder than everyone else. You're bigger than everyone else now, but you won't always be."

We had a good team, and Junior High Sports in a small town were reported with the same enthusiasm as High School sports. I loved reading the stories of our games in our local paper, and seeing my name in print. It was like reading my Dad's old high school newspaper clippings.

As much as I loved football, I loved basketball even more. I would shovel off the snow in the driveway to shoot baskets. My Dad would pull up in the driveway, takeoff his suit jacket and loosen his tie, and then he'd walk me through game situations. This was always how Dad and I connected, shooting baskets and talking in the driveway. I so wanted to be like him, and to make him proud of all I wanted to accomplish.

Hickory Hills Junior High was all I had wanted it to be. I had shattered the football school record for rushing yards and touchdowns scored. In basketball, I became the all-time leading scorer, and rebound record holder. I even finished the summer with our Blue Angels baseball team winning the city batting title.

Mom and Dad had started having nasty arguments to the point where they would call Tyler and me into the room to tell us that dad was leaving, and they'd ask us who we wanted to go live with? These arguments would blow over, and we would all go to the Queen City Drive-In to see a double feature.

My friends thought my parents were the perfect couple who acted like they were still high school sweethearts. Dad put Mom on a pedestal, and tried to give her whatever she wanted. At least that's how it appeared from my young perspective. Still, it seemed like their fights had picked up lately. Dad's best friend, Nick Fiorella, who was also an attorney, started showing up at the house to discuss some type of investigation, and the possibility that we should move out of Springfield. Nick was an incredibly funny guy who could make anyone in the room laugh. It seemed really out of place for him to be talking so seriously, and saying things that could not possibly be a good idea.

At the same time, Mom and Dad's friends, Doug and Gloria Wead, who were distributors for Amway, the health, beauty, and homecare products company, came for supper. But rather than a social visit, it seemed like they were looking at the house to buy it. A few weeks after the Wead's visit, I came home from basketball practice, and they were at the house again, this time with Jim and Tammy Baker, founders of the popular TV ministry called the Praise the Lord, or PTL Club. The guys were huddled around talking in the family room about something that Jim Baker was calling Heritage USA, a time-share resort for the TV followers of the PTL Club.

I was introduced to the Bakers before heading upstairs to take a shower, wondering what in the hell was going on. When I came downstairs, they said they were all going to Swenson's to get some ice-cream. They asked if I wanted to go. I said sure, so we all loaded up with the Bakers and headed to Swenson's.

I remember getting home and calling up my best friends, Eric Belk and Mark Hunter, to tell them about this whole bizarre ordeal.

The next thing I knew, the Weads were buying our house, and we were moving to a townhouse. I thought it was awfully sudden, and that my parents must have gotten a really good price to sell their dream home. It wasn't like we didn't move around a lot, but this seemed odd because Mom had just built the house she had always wanted. Things weren't all doom and gloom. In the new townhouse, my bedroom was in the basement with a walkout patio. My friends could just come around back and hangout. Mom might not have been happy, but I was.

Not long after, Dad sat Tyler and me down and told us that his ego had gotten the best of him, and that he had been charged with bank and tax fraud. He was now under Federal Investigation. He said he had told FDIC (Federal Deposit Insurance Corporation) investigators that he would run the bank he owned the way he wanted, and they could run the government. His statement, he said, had clearly incited the lead investigator and things had begun to snowball out of control.

He explained the details of the tax fraud and bank fraud he had been charged with, but I couldn't hear anything he was saying. How could this have happened to the guy with the golden touch who was larger than life in my eyes? The only way I could rationalize any of it was that he had spread himself too thin, and that he hadn't paid attention to details.

Dad told us that he had decided to plead to the two charges of tax fraud and bank fraud, otherwise this could go on for years, and deprive us of being together as a family. By doing this, he explained, he would get probation and he could put this behind him and rebuild our lives. He wanted the family to have a new start in a new city, St. Louis.

I sat in the court and heard Dad's guilty plea, but I have blocked it out of my memory. I remember seeing Grandma Ruth, knowing how upsetting this must have been for her. I also remember the sentencing hearing did not go as agreed. Dad had made a deal: He would plead guilty to two charges and get probation.

At the hearing, the US Attorney switched gears. He began to argue for prison time. When all was said and done, Dad was sentenced to six months in prison. It took everyone's breath away. It was bad enough that Dad was being disbarred as an attorney, losing all of his assets, and moving his family to St. Louis. He was now going to prison.

Somehow my parents located a house for rent in Ladue, the most expensive area in St. Louis. In our upscale neighborhood, mansions towered over their beautifully landscaped, manicured yards. There were no kids running around or riding bikes. There was no welcoming committee. We had made many moves in the past, but this time we were going into hiding in a place that could not have been more different than anything I had known previously.

My Dad was able to save one business out of the complete catastrophe. O.J. May, had come to dad's law firm in the late 1970s with a unique business idea. He was an insurance salesman and he had an idea about creating a company that sold prearranged funerals. He told my Dad that the Federal Trade Commission, FTC, had changed the rules for funeral home pricing. All funeral home goods and services now had to be itemized on their price lists.

O.J. said this opened up the opportunity to create a sales force that would meet with people at their homes, work with the lists, and let them pick out their casket and services ahead of time. The family would even have a booklet from the salesperson to help them fill out that would detail out the type of flowers, minister, music, pallbearers, etc. All of this would be paid for in one payment, or over time. The price would be frozen at the contract price. Dad told O.J. he thought the idea had some promise and would do all the legal work getting the company set-up. For his efforts, he would take a 50% interest in the company. They named the company National Prearranged Services Inc., known as NPS.

Dad set up 50% of NPS under the name Rhonda, Brent, and Tyler Trust (RBT Trust), so even with Dad's legal woes, NPS survived fully intact and was just getting started when we moved.

O.J May kept the NPS home office in Springfield. Dad rented a small space in the basement of a building in Clayton, in the suburbs of St. Louis. It would become the national home office eventually occupying all but one of six stories. Dad worked around the clock to get the company running well enough for us to survive while he was in prison.

CHAPTER 3:

The Basketball Life

Sports were my mental escape. We had been in St. Louis a few weeks, and Dad knew that I was really down. He said, "Brent, I talked to an old basketball buddy of mine who has a son your age. There's a summer basketball camp run by Coach Rich Grawer at DeSmet High School. I signed you up. It starts Monday."

I had heard of DeSmet because the 7foot center, Steve Stipanovich, who played for Mizzou, and went on to play for the Indiana Pacers, had gone to High School at DeSmet. Coach Grawer had won several state championships.

The first day of camp, I was asked by a lot of kids "Where are you from?" Up until that moment, I had never realized that I had a country accent. But, after a bit of teasing, I came to accept this as a badge of honor. Coach Grawer told us that he was devoted to teaching us to be better players. You could feel the energy he created in that gym. I wanted to prove to him that I belonged at this camp.

As the week went on, I got more and more attention from the other coaches at the camp. Coach Grawer pulled me aside during one of our drills and said he heard that I had just moved into town. He said, "Have you thought about a high school?" He said I was the type of player who could be an asset to his program at DeSmet. "You have a lot of talent," he said. "If you stay determined and work hard, I could make you a great player at DeSmet."

The week of camp was winding down, and I didn't want it to be over. The last day, I had made it through to the finals of the one-on-one tournament. Everyone was gathered around to see what would happen against the new country kid. I pulled out the win, and earned the title as DeSmet's one-on-one champion.

I decided to go to DeSmet, but I was beginning to get cold feet. It had nothing to do with basketball, or how impressed I was with Coach Grawer. DeSmet was an all-boys private Catholic school, and private schools were unheard of in my hometown. Also, add in the fact that I was not Catholic. But everything was different now, I thought. I might as well jump into the deep end.

I was finishing up playing a pick-up game at DeSmet with some of the older guys a couple of weeks before school officially started. Coach Grawer came into the gym and said he wanted to see me when I finished up. He told me that he had just made a tough decision. He had been offered the assistant coaching job by Norm Stewart, the head coach of the Mizzou Tigers. It was a great opportunity for Coach Grawer, but I was crushed. I had signed up to play at DeSmet because I wanted to play for this coach. I was already enrolled. There was no turning back now.

On the first day of school, schedule in hand, I walked into my homeroom class and took an open chair in the back of the room. I sat down and looked to my right, and there was a long-haired, full bearded guy who kind of looked like Jesus. Why was the teacher sitting in the back of the room? Once we introduced ourselves to each other, I found out that he was a new freshman just like me. Tony Giordano and his family were going through a media frenzy about his grandpa who had recently died. His grandfather was known to be the alleged head of the mafia in the St. Louis region. There had recently been several car bombings between the Leisure's and the Michael's for control of the alleged Giordano mafia throne.

I understood Tony's pain of a family being beaten down by the media. After we got to know each other, I opened up about Dad, about how everyone knew in Springfield, and about why we had moved. We became fast friends.

My big escape from all of this turmoil and worry was playing basketball. The new head basketball coach, Dale Burgman, called me to his office to tell me that I was going to be playing on the sophomore basketball team. I was torn about the promotion because my friends were on the freshman team. I also was not a fan of the sophomore basketball coach. He definitely was not a player's coach. I was no longer the tallest kid on the floor. I was having to work a lot harder on my ball handling skills because I needed to transition from a power forward to a guard. Maybe I really had stopped growing at 14 years of age. When the season started, I had made the starting five, but I was not the go to guy for scoring that I had been used to. This was a big adjustment for me. I still loved the big crowds at the games, but I was not having the best first season that I had hoped. This was the first time I had ever had a conflict with a coach in any sport. At Hickory, I wanted to be around Coach Greeves when we weren't at practices. The new sophomore coach and I got along like oil and water. It got worse as the season went on. Looking back on it, I might not have been an easy kid to coach with all of these emotions boiling up inside of me at this point in my life.

CHAPTER 4:

Dad Goes to Prison

The day finally came. Dad drove me to school and we parked in one of the visitor parking spots while the car idled. Mom and Grandma Jean would later drive him to the prison, a two and half hour drive from St. Louis to southern Illinois. This was going to be hard, he said, but I would have to step-up to the plate and be the man of the house. He told me to do whatever I could do to help Mom, and to be strong for Tyler. He didn't want me to get down about my coach. "Stay determined, and keep grinding," he said.

I tried to be big and not cry, but I did. We hugged and Dad said he was proud of me. I was embarrassed to get out of the car and walk into school because I had been crying. To my relief, no one but Tony knew.

Now, it was just Mom, Tyler, and me for the first time living in our dark, cavernous house. I told myself that I did not want to do anything to make my mom more stressed or sad. I knew she was scared, and she was trying to be strong for us. My Mom was all of 34 years old, and she was accustomed to living in a much different way. Dad was always there as her protector. The three of us were now left to navigate through this strange new world.

During the first few weeks, Mom would get in the car with us and drive, looking at houses all over the St. Louis area. This also gave us a chance to know the different areas of St. Louis, so that everything was not so unfamiliar. We only had a few more months on our lease and we needed to find a new place to live. Also, I think that subconsciously the exploring drives were a way for us to be together without being in a house we hated that constantly reminded us where Dad was.

Mom finally received the first phone call from Dad. He told us that we had been approved to go for a visit. The idea of prison was scary. Was it like prisons in the movies with dangerous characters and violence? How about the intimidating prison guards? How sad was it going to be to see my own dad in a federal prison uniform?

That weekend, we got on the road early. Dad had purchased a company car before he left us that came with a CB radio. A CB was how most truckers and some cars communicated on the highway before cell phones. The truckers would alert each other where the speed traps were. It was entertaining listening to these truckers talk, but it also meant we were making good time.

It seemed like it took forever once we pulled off the highway onto 'Prison Road.' I thought we were lost as we drove through the scrappy countryside. And then we were finally at a gate, with a guard, sitting in what looked like no more than a shack. He waved us through. Along the road were small ranch style houses. We assumed this must be where some of the prison staff lived. As we drove further, we saw the intimidating maximum security prison, with tall double spaced chain-link fence topped with rolled barb wire. There were tall guard towers everywhere with men holding rifles, but luckily Dad wasn't there. We turned left and drove to the prison, a group of metal buildings that looked more like an army barracks with no fence.

When we arrived at our stop, we got out of the car and walked into a room that looked like an old teacher's lounge with tables and folding chairs. The prison guard gave us paperwork to fill out, and we waited for what seemed like a long time. Finally, Dad came through the hallway door with his big white smile, his hair longer, wearing a white t-shirt, khakis, and black prison boots.

He grabbed each one of us and gave us big hugs. We all dissolved into tears, relieved that Dad looked good. I had had this subconscious fear that he would come out and not look like my dad. Almost as if he was going to turn into some scary prison creature. We sat around a small folding table trying to catch each other up on all that had been going on in each other's lives. It felt oddly secure and normal to have the family back together as a whole, even if it meant we had to meet in this strange prison visiting room.

Dad introduced us to some of the inmates who were sitting at the other tables with their families. One of the families even offered to share some of their prison nachos, which they had made in the microwave. The inmates seemed friendly and were nice to Dad who told us that he had gotten a job cutting up vegetables for salads in the maximum security prison. He told us that the maximum security inmates had gone on a work strike, so the authorities had bussed over him and his fellow minimum security inmates do the work in the kitchen.

Dad acted like it was not a big deal, but it worried me. I was surprised the prison staff allowed the two prison populations to mix. He told us his bunkmate was a young kid in his early 20's who had played tennis at Arizona State. The kid had supposedly gotten swept up in a drug bust of his roommate who was dealing. Dad said the kid was a good guy, and he had encouraged Dad to get in shape by working out with him. All in all, it appeared like Dad had settled in as best as one could into prison life.

We couldn't wrap our minds around the fact that we were now one of those families who went to a prison on the weekends to visit their Dads, or their husbands. Yet as the weeks went by, the visits became more comfortable. We also got to know the staff, and become more at ease with the other family members who came to visit. We would sometimes make a whole weekend out of it and stay at the Holiday Inn in Marion. We found restaurants we liked, and a movie theatre that was close by. We were a prison family now. This routine became our new bizarre normal.

CHAPTER 5:

Move West

In the spring of 1982. Mom, Tyler, and I finally settled on a newer, developed neighborhood with younger families and kids playing outside. It felt like Springfield. Mom had been so strong these last few months. Now she was going to attempt to do something that she had never done before. She was going to put a contract in on a house. Dad tried to help as best he could over the phone, but we heard inmates yelling at him that he was taking too long.

The move gave us a new sense of energy. We were still carrying the secret that my Dad was in prison, and the chatty neighbors would ask Mom leading questions to try to figure out if she was a widow or divorced. Mom stayed true to the story that Dad's job kept him out of town while he expanded his new company.

My brother was finishing up the 6th grade in a Ladue Elementary school. He loved science and nature activities. He was able to catch bumble bees by the wings and tie a string around them. He would walk around like he was flying a bumble bee kite. He was into computers before I knew there were computers. And he had a true talent for writing. He had decided he wanted to attend John Burroughs middle school and High School. It is one of the best, most respected private schools in the Midwest. It was also a very expensive school to attend. He had submitted his scholarship application with an emotionally compelling essay about our Dad, and how he was surviving as a 12-year-old son. The school said it was one of the best essays they had ever received from a potential student, and they created a special payment arrangement so he could attend.

CHAPTER 6:

Forever My Girl

I was outside oneday shooting baskets into the hoop Mom had bought me, and making up a game where I had the winning shot for the 100th time. I kept noticing two girls riding their bikes around the block. One of them caught my eye. She wore khaki shorts and a dark green polo shirt looked like a young Farrah Fawcett; every schoolboy's dream girl.

I decided it was time to make my move when they came around the block the second time. I shot the basketball, and acted like I couldn't catch it, letting it roll into the street where they were.

I know you must be thinking, "What a smooth move." Well, it was the best I had at the time.

I walked up to the girls and introduced myself. My young teenager heart started racing the moment I met Julie. I tried to create enough conversation to keep her from being bored and moving on. She told me she lived right up the street and asked if I went to the local high school. I told her the whole story about why I was going to DeSmet. We figured out that I was a grade ahead of her. She was 13 and finishing up 8th grade. I was a 15-year-old freshman who desperately wanted to have my driver's license. Julie laughed because she had seen me driving around the block in our car. My Mom let me do this sometimes to practice my driving skills. She had assumed I was older. We stood by the driveway and talked for quite a while. Julie was so easy to talk to, and I felt an instant connection with her. Julie was like no other girl I had ever met. I even liked the way she said my name. I finally mustered up the courage to ask her for her phone number. As the girls got on their bikes and rode away, I couldn't have imagined that I had just met my future wife.

CHAPTER 7:

A Second Wind

The day before Dad was released, we drove down to Marion to make sure we were there the minute the prison released him. At dinner that night in our favorite restaurant, we talked about how proud we were that we had stood tall together. We had leaned on each other when we were having bad days. This prison nightmare was over, but I couldn't fight back the feeling of paranoia that something was going to go wrong. Could we get there and hear the prison officials say that they were not going to release him?

When morning arrived, we packed everything up, and I loaded our bags in the trunk like I did every weekend. I slammed it shut. A hot flash went through my body. Where were the keys to the car? Oh my god! I had locked them in the trunk.

I went inside to tell my brother and Mom what had just happened. They thought I was joking. We were all in a sudden panic. There was a man in a truck that was parked next to us that was getting ready to leave. I was hoping that maybe he had some tools, or an idea of how to get into the locked trunk. I told him that we were in town to pick up my Dad from prison. He had tools in his truck and thought he might be able to get inside by removing the back seat. Finally, he created enough room for me to crawl through the space into the trunk. I found the keys in the dark, cramped space, and crawled back out.

We were now over an hour late to get to the prison. Dad had been sitting at the release area probably with the worst thoughts going through his mind wondering where his family was. When we parked and he came out to us. It was like Christmas morning. The Cassity family was whole again!

Dad had a lot of work to do with his new company. Just two months before, while Dad was still in prison, his partner O.J. May, had a massive heart attack and died while working at his desk. The company had been rudderless since. Plus, the company's account was overdrawn by $80,000, with only fifteen NPS salesmen remaining. Dad was now co-owner with O.J.'s widow, and he had to come up with a plan to sell himself out of this crisis.

He called a company meeting with the remaining fifteen salesmen. The opportunity was there to be had if they would dig in and grow with him, he told them. His boyish, charismatic charm made most people believe they could accomplish it all if they would hitch a ride with him. And his new team was all in.

Truth is, if you could sell and build a team, you were going to make good money at NPS. Dad had experienced a well-run company in the past. Doug Wead invited Dad to attend one of Amway's national sales meetings to get a feel for multi-level marketing. Dad learned that building a good sales company was not only about selling the dream and delivering, but you had to create the right compensation to reward your rock star producers and managers so they could motivate the new rookies. Recruiting, training, goal setting, and promoting was the lifeblood of a successful sales company. In 1982, under Dad's guidance NPS started to become a player in the pre-arrangement market.

Dad met regularly with O.J.'s widow to negotiate a buyout of her 50% ownership that did not involve an upfront cash payment. After a few meetings, they came to an agreement on a longer term monthly payment. This added more internal pressure for Dad to keep the sales growing to keep these payments current.

Mom had planned a coming home party for Dad at the Lake of the Ozarks with my grandparents, uncles, aunts, and cousins. I always loved these family gatherings, but this was by far extra meaningful to have Dad back in the mix. Everything seemed to be moving back into the optimistic, positive column for our family.

After the party at the lake, Grandma Jean called to tell Mom that she had just returned from the doctor, and they told her she had lung cancer. Grandma was only 55 years of age, but a heavy smoker like many women her age. Things did not sound good.

When Dad got home he went straight to his medical books that he had when he defended medical malpractice cases for his client doctors. We wanted to find out everything we could about the seriousness of her lung cancer. Less than a week after being back from the Lake of the Ozarks, and Mom was packing her suitcase to go be with her mom.

I was heading down to the Mizzou basketball camp. Coach Grawer, who was now the Mizzou assistant basketball coach, had insisted that most of the DeSmet team participate in the week-long Mizzou camp. Basketball was still my go-to escape for all things challenging in my life.

The camp was competitive as I had imagined it would be. One day my teammate, Brad Stallings and I were trying to dunk the basketball. We spent hours working to accomplish the task. We heard someone say, "You guys are taking off too soon."

It was Jon Sundvold, Mizzou point guard and later first round draft pick of Seattle Super Sonics. He pointed out that we were all about the same height, so we needed to plant and go straight up at the rim. If we stayed focused and practiced, we would eventually be able to float like the guys on TV. We tried it, and what seemed like suddenly, we were dunking the basketball. This was a dream I could hold onto, and my basketball idol had shown me how to do it.

The one-on-one tournament was a place to make a name for yourself. I had worked my way back into the finals. It was the last day of camp, and I couldn't have been any more nervous. The big kid from Southeast Missouri in Cape Girardeau jumped three points ahead of me. My scoring was cold as ice. Dad, always said when you are cold, drive to the basket. I had a small advantage when someone was guarding me because I was left-handed. I thought of what Dad had taught me, and soon felt my nervous jitters fade. I faked right, drove to the basket, and won.

Norm Stewart was being interviewed by a local radio station about the camp, and motioned for me to come over. He told the radio audience that I had just won a hard fought battle to win the one on one tournament. He said,

"We are going to keep our eye on young Cassity out of St. Louis Missouri from DeSmet." That might be the best moment I have ever had in basketball, and it wasn't in a game.

I couldn't wait to get home and tell Dad. I also knew I was coming back home to the uncertainty about my Grandma Jean. Mom would make many more trips, but in the end, Grandma died within a year of her diagnosis.

Learning from Death

When the funeral director taking care of Grandma's arrangements moved to the details of the funeral itself, Mom asked for a closed casket, and added that Grandma had told her she wanted to be buried in her favorite pajamas. This did not sit well with the rest of Mom's family. In a small town, there was always an open casket. Grandma laid out in her pajamas was not going to happen. More important, none of Grandma's wishes had been recorded in a pre-arrangement document. Dad had tried to do this for Grandma Jean early on, but he decided because it was family he did not want to pressure her.

It was not lost on us that our family owned a pre-arrangement company. Mom was devastated that Grandma Jean's wishes weren't honored. Family members start with the best intentions when trying to make funeral arrangements,but when emotions run high, the best of families may end up disagreeing.

Friends, family, and clients Grandma had helped over the years at the shoe store came to pay their respects. I kept thinking that my Grandma would turn over in her grave knowing that she was laid out with an open casket, in a dress I had never seen her wear before. The treatments in her last days had made her face swollen. She did not look like the grandma I had known my whole life.

As we drove back to St. Louis, we talked about how important it was to have all our NPS families fill out their "Gift of Love Booklet" detailing all their wishes. As a fifteen-year-old boy, I didn't know much about the company Dad was building. For the first time, I realized filling out your wishes for your funeral could be a real gift to the family members left behind. If Grandma would have listed all her wishes in the booklet, the family would never have gone against what she had written down.

When we pulled in the driveway, all of us noticed that our yard had been freshly cut and looked immaculate. We did not have any idea who would have done this for us. I called Julie to tell her we were home, and I told her that someone had cut our grass while we were gone.

Julie said, "That was me."

CHAPTER 8:

High School Lessons

The summer before I got my driver's license, Dad needed help setting up leads for his salesmen. My job was to cold call a list of people that NPS bought containing zip codes with people aged 55 and older. I am not sure if anyone jumps for joy to make cold calls on the phone, but it was an incredible education of how to handle the phone, and to try out different scripts in order to make a successful appointment. I was paid a small amount if I was able to set an appointment. I then got paid more if the appointment resulted in a presentation.

I was good at setting appointments and gained a true appreciation for the people who made cold calls. It also showed me that certain word tracks worked, and that training was an essential ingredient to improving your percentage of successful results. When the summer was over, I shared my edited and improved phone scripts with Dad. He liked them so much that he incorporated them into the NPS training school. Dad and I had always revolved our conversations around sports, but this was different. I was only 15 years old, but earning his respect in business was better than any three-point shot.

My sophomore year of basketball was heading in the wrong direction. I bounced between varsity and sophomore teams to get playing time. It was a real bust to my ego. I could not break into the starting varsity lineup, and it felt like a demotion to move down to the sophomore team even though it was my age group. I was feeling sorry for myself, like I was getting the raw end of the deal from the coach. It was the first time that I questioned myself about my skills. So much of my identity was tied into becoming top basketball player.

I had clearly thought in 8th grade at 6'1" that I would at least grow a couple more inches. By high school, just about everyone had caught up with me, or had grown taller than me. My days of being the star "go to" player were quickly fading. I needed to create a different identity.

I started thinking about what I wanted to do with myself for a career. Dad had been an attorney. I liked the idea of the courtroom with the jury, and in using my abilities to persuade someone to my point of view. I was always drawn to history and politics. I thought this could be a good career fit for me. I decided to sign up for Father Craig's theatre class. It seemed that if you wanted to be good in the courtroom, theatre could be a useful tool.

Theatre taught me how to keep the audience engaged by building emotion. It was also a great experience to step through the nerves of performing in front of people.

CHAPTER 9:

Mizzou Strong

As long as I could remember, I had always wanted to attend the University of Missouri, affectionately known as Mizzou. I chose to major in Political Science and minor in Theatre. My plan was to be a great trial attorney, and my emphasis with my major and minor would get me exactly where I wanted to be.

I was lucky to have an engaging smart advisor named Professor Hardy, who later ran for Congress. He was also the Professor for my State Government class. He was known for dividing up the class into the House of Representatives and Senate. You then had to nominate your leadership positions, and write and pass bills. I loved the way he engaged the class in the process of how things in government worked. I was nominated as Speaker of the House. In the back of my mind, I thought that I might like to go into politics.

One day after class, Professor Hardy told me to meet him in his office. I knew I was doing well in his class, but I couldn't imagine what he wanted to talk to me about. When I arrived, he told me there was an internship for two people in the Missouri Attorney General's office. It was competitive, but he thought I should apply. If I was lucky enough to win one of the two spots, I would work in the capitol, Jefferson City, Missouri, over the summer break. Dad told me this was an incredible opportunity, and it would be impressive to have on my resume when applying to a law school.

After the interview and application process, I got the call from Professor Hardy. I had been selected. This was going to mean that I wouldn't be coming home for the summer. Julie was finishing up her senior year in high school.

We had already been apart during my first year of college. We were going to have to make it work.

On the first day at the Attorney General's office, I couldn't believe how many attorneys were working in a single building. The secretary who oversaw the interns introduced me to my colleagues. She then opened an office door and said, "This is your office."

I hadn't expected to have my own office. We kept strolling down the hallway, and the Attorney General, Bill Webster came out of his office. The secretary stopped him and said, "Mr. Webster I want you to meet one of our new summer interns from the University of Missouri."

He was one of those politicians that had a charismatic "it" factor whenever he walked into a room. As I was shaking his hand, I could not get over how young he was. I later found out that at 31, he was the youngest elected Attorney General in Missouri. Everyone believed he had what it took to run for President one day.

In 1992, Webster eventually ran for Governor, knocking out Roy Blunt in the Republican primaries. Then things fell into a nightmare for him. His political and personal world crumbled by what appeared to be an ugly partisan scandal during the election. He was accused of using the government printer for campaign flyers. He lost the Governor's race in a landslide to Mel Carnahan. Webster's legal troubles cascaded into criminal charges, and he eventually pled guilty to felony embezzlement, and was sentenced to two years in prison.

When the news hit that Webster had pled guilty, and was sentenced to prison, I couldn't believe it. If there was a picture in the dictionary for an all-American man, Bill Webster would be it. Everyone who knew him believed he was an incredibly good, and generous man. It appeared to me that there was no escaping if the United States of America made you a target. This was burned into my soul as a belief. You cannot ever get on their radar. Of those who are federally indicted in the United States, 97% plead guilty.

When my brother Tyler was a little boy, he had a tape recorder. Part of his entertainment was to sneak his recorder in a room when family or friends were having a conversation. He would secretly record their conversations. He had done this years ago when my Mom and my Grandma Jean were at the kitchen table talking, laughing, and gossiping about all of life's events.

On my first winter break at home, Tyler was cleaning out some things in his room and ran across this old tape not knowing exactly what it was. He hit the play button, and there was Grandma Jean's voice. Tyler brought the tape downstairs to the kitchen table. He hit the play button. Like magic, Grandma Jean's voice filled the room. She had been gone for about four years, but it felt sad how fast we had lost the memory of idiosyncratic inflections in someone's voice, or their distinctive laugh.

That led us into a deep, thoughtful family discussion about what a family is left with when someone dies. The deceased has a name, a date of birth, and date of death marked on a cold stone. They have stories that fade with time, and pictures that get misplaced or lost as the years move on. Why didn't average people like us have the same luxury of Presidents or movie stars, who were given films and recordings, we wondered.?

Dad pointed out that the public expects to view the highlights of a celebrity's life when they die. Their life has already been chronicled, so it wasn't that difficult to produce a film for the whole world to remember them.

Tyler said, "But, no one is making it their job to film and store the life stories of our own families!"

Then, I said, "Well, someone *should* be the filmmaker of filling in the dash between the date of birth and date of death."

Dad added that maybe this could be something we offered our families who prearranged their funerals. In that moment, a Cassity family idea was born from Tyler's cassette tape. We decided that we were going to try to build this idea into a business that could revolutionize the way that a family remembered the life of a loved one.

There is an old African proverb, "When someone dies, a library burns."

I said we could be known for creating a "Library of Lives." I still wanted to make my mark as a notable trial attorney, but this seemed like a big idea to me, and I didn't want to give up on it.

Dad jumped on the idea and named the new company that would film stories about people's lives,' The National Heritage Foundation.' He hired interviewers, purchased some cameras, and an editing suite.

When I came home that summer, the company needed a salesman. I was passionate about the idea, so I thought this would be a great experience for me.

We tried several ideas on how to introduce the new concept to clients. One idea was to offer the prospective customer a honey baked ham if they would allow me to make a presentation in their home. The honey baked hams worked, creating a good deal of leads.

I would bring a small, TV-VCR player and play a tape showing what we offered. At the end of the presentation, I would set-up one of our staff interviewers to arrive at the family's home and interview them, recording their stories, and incorporating family pictures. The interviews were professionally edited to music.

When I made my second visit, I would watch the interview with the family. We offered copies of the tapes, along with an agreement to store their tapes in our company archives. The tapes cost the family $1395.00. Once I had the completed interview in hand, I had a 70% closing percentage after the families had viewed their interview. I made $250.00 for each sale.

I was making an average of two presentations a day, and loved sitting down and watching these stories with the clients. The interviews were emotional, and extremely moving. Sometimes, a couple would share emotions or feelings about their spouse that they had not verbalized for years. In some cases, maybe never.

I was passionate about how important this was for families. I was also learning that I had a talent to perform in a sales environment, regardless of my age. There was no doubt in my mind that we were on to something big. But how could we create the best marketing platform to reach out to prospective customers?

That summer I was also taking night classes to prepare for the LSAT, Law School entrance exam. I was struggling. This was nothing new for me, I had struggled my whole life taking standardized tests. I had always used the excuse that I was left-handed, and I was thinking from the right side of my brain. I also knew there were successful left-handed attorneys who were practicing law. It seemed the harder I pressed on practice tests, the worse I performed. Becoming a successful trial attorney was the only plan I had been working towards. What would I do if I could not pass the LSAT?

My acting classes were supposed to hone my skills as an effective trial attorney. But, I excelled in my directing classes. I loved the challenge of getting the actors to align with my vision. Ultimately, a scene was directed successfully if the audience was persuaded to believe the actions, words, and emotions from the actors.

It would be smart for anyone wanting to be in management to take a directing class. Theatre Directing encompasses all the tools that successful managers need to successfully build the "buy-in" belief with a big picture vision or goal for a company.

Professor Miller taught my senior Directing class. Each year he would select a few senior student actors he believed should pursue an acting career beyond college. Professor Miller was a thoughtful, talented, experienced, and respected Professor. Everyone in the Mizzou theatre world was hoping to be recognized or complimented by him. One day, he called me to his office. The meeting was not to convince me to continue to pursue my acting career. He wanted to talk to me about directing. He told me that I had a unique imagination to create a compelling, believable story with my directing skills. He told me a director must have that ability to get actors to perform what is only in his mind. He said, "You have that ability, and could have a successful career in directing if you are willing to take the leap and suffer through the hard knocks to make it in a tough business."

He said so many people with my kind of talent never crossed the line to compete, so the number of talented people I would compete against would not be as overwhelming as I would think. I really let his words sink in. I knew that I was coming to a fork in the road.

CHAPTER 10:

Tyler

Tyler and I were three years apart in age, had the same parents, lived in the same house, and could not have been more different. My life centered around sports. Tyler loved science, writing, and anything his creative mind could dream up. Tall, good-looking, Tyler had a solid group of friends and went out with girls, but never had a long serious relationship.

My friends would say, "Cassity, why doesn't your little brother want to play sports?"

For the longest time, I thought it was because he wanted to do the opposite of anything that I did. I know that sounds insecure on my part, but I subconsciously had come to believe it to be true.

Tyler's high school encouraged the student body to play a sport, so Tyler tried out for the football team and became an All-Metro first team defensive end. He had never been a fan of football, and still isn't today, but he became a tough-nosed defensive end, and sacked quarterbacks like they deserved punishment. I wanted us to be closer as brothers like the other friends who had little brothers. We just seemed to be missing something between us.

My senior year in college, Dad planned a family trip to Acapulco, Mexico, for Spring Break. Tyler was in his first year at Columbia University in New York City. Dad was always big on planning family vacations, and it was his way to get everyone together.

We were sitting in a restaurant where the music was loud, the crowd full of fun, and the drinks flowed, when I noticed that my mom and Tyler seemed to be in a serious discussion. Everything was so loud and distracting, that we hardly noticed the two of them slipping outside to continue their conversation.

Since Acapulco can be dangerous, Dad finally settled our bill, and we set out to find them. They were sitting on a street bench, still talking. "What are you doing?" we asked.

Tyler looked up at us, and without a moment's hesitation said, "I just told Mom I'm gay."

I would later learn that Mom had found a note from a college friend in the pocket of Tyler's jeans while doing his laundry, and had already figured it out.

Dad and Tyler got up the next morning and went on a chartered fishing boat to be together. I told Mom that I was relieved with Tyler coming out. Selfishly, our childhood made so much more sense to me now. Tyler didn't hate me. He was different than the brothers of my friends. He was just trying to find his way, and to figure out who he was. I wanted to figure out how I could support him in the best way I could, so he knew I loved him whether gay or straight. I immediately started to scan back in my memory bank hoping I had not said something stupid with a gay teenager joke, or making some kind of slang reference to being gay. I knew I probably had, and I knew that it would have been hurtful. Mom was scared of the AIDS epidemic that had taken so many lives in the 80's. This was a real fear.

When Tyler returned, I met him in his room., "Tyler I love you because you are you," I said. "It doesn't make one bit of difference whether you are gay or straight. I just want you to be happy." I also told him that I may have made some insensitive gay teenager jokes in the past and I wanted to apologize.

We stood and hugged each other tightly. Tyler's coming out shed an invisible barrier between us, bonding us closer as brothers.

Dad handled the event like he did any crisis, whether it was health, business, or personal. He hit the books to find out everything there was to know on the subject. I honestly think that his first thought was that he had done something as a father to 'make' Tyler gay. Many people have differing opinions, but our firm Cassity opinion is that no one chooses to be gay. No one chooses to be straight. Your brain is wired a certain way, and you are who you are.

CHAPTER 11:

Joining the Family Business

My career fork in the road arrived in my mailbox. My LSAT scores were horrible. It shouldn't have been a surprise, but I had held out hope that I was going to get the score I needed. I was so embarrassed and humiliated because everyone knew that my plan was to go to law school and to be an attorney. I did not have a plan B.

I think there's always some sense of competition between a father and son. Dad had become a successful attorney. I was trying to follow in his footsteps, and I had failed to even get into law school. Failure never tastes good however you choose to wash it down. There was only one way for me to shake it off. I would pick myself up, dust myself off, and come up with a new plan. Someone once said that a goal without a plan is like having a destination without a map. It was time for me to find a new map with a new destination.

As much as I loved the idea of moving to New York or California to take a stab at being a director in theatre or movies, I knew my heart was not in it. I lacked the confidence I needed to tackle that unknown world. The one thing that kept rolling through my mind was the idea of creating a competitive successful sales team. I liked the idea because it felt like playing a sport. Just like in sports, you keep score. If you outperform everyone else, you win, and sometimes you win big! There was some comfort in knowing that I had a decent amount of sales experience for someone my age. I had made cold calls setting up leads for NPS salesmen as a teenager, and had sold the life story video tapes to families.

Up until then, I had not considered going to work in the family business. I wanted to succeed on my own. If I went into my Dad's company, people would say, "Oh, he's just the founder's son. It was just all given to him. He had to work at his Dad's company because he couldn't get a job anywhere else." I didn't know if I could get past thinking about what others might think of me.

I decided it was time to talk to Dad. We sat down in his office, and I ran through all the reasons why I thought NPS could be a good fit. He listened intently, and finally said, "Brent, I don't have any doubt in my mind that you would be outstanding if you came to work for NPS."

Dad was always my biggest cheerleader with whatever I was trying to accomplish. I have to admit I was not as confident as him. I told him the one thing I did not want was special treatment because I was the son of the founder of the company. I told him I would rather move away from the St. Louis area and make it pass or fail in a new area or territory. That way I would know that I made it on my own, or not. It was important to me that the people in the company knew I started at the bottom and worked my way up.

He stared at me for a while, and said, "We actually have a brand new area, Austin, Texas, with a funeral home that NPS has just signed to represent. We need someone to represent it."

That sounded perfect to me. NPS had become a big player in Missouri. Illinois was becoming a strong second in sales. Texas was the new kid on the block, and so was I. I knew I had a lot to learn, but I had a burning desire to prove to myself and to everyone else that I could be a success. "I'll take it," I said.

Julie and I had talked about the pros and cons of me going into the family business. I was anxious to talk to her about my conversation with my Dad. She agreed that this would be the best way, so that I could earn respect away from the shadow of my Dad.

Since, my original plan was to go to the Law School at the University of Missouri. Julie and I had planned to be in Columbia, Missouri, while she finished her senior year in college. We had undergone a few break-ups over the course of our seven years together, but had worked through them. We had taken the next step and gotten engaged at the end of my senior year in college, and had devised a new plan. Julie liked the idea of getting a new start in Texas, and decided to finish her last year at a small Texas College.

I enrolled in the next NPS three-day training school. The training was strict about goal setting and planning your day properly with your leads. There was also situational storytelling that helped the salesforce overcome objections. The cloud story had particular resonance. It told of the husband looking down from the clouds watching his wife go through all the difficult funeral decisions by herself. Decisions that the couple should have made together.

Our role was to ask the husband if he were given just a few minutes back to go down and assist his wife with those decisions, would he do it? By pre-arranging and making these decisions now, they essentially were doing that, giving them the peace of mind that they made these most important, difficult decisions together just like they always had.

We planned our days with enough leads to make three presentations a day. The numbers would work if we closed at least one of those presentations. This was important, because if we were able to average three accounts a week in a four- week period we would promote ourselves to senior counselor, earning a couple of extra percentage points per account. To become a marketing director, we would need to recruit and train new team members to average eight accounts a week in a four- week period. We then earned the right to an override from the team's production.

To earn the prestigious, respected, Regional Vice President position, a manager would either successfully promote three marketing directors, or would average $100,000 of weekly business for four weeks. As I completed my last day of school, I was extremely impressed with the company my Dad had built in the seven years since his release from prison.

I also loved the egalitarian sales structure. I had my 22-year-old eyes set on becoming Regional Vice President. This was a commission only business. My most important job was going to be hiring and motivating people so that they could be part of my team and succeed. The company had a built in weekly scoreboard with our weekly newsletter called, *The NPS Roadrunner*. This newsletter scored all the weekly production by each region, including motivating success stories. This structure was right in my wheelhouse.

I needed to spend a week in the field before I moved down to Texas. I was assigned to Illinois to work with Mark Monia's team. Mark was a nice soft-spoken guy with a good sense of humor.

I arrived at 7:30 am at a local coffee shop. Eight people were gathered around the table drinking coffee. I didn't drink coffee, but I did that day because I wanted to blend in like all the other adults. I was struck by the fact that there was no discussion about the successes of the day before, or who had their day planned for the day. It was just a bunch of people talking, gossiping, and telling jokes while they drank coffee. This meeting made a strong impression on me. I was a rookie, but I knew how important it was to be a role model who inspired people to be the best they could be. My meetings would be structured, organized, and motivational. These meetings needed to be the spark that built confidence in my team to go out and make sales for the day.

Almost 90% of the funeral homes that NPS represented were in rural areas. The ideal situation was to hire people who were well known in the small towns. This made it much easier for them to call on their friends. I teamed up with Dennis Boeker. He was a natural; able to put people immediately at ease. He was very comfortable knocking on people's doors, and telling them that he was from the funeral home. In the back of my mind, I thought if you can sell funerals door to door you can sell anything.

Dennis was at ease talking to couples in any situation about their family, home, and activities, just as we were taught in class. Once he finished his warm-up, he would ask if we could move to their kitchen table so he could open his presentation kit. As everyone got situated around the table, Dennis said to the couple, "Brent is new, would you mind if he read through the presentation pages to get some practice?"

Little did I know that this was also part of the company training. I thought I was there to observe. The training idea was that the new counselor would read through the presentation, and the senior counselor could also jump in and close the sale at the end if he was needed. You learn a lot more when you are part of the presentation. This training technique gave the new counselor the confidence that he had given a presentation. If the family bought the pre-need policy, all the better. I was about to make my first sale.

CHAPTER 12:

As Big as Texas

Lake Travis was nestled in the Texas hill country only ten miles from Austin. For a twenty- two-year-old, the 6th street night life next door to the University of Texas could not have been drawn up any better. On top of all that, the spicy Tex-Mex cuisine coupled with mouthwatering barbeque was heaven.

My first order of business was to meet Arvin Harrell at Harrell funeral home. Jeff Stevens, the Texas State Manager, had come down to Austin to make the introduction. My Dad had hired Jeff a few years back from Monsanto. I liked Jeff, and had known him since my high school days. Jeff was a smart, quick witted, funny guy, and like an older brother I never had. I was genuinely excited that he and I would be working together.

Jeff was pleased with how the meeting with Mr. Harrell had gone. He told me I needed to get some business written to show Arvin that we were for real. I said maybe we should take some time to map out the territory with the funeral homes in the surrounding area. I could feel the vibe of a push back from this idea.

Jeff said, "Let's get you focused on getting your senior counselor promotion."

I asked Jeff how I should plan for running some ads, so I could start building a team. Jeff said, "Don't get ahead of yourself. You have to do this a step at a time."

What he was saying made sense, but this certainly wasn't the big picture rah, rah conversation I was trying to nudge out of him. For the first time, it occurred to me that I might be a threat to Jeff in Texas. This was his state, and I just might have punctured his Texas world order.

When my first check arrived in the mail along with my *Roadrunner* newsletter, I was surprised to find that this edition was not the official NPS newsletter, but a newsletter that had edited out all the other company numbers, except for Texas. I got on the phone with Jeff who said he didn't want to deflate the state of Texas until the State had time to grow their numbers to compete with the rest of the company. I told him that everyone could only compete by seeing the whole picture. We couldn't just pick and choose the numbers we liked. I could not bring Jeff around to my way of thinking, and it became clear that he and I had two completely different beliefs on what motivated people and a team.

Up until this point, Jim Crawford NPS CEO, had stayed out of the state of Texas. Mostly because Jeff and Jim didn't see eye to eye. I picked up the phone and called Jim. I was stirring the pot, but I believed the pot should be stirred on an issue as big as having competing newsletters. There is not a more competitive individual I know than Jim Crawford. He had been with the company from the beginning, and was widely known as "Mr. NPS" to the funeral directors and the politicians in Jefferson City Missouri. He was what an old salesman would call a real closer with the low voice and the looks of Charlton Heston.

After I explained the situation, Jim replied, "Young nephew what in the hell are you talking about?" Jim always referred to me as young nephew "This won't stand. This is a damn sales company that has one big scoreboard for everyone to compete." I am not sure what happened with the phone call between Jim and Jeff, but Texas began receiving the unedited NPS *Roadrunner* the following week.

Jim called and told me that he was coming to Austin to get a lay of the land. We met in the Four Seasons hotel bar, a happening place filled with politicians, businessmen, and celebrities. I brought my map of 25 funeral homes in the surrounding rural areas, and we plotted our Central Texas strategy.

I explained that if we signed up half of those funeral homes we would quickly become a $100,000 a week region. Jim said, "I can sign up the damn funeral homes. You just hurry up and get the people trained to write the business." We both went to work on our plan. The Four Seasons hotel bar became our de-facto office where we strategized and celebrated over the course of the next year.

Julie and I had only been in Austin for a few weeks. While I was working long hour days, she gotten a waitressing job at Chili's, and had enrolled in school. I was not quite 23 years old, and it was time for me to make a terrible decision. I started thinking that maybe I was too young to be engaged. I was in a very selfish stage of my life, only focused on building a region to make a name for myself. An old girlfriend kept trying to contact me. Plus, there were a lot of girls in Austin. All of these thoughts were rolling around in my head causing me to ask the question, "Was it the right time for me to be in a committed relationship?"

I decided to do the unthinkable, and broke off the engagement to Julie. Just like Dad had done years before with Mom. I became enemy number one with Julie's parents. They made a trip down to Austin and moved their daughter back home.

CHAPTER 13:

Building and Winning

Jeff and I never had the same close relationship we once had, and I wasn't going to wait around for someone to tell me when I could start building my region. I had a plan, and Jim Crawford was fully invested in filling my schedule with funeral homes to represent.

I named my team the 'Cassity Crusaders.' I wrote a newspaper job ad titled 'Small-Town Hometown Values' that pulled in the exact people I wanted to interview. I was also able to recruit a couple of my best friends (Steve Hearn, and Brett Gaither) from my Fraternity days who were looking for an opportunity.

We were creating company stars with Sherry Elstner in Caldwell, James Bohanon in Luling, Fred Feelan in Burnet, Jan Cobb in Austin, Mike Fleming in Austin, and Ignacio Moreno on the outskirts of San Antonio. They would drive every Monday morning to have our team meeting in Austin. Everyone couldn't wait to take a seat and see where their names were on the scoreboard. I made sure this meeting was always entertaining with heaps of praise for promotions, hitting personal goals, and sharing success stories with how we were creeping up on the company competition. I purposely made us the underdog taking on the world because I'm a big believer that you always need to have a competitor bigger than you whom you are trying to catch. I knew if I could get a new recruit to one of these meetings, I would have their full commitment.

I sat down with each one of these team members when we hired them and found out what they wanted. What was their big 'why' of what motivated them? Was it a new house, saving to pay for the kid's college education? Was it having enough money so your spouse could stay home with the kids? What about finally having enough money to make renovations to your home? I needed to get inside each person's head to motivate them to their goals.

We not only celebrated when someone received a promotion, but we also had a big celebration when someone achieved a personal goal. The competition and the success of this group became contagious. Everyone thought they had a shot to do more than they had ever done because everyone around them was reaching their goals. We were a tight knit team who felt a lot like a family.

Our team also loved their job. And felt they were making a difference in the world by giving a senior couple peace of mind about what would happen after they died. I also knew how important it was for my team members to see their name in print. I knew the numbers better than anyone, and I knew the great success stories behind each one of the numbers. I was the 'writer in chief' promoting my team in the company newsletter for all to see.

There was one thing that bothered me when I visited with funeral directors. They would comment that, "All you preneed people destroy my casket averages by what you sell."

We sold by pictures in our kit, but that wasn't making us sell cheaper caskets. I needed to figure this out. We were selling the wrong way. We were presenting the cheapest casket first, and both the customer and counselor would get stuck on that. We needed to flip the pages around and show the most expensive casket first. In any other business this is called giving a customer sticker shock. When you are selling a car, you don't show the customer the stripped down car on the back lot. You start on the showroom floor where the shiny beautiful cars sit with all the preferred features.

I decided my team would remind their customers that "some people work hard all their life and want the very best, and you might like the bronze casket, costing $15,000. Others like the precious metal copper at about half the price of the bronze…Well, maybe you are like most people we talk to…you prefer the middle of the road and these are our middle of the road caskets."

With this strategy, you never even make it all the way down to the cheapest. My team's casket averages immediately went up. Everyone was happy. The customer bought a better casket, the counselor made more money, and the funeral director found a preneed company that didn't destroy his casket averages. This eventually became the way that we sold nationally, and the strategy we taught in every NPS training school.

Three times a year NPS would have a big national contest broken down into the company divisions, so everyone was eligible to qualify. When you qualified, you earned an all-expense paid trip for the weekend, culminating with an award show meeting that rivaled the award shows you would see on TV. There were many NPSers who had never been recognized like this in their entire lives. It became part of our culture, an incredible way for spouses to be a part of the recognition, and take pride in what their husband or wife had accomplished.

I decided to make Champion t-shirts with a logo that recognized each of the divisions of the contest for my Cassity Crusader team. At the next Monday morning meeting, I had the t-shirts hanging on the board. I explained how the contest worked with the qualifications. I told my team that these t-shirts could represent who wins here on our individual team, but I believed it was our time to shine. The underdogs were going to take down the old veterans. I believed I could hand out these t-shirts in St. Louis because this team would win every division of the contest nationally. No team had ever one each division nationally. The team loved the idea, and that became our team goal.

It ended up being one hell of a close national contest, but my team pulled it out. A new Illinois manager, Mike McCoy, had a strong team that gave us a run for our money in some of the divisions. From that contest on Mike McCoy and I would always be in competition about how best to grow an NPS team. Later, I would learn that Mike had a much darker side.

In the process, I had earned a promotion to Regional Vice President in just ten months' time, the youngest to earn it. I also set a company record for the fastest promotion to Regional Vice President.

Dad introduced me. When I accepted my award, we hugged tightly, and he whispered in my ear, "I am proud of you son."

I made a point to thank Jim Crawford in my speech, and later that night I told Jim that none of it would have been possible without him. He said, "Young nephew, all those nights strategizing with you at the Four Seasons lobby bar, I have never had more fun in my entire business life."

That original Texas map with the circles around the 25 towns has hung framed in my office for years to remind me how important it is to have a plan, and to plan big.

The national contest truly felt like a personal victory lap after falling flat on my face by not getting into law school. Directing, motivating, goal setting, and creating a duplicable system was my natural comfort zone.

CHAPTER 14:

Building an Idea

Dad had been busy while I was making a name for myself in Texas. A funeral home had become available in Springfield, Missouri. The funeral director for Ayre Goodwin Funeral Home had gotten himself into trouble with his own prearrangement trust fund. He needed someone to save him from future unfunded preneed accounts. Dad agreed to acquire the funeral home for no money with the agreement to fund all the remaining unfunded accounts.

The Lee family, who were family friends, agreed to run the funeral home. Jimmy Lee was well-known and respected in Springfield, so we decided to change the name to Ayre Goodwin Lee Funeral home. Randy Murray, the manager of the state of Missouri, was a true believer in the life story concept. Randy and I had been in contact while I was in Texas. He was doing a great job of putting procedures in place to introduce families to the new video concept.

Randy incorporated the process of getting pictures before every funeral service, so our video editors could put together a highlight film edited to the family's favorite music to show at the visitation and the service.

Families were hesitant at first because it was not the traditional way of doing things. We told the family there was no charge for this service. If they viewed the video and didn't want it shown, we would just give it to them as a keepsake. Once a family saw the video, however, they wanted all visitors to see it and wanted it played on an endless loop. The video created a warm, sharing atmosphere in the room, giving visitors the ability to celebrate the life of the loved one.

Thirty years ago, you would have thought that we were doing something sacrilegious by playing a video in a funeral home. Other funeral directors said we were destroying traditions of a funeral for a family. The Springfield paper wrote a story about the new concept, and interviewed several of the families who described how meaningful of a keepsake it was to their family. The other half of the article reported on local funeral directors saying they would not provide this video service at their funeral homes. How dare someone come into this business and try to change their traditions?

What an odd thing to say when you are in the customer service business, and the customer is saying how meaningful this was for their family, I thought. You have to evolve to meet the needs of your clients. If the technology is there to provide a more meaningful experience to remember your loved one…then why wouldn't you do that?

The article made one thing very clear to me, we were going to be the rebels of a stale, staid funeral industry. These were people who had owned funeral homes that had been handed down to them for generations, and they were either too scared or too stubborn to change.

Dad had been working on several acquisition opportunities in St. Louis. I knew if we took the next step, I would need to leave Texas to pursue our dream of truly revolutionizing the death care business. I had gained some valuable insights by representing so many funeral homes in Texas, and I hated the idea of leaving my close-knit team. But, I knew we had solid managers who were working our systems to expand and grow the region. It was time to move on.

CHAPTER 15:

Coming to My Senses

My business life was on a high when Mom told me she had breast cancer. I was devastated by this news. My Mom was only 43 years old. It seemed like yesterday that we had gotten the cancer news about Grandma Jean. The doctor believed the cancer was contained and had not spread to any other areas of her body, but we were worried.

I desperately needed to talk to Julie. She had been my emotional touchstone since our early teens. Now, I was in the open sea navigating all of this on my own. I picked up the phone and there she was on the other end of the line. I could barely get the words out of my mouth before I broke down. Julie had her own unique way to make me feel like I could stand tall to anything. We began talking on the phone daily.

When I flew in from Austin for Mom's operation, Julie was right by my side. This was the girl I had always loved. I knew I had to do whatever it was going to take to build back the trust I had so badly broken.

Mom went through her operation as strong as she had always been in dark times. The doctor said he believed she was going to be okay. Mom said she was happy that I had Julie to help me through this. I told her that this whole experience had brought me to my senses that Julie has always been the one for me. Mom said that her cancer diagnosis had proven that you can't assume you can wait for what you want until tomorrow. "If Julie is the one," she said, "You had better make sure you don't lose her."

Julie agreed to go on a Caribbean cruise with me. It was a way for us to get away from everything, and enjoy being with each other. We were by far the youngest couple, but it was an adventure exploring the islands. I knew Julie was scarred by my past actions, but our relationship was real. When I proposed to Julie the second time, we knew it was for real.

I moved back to St. Louis, and we began planning our wedding. There was one problem. Julie's parents did not want anything to do with me. I knew I had a mountain to climb to earn my way back. We had chosen a church, and were required to go to premarital counseling. The minister had bullfrog eyes when we started discussing all the issues with me and our parents. Our parents had been close friends early on in our relationship, and then had a falling out a few years earlier. It clearly did not sound like the way you were supposed to begin a marriage. The minister finally said, "I am recommending that the two of you do not get married. I just don't think you can make it and overcome all of these issues."

He was right that we had a lot of issues, but we went full steam ahead with the wedding plans. Eventually, Julie's parents started to break down a little at a time. June, Julie's Mom, got more involved with the planning of the wedding with flowers, the wedding dress, and the maids of honor dresses.

We knew things were going to be okay once they started inviting friends and family to the wedding. The day of the wedding, Larry, Julie's dad, walked her down the aisle, and gave Julie away like any other wedding ceremony. Julie and I looked into each other's eyes and turned to the minister. We were only 22 and 24 years old, but we were sure that everything would be okay.

CHAPTER 16:

eral Home Owner

Julie and I stopped by the airport bookstore before we boarded our plane for our honeymoon to St. John in the Caribbean. While Julie went in search of her favorite magazines, I found a book that interested me, *Customers for Life*, written by Carl Sewell, a Dallas car dealership owner. Little did I know this book would become my bible, whose example I followed when I created the culture, scoring, and competition in operating our funeral homes and cemeteries.

Carl Sewell inherited an underperforming car dealership from his father, and through his innovative leadership he built the top performing GM dealership in the nation. His belief was that you first have to decide to be the very best. Sewell didn't just want to be the best car business in town. He set his goal to be the best business in town. His message was simple: Figure out what the customer wants and provide that service, and be the best at doing what you do.

Sewell broke down all the numbers that were important in his business. He was a big believer in keeping scores designed to keep track of measurement, feedback, and recognition. He figured out four ways he wanted to keep score:

1. Quantity
2. Quality
3. Cost
4. Timeliness.

When putting his program together he asked:

1. Is the measurement important?
2. Is it easy to track?
3. Will my employees understand the measurement?

His analogy was how baseball kept statistics. It mattered that the team knew and understood the numbers. He believed that people would rather shoot for a goal than avoid making a mistake. He wanted to make business not only personal, but fun, enabling employees to know when and how they were making a difference. Sewell even timed the car porters when they returned a customer's car after it had been serviced.

In those days, dealerships would close the service department at 5pm week days, and remain closed on weekends. Sewell became the first dealership to open his service department until 6pm on Saturdays and stay open on week-days until 9pm. When customers complained about having to wait to get a ride when their car was in for service, Sewell provided a fleet of free loaner cars. These were slap your forehead simple decisions that brought satisfaction to his clients and staff, and immediate new revenue to the bottom line.

He believed in field trips every six months to visit other exemplary businesses he would read or hear about to glean ideas to implement for his customers. He believed in having a 'wow' factor to differentiate yourself from your competition. For example, Sewell decorated his restrooms like a five-star hotel restroom. People would go home and tell their friends about the dealership that cared enough to have spectacular restrooms. Sewell knew that people compared visiting a car dealership to a trip to the dentist. He wanted to provide his customers 'more than expected'- making him different than all the other dealerships in town.

We, too, had to have a good system that created avid disciples for our cause. The difference was that ours wasn't any other business or sport, we were dealing with someone's death. It required compassion in everything we set out to do. At our weekly operations meetings, we read letters and shared the stories of families who were so touched with how our staff made the extra effort to honor the life of their loved one.

Time and time again, a family member would say the video tribute captured the essence of their dad or grandma. This would be a keepsake their family would treasure. These comments built the heartbeat of our company culture. If an attendee at one of our services walked away thinking that their experience was more than they had expected, we had achieved our goal.

Sewell's book spoke to my soul. I read and highlighted it like I was going to have a test when I'd finished. I was open to any idea that could set us apart as a funeral home. We were responsible for one of the most important life events a family would ever experience. So we needed to do everything possible to create an experience where people walked away from the funeral thinking, "That was the best funeral experience I have ever attended."

People do not sit around the table and discuss how important funerals are, but most would agree they are just as meaningful as weddings. I wanted us to be known as the people who were compassionate; people who were the very the best at helping someone grieve and remembering and honoring a life.

In the early 90s, Cassity Heritage Funeral Homes had acquired four funeral homes and one cemetery. Dad had worked his magic by negotiating deals that were all owner financed. In most of these deals, the funeral home owners were able to retain ownership of the property, and we bought the business. My dad and I made a great team. There was no one better at negotiating a deal than him, and I was right in my wheelhouse by implementing my systems.

The funeral homes kept their original name, and we added the brand name, "A Cassity Heritage Funeral Home." For example: Ambruster Donnelly, A Cassity Heritage Funeral Home. Branding was a new concept in the funeral home business. Service Corporation International, a publicly traded funeral home acquisition company, did not change any of the names of the 2500 funeral homes that they owned. They didn't want the public to know that their funeral homes were owned by a National Corporation. I wanted people to know if they saw our branded name that they were going to have a different experience in the service we offered. Our motto was that we were providing 'more than expected service.' The common belief in the funeral home business was that a funeral home cannot grow market share. People go to the same funeral home their family has always gone to, much like a church. Why would you change funeral homes if they all offered the same service? I believed you had to create a reason for people to make a change.

I liked to sit down and interview the funeral home owner. I sat down with Mrs. Ambruster, a sweet lady in her 80's. Prim and proper, with neatly coiffed hair, she was a third generation owner. I asked her, "Is there a popular service the funeral home offered families in the past that is no longer offered?"

She said, "Let me think about that, Brent. Yes, there was a service we had that everyone loved. We had a sweet older lady who made homemade baked goods and served them on a silver rolling cart to the visitors. She also served coffee and tea."

"Why did you stop providing that service?" I asked.

"She died about 35 years ago," said Mrs. Ambruster.

Needless to say, we incorporated the silver tea service with the homemade baked goods at every visitation service at every Cassity heritage funeral home. I am not going to say this was easy to implement with some of our old time funeral directors. I got a call one night from one of my funeral directors. He told me that we had a problem. One of the directors was running people out of the visitation room if they drank or ate near the casket.

I called the old funeral director. He said, "Brent, they're going to ruin the carpet if we let the people eat and drink in there. It just isn't right."

"I will buy new carpet if it gets ruined," I said. "But we're offering this service to make people feel more comfortable."

Reid Millard was a funeral director who thought outside the box. We borrowed his idea of offering valet parking at our funeral services. This was very much appreciated by the older folks, and there was usually a good number of them attending a visitation or funeral service. This allowed us to offer a card of appreciation on behalf of the family, with a mint attached to it as they received their car from the valet attendant.

We also provided each family with an aftercare counselor who would follow-up with the family after the service. Usually the aftercare counselor would deliver the extra copies of the life story video. We always made sure we completed an evaluation of how we performed with the funeral service.

As Carl Sewell said in his book, "Being nice is twenty percent of providing good service. The key is to devise systems that allow you to give the customer what they want every time."

I was able to build a very talented group of managers. Sue Kroupa, Chief Operating Officer, had grown up in the funeral home business. We had acquired the Lang Fendler Funeral Home, which was a funeral home her Dad had owned, and Sue had helped operate. Sue had a great eye for detail, and had a work ethic second to none. Once Sue believed in you, you could not find a person more loyal.

Chris Buckley, Vice President of Operations and Training, was the brother-in-law to the Pfitzinger brothers. The brothers had Chris doing every type of chore around the funeral home from mowing the grass to picking up bodies in the middle of the night. Chris wasn't scared to try something that had never been done before. He trained our staff on every aspect of our systems. Chris trained everyone from how to ask and receive the pictures for the video tributes, and how to answer the phone, to sitting in on our funeral arrangements with funeral directors to make sure they were doing it our way.

Randy Murray, Chief Marketing Officer had marketing and sales running through his blood. Randy was always seeing things in the big picture, and believed we were in the business to revolutionize the way someone remembered a life.

This management team would meet on Tuesday to prepare for Wednesday's weekly operations meeting. This gave me the opportunity in the Wednesday operations meeting to recognize someone with specific details with why they did a great job. We did not believe in empty praise because empty praise was lazy, and eventually meaningless.

Randy Sutton had been my Dad's Chief Financial Officer for NPS for years, but I felt it was important to have my own numbers guy. I needed someone who could break down the financials for me, so I could easily understand where we stood as we were growing the business. I had only one name in mind.

Will Hawkins was not easy to hire. He had been my fraternity brother at the Phi Delt house. He was rocket scientist smart. On a fast track at Price Waterhouse, he had run all the finances at our fraternity house with one hand, and got his 4.0 in finance on the other. He was a good friend of mine, and I had been talking to him about the video life stories ever since the summer I sold the videos.

We were both 24, and when I went to lunch to try to recruit him, I knew he liked the stability of a big company. But I was offering him something big, the chance to make a difference and to change an entire industry. He told me he was intrigued and would get back to me. Later that night, he called me and said, "I'm in, let's go big and make a difference."

Will made an immediate impact with the company. He was very well-liked because he wanted to delve into every aspect of what we were doing, learning how systems worked, and where we could save money.

In September 1992, a year after Will joined the company, he called me to tell me his brother had two extra tickets for the Mizzou football game. Our first born, Courtney, was only four months old, and Julie had been up with her that night. Julie was tired, and it was forecasted to rain off and on that day. I told Will I would take a pass.

"Okay," he said, "I think I'll go, anyway, to see my brother."

Driving back after the game, Will went up a steep hill in the passing lane. His Mustang convertible hydroplaned and went into oncoming traffic. He was instantly killed. I often wonder if things would have worked out differently for our companies if Will had survived that car accident.

CHAPTER 17:

Kicked Out Before I was In

When we acquired the two Pfitzinger funeral homes, the owners belonged to an association named, 'An Association of St. Louis Owned and Operated Funeral Homes.' They had a little St. Louis logo next to each of their obituaries that signified their membership. They met once a month for lunch. The group was trying to distinguish themselves from the publicly owned SCI funeral homes.

I also was aware that these funeral directors did not like the idea of a preneed company getting in the business of funeral home ownership. I thought it would be fun to stop by their meeting to gauge their reaction. After all, I was a St. Louis guy whose family now owned funeral homes.

From the stares I got when I walked into the room, you would have thought I had murdered one of their family members. Del Sherman, the President of the association, asked why I was there. I told them we had just acquired the Pfitzinger funeral homes, and I knew they were a member of this association, so I thought I would come by and introduce myself as a new family- owned St. Louis funeral home owner.

Suddenly, an overweight man in a too-small suit, yelled, "How dare you come here. There isn't a chance in hell we'll ever allow you to be a part of this group. You should get the hell out of here!"

Del Sherman was more civilized. He told me I would need to step out of the room while they voted on my membership. It was a lightning quick vote. Del opened the door and ushered me back into the room. He said the vote was unanimous not to allow me membership. I told them that I appreciated the opportunity to meet everyone, and I looked forward to competing against them in the St. Louis market.

It was cocky of me to go, but I wanted them to know there was a new kid in their market. Change was on the horizon, and they were not going to like it. If they didn't like me now, they were really not going to like me once they started competing against me.

When I got back to the office, I gathered the management team to tell them about my association meeting. I was invigorated by the idea of revolutionizing the funeral business. I told the team we needed to come up with our own logo. We decided to use the Cassity family crest. Underneath the logo, it proclaimed that we were St. Louis Family Owned and Operated.

I told them that in the Kansas City Newspaper, I had been noticing pictures of the deceased pictures along with the obits. We needed to talk to the St. Louis newspaper about this feature because our funeral homes were already gathering pictures for every service to produce the video tributes. This would not only differentiate us in the obituary for our funeral homes, but this would also create a more personal obituary for the families we were serving, and the paper in turn would sell more ad space.

CHAPTER 18:

The Secret Growth Formula

My Dad always told me, "Brent, if you work hard enough to become successful in life, your critics will always say you either:

1. Inherited it.
2. Stole it.
3. Or got lucky.

Otherwise they could have done it too."

Every time we had a funeral service it would bring at least 50 to 150 visitors to experience how different we were. I needed to find a missing puzzle piece that would drive more people to call our funeral homes. The next two marketing ideas we implemented allowed us to double the market share of our funeral homes, and established me as enemy number one to my funeral home competitors. Those ideas came from two 70-something seniors, one a wise Irishman, John Flanagan, known as the West Coast Funeral Home Price advertiser; and the other, Helen Holmeyer, who had created a senior citizen's group called New Beginnings.

Death care magazines probably do not get that much circulation, but I sometimes would get ideas from the articles. I was reading about a wealthy California funeral director, John Flanagan, who was constantly being bought out by the Public acquisition companies, and then would start a new location to later be bought out again. Buried deep in the article was the fact that John Flanagan was growing his market share. Many times he would double the market share with a new start up funeral home. No one in the industry was doing this.

I was intrigued by the Flanagan article. So, I picked up the phone and called the funeral home. Lo and behold, John Flanagan answered. I told him who I was, and that I had just read the article about him. He seemed flattered that a young guy in the business would call him. I explained what I was doing with the video highlight films, and the other services we were providing. What I needed was more foot traffic to show off how different and better our service was.

I said, "Mr. Flanagan, you're doubling market share in a business where all the experts say this is impossible. They didn't even focus the article on this incredible fact. It was buried in the last paragraph."

"Well, young Cassity," he said. "You're the only one who seemed to have noticed that fact, and you are the first call I have ever received that has asked me how it is done." He added, "I will tell you this…If you are a traditional funeral director you won't do it even if I can prove it works."

Now he really had my attention because I was not a traditional funeral director. I was also not a funeral director at all.

Mr. Flanagan said, "Why don't you hop on a plane and come see me?"

I was on the next flight out the following morning.

I pulled into the parking lot of a beautifully, manicured, expansive new Palm Springs funeral home. There was a cemetery across the street, but Mr. Flanagan was building a stunningly large outdoor community mausoleum building directly next to his funeral home on his property. I had never seen this type of development with a combination funeral home/mausoleum development. It made total sense to me.

I walked in and immediately recognized him from his picture in the article. He did not look like a Palm Springs multi-millionaire. He was tall with white hair and coke-bottle, black- rimmed glasses, and old man soft soled shoes. He walked a little slumped over with a slight limp from bad knees. He saw me and immediately came out to greet me.

I don't know if it was because we were two Irishman, but we immediately hit it off. He introduced me to his wife, Honorine, who was attractive and considerably younger. He told me that there was no one better than Honorine on the phone, saying, "The phone is the secret ingredient to our success."

We sat down in his perfectly appointed visitation room, "If you think I'm growing market share by building magnificent facilities, you couldn't be more wrong," he said. "I simply like to work in a beautiful place. You probably know this, but 70% of your costs are fixed when you operate a funeral home, so it's much like a hotel. The more you rent out the visitation rooms the more profit you can make. Your costs will be the same whether you have five funeral services a week, or fifty. So, how do you drive more business to a funeral home?"

I advertise every day in the obituary section with an ad that reads, 'The Truth About Funeral Prices.' The ad listed his price, $988 and showed the phone number in big print, and a coupon to cut out and send. Mr. Flanagan said the beauty of this strategy was that other funeral homes hated price advertising, and hated to be asked about how much funerals cost. He said the secret ingredient was to be prepared to handle the phone call. He said, "Let's role play the phone call."

"Okay," I said. "I'll be the customer calling. I am calling about your $988 funeral service."

Mr. Flanagan said, "Of course! We offer a complete funeral service for $988. Would you be calling about a family member?" I said, "Yes, my Dad." Mr. Flanagan responded, "Was your dad a veteran? I said, "Yes." "Then your family is entitled to a $355 death benefit. We work with these forms every day and we will file the proper paperwork to make sure your family receives it. Also, I am assuming your Dad was on social security. There is also a $155 social security benefit he is entitled to, and we will also make sure we file the proper forms for your family to receive that benefit. Mr. Cassity, will you be having family coming in from out of town?"

I responded, "Yes, we have several family members out of town who will be attending the service."

Mr. Flanagan said, "We've worked out a 10% bereavement discount with the airlines for your family members. We just need the names and we will make sure that is all taken care of for you. Also, we have a 10% bereavement discount with the area hotels that we would be glad to set up as well. Finally, Mr. Cassity, have you ever been to our funeral home?"

"No," I said.

"We'd like to send a limousine to your house to pick up whomever you wish to come to our funeral home to meet our staff and see the homelike atmosphere we provide to families. What time would work for you?"

Mr. Flanagan said that person might now pick up the phone and call the competition, and ask them where their funeral prices begin. They will say our prices begin at $2,300, and the call is over. Mr. Flanagan added that very few people want a $988 funeral service, but if they do…70% of my costs are fixed, and if a funeral ad can bring 50 to 150 visitors for additional foot traffic to see what a beautiful facility I have at that funeral service… It might as well be me having the service than my competition."

Then Mr. Flanagan said, "That's how you double market share, young Cassity."

This was a brilliant strategy. Traditional funeral homes believed funeral price advertising was disgraceful. I loved it!

Mr. Flanagan told me I had to make a commitment to advertise every day, and train my staff non-stop with phone language. We grew very close over the next few years as we implemented his system. We developed a grandfather/grandson relationship. He loved seeing his system come to life with a young apprentice in the Midwest who believed in his brilliance.

The second idea was something we created on our own. At the Pfitzinger Funeral home, Helen Holmeyer had created a small senior social group called New Beginnings of mostly twenty to thirty widows and widowers who would travel together. Randy wanted me to meet Helen who was looking for money to help to advertise her group. I took a liking to this feisty senior. I said, "Helen, what if we team up with you?"

I proposed we do a monthly New Beginnings meeting. I would provide our funeral staff to work the meeting. The attendees would pay for their lunch, and we would provide the entertainment. New Beginnings would invite every widow and widower who was in the daily obituary, regardless of what funeral home they went to for their service. With this program they would meet our Cassity Heritage Funeral staff every month in a fun social environment.

New Beginnings was a huge success. The program grew to over 5,000 people meeting on a monthly basis at three different locations across the city. We would provide activities. Dance lessons were popular. The local weatherman might come to talk to the group about gardening season. New romances blossomed. We were also able to use our filming department to record the monthly meetings. People loved to see themselves on the big screen. We handed out prizes for all birthdays each month, and created a short video interviewing the birthday members also.

Each person who attended received a New Beginnings membership card. On the back it had emergency information to record, and had the Cassity Heritage funeral home number to call. Our competing Funeral Directors called and told us that we did not have the right to interfere with their families by inviting them to New Beginnings. But, we were beginning to convert several of these New Beginnings members, as new preneed funeral customers because they had become so familiar with our staff.

If our competitors didn't like me after I attended their St. Louis Association of Owned and Operated funeral homes, the daily price advertising, along with New Beginnings put me in a new league. But, my job was not to try to be friends with my competitors. My job was to grow our company and prove to our families that we were the best at what we did. I didn't realize at the time that these competitors were not going to play fair. The next step they took was ugly and nearly put our company out of business.

CHAPTER 19:

Competitors Revenge

The funeral home business is an odd business, but it's made odder by the fact that the business is regulated by competitors. In Missouri, the State Board of Embalmers and Funeral Directors rules and regulations require licensure for 'individuals engaged in the practice of embalming, funeral directing, and pre-need agent/funeral director agent and licensure of funeral establishments, pre-need sellers and preneed providers, in order to ensure the good of the public.' Board members are appointed by the Governor with the advice and consent of the Senate.

The Chairman of this Board was John Bopp, of Bopp Funeral Home about two miles up the street from Pfitzinger, A Cassity Heritage Funeral Home. Pfitzinger Funeral Home had been gaining significant market share with our head-to-head competition with Bopp. We were also renting a large billboard that shadowed Bopp funeral home at a major intersection. It was a beautiful picture of our funeral home with our water fountain spraying in the air, and a burst of colorful azaleas. In big letters it read, 'Funerals from $988 with a big arrow pointing down the street.

The Funeral Board decided they would conduct a 'random' audit of NPS. NPS was notified by the State Board that they were coming to our office. The Missouri statute required that when you collected the funds for a funeral pre-need, 80% of the funds were required to go into trust, and 20% could be used for overheads. (Example: For a $5000 funeral, $4,000 is required to go into trust, while $1,000 can be used for overhead.)

We were required to have an investment advisor make prudent investments with the trust funds. These investments could include stocks, commodities, even cattle. Some funeral directors had gotten hurt in the past investing in stocks, which made their trust underfunded. Regardless, how your investments performed, the funeral home was required to provide the funeral.

NPS chose to buy an insurance policy. If the funeral cost $5,000, NPS bought a $5,000 policy so the policy wouldn't go down in value and would cover the cost of the funeral. Our family eventually purchased an Insurance company that issued those policies. The money that went into the funeral trust either bought new policies, or paid premiums on existing policies.

The Attorney who represented the State Board of Embalmers and Funeral Directors was from the Missouri Attorney General's office. After the extensive audit was conducted, NPS received the report claiming that our trust fund was $22 million underfunded. How could this be?

Actually it was simple. Many of our NPS customers were on payment plans for their funerals.

Our lawyer, Howard Wittner, told me we could either value the policy at its cash value, the amount that had been paid in--Let's say a person was making payments and had paid $1,000 of the $5,000 policy. Its value was now $1,000—or the face value, the total amount of the policy.

In our example, a $5,000 policy would be valued at $5,000, which is how NPS valued the policy. If the customer died early and had not paid the full amount, NPS would still pay the full $5,000.

The funeral director board now had exactly what they needed. An explosive scary report to leak to the press that had been produced by a regulatory body. Jim Dixon, the new Attorney General, had just been elected and was hungry for a big statewide case. Ours was not only statewide, but it involved old people and funerals. We also drew an attention-seeking reporter at NBC Channel 5 in St. Louis, Miles Olsen, who made it his mission to bring the Cassity family down. Only ten years removed from Dad's release from prison, our family was gearing up to live through another nightmare.

Howard Wittner, our attorney, immediately filed for a Declaratory Judgement. This would put the matter before a judge to interpret the Missouri Preneed Statute Chapter 436. In the meantime, Miles Olsen made sure that he showed all our funeral home locations with each lead story. He featured each newscast with my dad as the shadowy figure who was a convicted felon. My parents' house was prominently featured in the news articles and on nightly TV.

One night my Dad was driving home from work. He stopped at a light and Miles Olsen jumped out of the TV van. Olsen approached Dad's car knocking on the window with his microphone and cameras rolling, demanding an interview. Dad said, 'Let me pull over, and I will talk to you.' This made for very entertaining TV and incredible ratings. Dad did a very good job with the interview with no preparation.

This press coverage went on for months with interviews of funeral directors, the Attorney General, and clients who said they were going to cancel their funerals. We were overwhelmed and defenseless while the issue was before the judge. Their plan was to bleed the company out before we could get a ruling. We had to fight back because the reports neglected to say that NPS had never failed to pay for a funeral.

We had mountains of letters from our customers who were more than satisfied with our service. Customers received exactly what they had paid for. Howard, Dad, Jim Crawford, and I met to discuss how to combat and fight back. We decided we would run some large ads in the newspaper to get our side of the story out.

Howard and my Dad thought it might be a good idea for Jim Crawford and me to sit down for an interview with Olsen. I was only 25 years old and frustrated. I wanted to do an interview. Down deep I wanted to show my Dad that I was up for the task of defending our family and our company. Before the interview, we paid a media expert to come in to train us on how to handle a hostile interviewer. That prep work helped calm my nerves.

In the interview, I did my best to show that this was an issue drummed up by our competitors who did not want to compete against someone who was taking market share away from the State Board Chairman, and other members on the State board. Our competitors wanted us out of business. Ultimately, it did not really matter what we said because Olsen had his own narrative, and he didn't want to hear the other side.

He edited the interview to achieve his objective. He mostly wanted our faces on camera, so he could voice over with his reporting. We did something different when the interview took place. We had our own film crew film there to film the interview knowing that the network would edit out most of our answers. We used our tape to send to customers when they called our office. The tape was the whole story, and it helped us retain customers from canceling their contracts.

NPS took an incredible loss with cancelations during those months. Surprisingly, our funeral home numbers were staying strong through all the bad press. It was a testament to our loyal employees who kept fighting, and the exceptionally unique service we were providing families.

Finally, after months of filings and hearings, Judge McHenry was ready to hear oral arguments. He attentively listened to both sides, and then said, "I'm thinking that buying a preneed funeral is something akin to buying car insurance. You do not buy the car insurance for an investment. You buy it to pay off if you have a wreck. I see the preneed funeral much the same. The family is buying the funeral not as an investment, but to pay off at the time of death." The judge had just tipped his hand that he was leaning towards our argument to value the policy at face value.

This was a huge blow to the Attorney General and the Missouri State Board of Embalmers and Funeral Directors. The Attorney General, was not going to be seen as losing the argument, so both parties immediately went into discussions to find a solution for a settlement. The assistant attorney general and Wittner eventually arrived to a negotiated settlement.

The Consent Agreement recognized that we would have our policies in trust valued at their face value. The company also had to agree to have a monitor at our offices to watch how we put the money into the trust. Bob Locke, the monitor, would be a fixture in our NPS home office for the next six years.

Miles Olsen, the NBC Channel 5 reporter, however, was not satisfied. He lay in wait to seize the day years later.

CHAPTER 20:

New Focus

I felt like I had just come home from war and I craved getting back to a normal life with Julie and our growing family. Carly was our new addition. Larry, Julie's Dad, and I joked that I was now a Dad with two girls just like he was. I had caused Larry a lot of early heartache with my shenanigans in Austin. Now I would be dealing with the boys in my girl's life. I loved being a girl Dad, but Julie and I thought we might try one more time for a boy.

I also focused on growing our funeral home business, but found myself spending more time at Bellerive Cemetery. This cemetery was a hidden gem, sixty two acres with the best location of any cemetery in the St. Louis area, located not far from the well-known Bellerive Country Club that had hosted several professional golf tournaments. The problem was that no one knew this cemetery existed. When we purchased the cemetery, it had a six- foot fence facing the main road. You literally could not see what was beyond the fence. The name of the cemetery was Hiram Cemetery, which was actually a Masonic name, but people assumed it was a Jewish cemetery.

The first thing I did was remove the fence fronting the main road, replacing it with landscaped flower beds the length of the property along the road. I formally changed the name to Bellerive. I was told by everyone who owned cemeteries that you cannot change the name of a cemetery that had been around since 1925. I never gave it a second thought. The previous owner only allowed flat markers for memorialization. I was going to create a cemetery with every type of memorialization available. This included cremation areas, private mausoleums, private estate gardens, large upright monuments gardens, and eventually a beautifully timeless white, Georgia marble community mausoleum.

I traveled the country to find the most unique ideas at other cemeteries. I probably got the love of developing properties from my mom, but I really felt I was in my element. I loved creating a beautiful space for the living and the dead, and I loved walking the property and imagining new memorial areas. I also loved watching families use the new memorial areas for peace, reflection, and connection. What I was creating had permanence that would be there long after I was gone.

Developing a cemetery is much like developing a neighborhood with much smaller lots. I later came up with the idea to create street signs with family names. Memorialization in cemeteries was a place to let your imagination run wild.

My all-time favorite idea at Bellerive was creating the Isle of Memories. The area was located in the middle of the cemetery with the small original stone bridge in the middle of a grass ditch that had two streets running down both sides of the ditch. This area was completely unmarketable the way it was laid out. I did not need both streets, so I removed one. We designed a meandering creek with a large waterfall at the top of the creek, and a fountain at the bottom pool. The creek created four private islands for estate mausoleums, and landscaped areas for cremation benches, along with cremation boulders. We spent $67,000 to create the area, and sold over $2million of memorialization.

It was invigorating to see an idea come to life, and become something that families loved. I later created a golf green to accommodate the golf lovers who lived around our cemetery. The manicured golf green was surrounded by upscale private family mausoleums. Our sales ad for the golf green at Bellerive cemetery was mentioned in a joke on the 'Tonight Show' with Jay Leno.

Bellerive became the prominent cemetery in St. Louis, with an impressive list of well-known families, business leaders, and famous individuals, including the beloved, legendary baseball player and St. Louis Cardinal, Stan Musial; and the pioneer of rock n' roll Chuck Berry. Bellerive had yearly revenues of

$325,000 a year when we purchased it. After developing the land and creating innovative marketing, Bellerive grew its revenues to over $4.2 million annually.

Tyler had now graduated from Columbia University, and had decided to move back to St. Louis and join the family business. He had a new idea he had been working on that could incorporate new technology with how we filmed, displayed, and marketed our life stories. Up to this point we filmed families and gave them copies of the interviews on VHS tapes. We continued to store the original, creating 1,000's of interviews in our library of tapes. Tyler's idea was to digitalize the interviews and load all the interviews on a touchscreen console at the cemetery. He believed we would eventually be able to use the new medium called the Internet to house life stories that could be viewed by families. This would truly create a 'library of lives.'

Instead of a visit to the grave, a visitor could have an option to sit at the touchscreen console to watch, listen, and possibly meet an ancestor for the first time. It was a big idea. It made more sense that someone would go to the cemetery, and not the funeral home to experience this. His idea had the possibility of taking us and the client a giant leap forward.

Our funeral homes and cemeteries had become known for unique, and impressive customer service. The 90's created the era of consolidation of funeral homes and cemeteries by public companies. The funeral business seemed to be one of the last businesses to be consolidated. The big public companies were offering crazy prices for buyouts, with their stock trading at $40 to $50 a share so they could afford to pay sky-high asking prices. They needed new inventory to continue to drive their new revenue and stock price. Houston-based Service Corporation International, SCI, was the largest consolidation player in the world, not only in the U.S., but also in Canada, South America, and Europe. The Loewen Group was not far behind. Another reason they needed to aggressively buy new properties was because they were awful operators. They were losing market share across the nation.

Both companies eventually came calling. Dad and I began talking about the phone calls I was receiving., "Brent," he said. "You know NPS has not fully recovered from the hit we took with the Attorney General battle. It could put our family in a much improved position if we accepted one of these offers. This market of consolidators offering buyout prices is not going to be sustainable."

This was true because it was a bad formula to chase revenue while losing market share. Their share prices would eventually take a hit. Tyler agreed to sell the funeral homes, but we had to keep Bellerive as our beta site for testing what he was working on.

I returned the call to SCI. It felt strange because I had used SCI in all my company meetings as the foil, the ugly company making us the beloved underdogs giving exemplary service, while revolutionizing the industry with our ideas. Now I was calling them to possibly surrender my funeral homes for them. It made me sick to my stomach, but I didn't want to stand in the way if NPS needed a cash infusion.

The romancing began at the Funeral Convention in Vegas where acquisition firms rented out elaborate suites for cocktail hours and schmoozing. This arena was right in my Dad's wheelhouse. He was the master at bluffing and sniffing out a bluff in negotiations.

We first met with Loewen Group. They were anxious to enter St. Louis and Springfield. We gathered in one of the gaudy hotel suites. Loewen threw out a bigger number than what I was expecting. You would not have known it from Dad's reaction. He told them that he appreciated the meeting, but we were meeting SCI. He needed to know if this was their best opening offer. The Loewen executives looked at each other, and increased their offer by almost $1 million, just like the movies, or a high stakes game of poker downstairs on the gambling floor. I had never experienced a meeting like this.

The next night, we met SCI who was aware that we had met with the Loewen Group the night before. Over drinks, we casually talked about our operation in their monstrosity of a suite, with servers offering caviar and cocktails. I felt like I was in a scene from Dallas, the TV series. Surely, J.R Ewing would drop by at any minute.

Dad took notes on his yellow legal pad while they discussed buyout numbers. As Dad flipped the yellow pad page, on the back was the Loewen name scribbled with their offer number. I noticed this move as all the players continued to talk. The SCI offer ended up being almost $2.5 million more than the Loewen offer. I am convinced that the open backside of the yellow pad had a lot to do with how SCI arrived at their final number. There were not a lot of negotiators like Doug Cassity in the funeral home industry. He had just negotiated a monster deal.

There are always crazy things that happen before a deal closes. We had something come out of the woodwork as SCI was doing their due diligence. We did not own the Pfitzinger building, so we were not notified by the city that our business was going to be demolished as part of a Tax Increment Financing district. We were potentially selling a business without a building to operate. We began negotiations with the city to find a solution. It was finally resolved that we would build a new funeral home across the street in a blighted area, and SCI would lease the building from us going forward. In the end, we took no stock. It was an all-cash deal with 10-year non-competes, except for Bellerive cemetery.

I was getting ready to turn 30 years old. After we banked the sales proceeds, and caught up on critical bills, my third of the buyout was $1 million to put in my bank account. This made me think about what I wanted to do with the rest of my business life. This would be the natural time to break away from the family business and break out on my own.

CHAPTER 21:

Good Times

Truth is, I loved what I was doing. There was nowhere I could go where I felt we were doing big things as a company and making a positive difference in people's lives.

Our third daughter, Connor, (aka The Baby), was on her way. Julie and I decided it would be a good time to find a bigger house for our growing family. As a child who moved from home to home throughout my young life, I wanted this new house in Clayton to be our last move, the house our family would call home.

Our girls were always busy with after school activities, but Julie made sure on most nights our family gathered around the table for supper. This event was the magic family glue that kept us all plugged into each other's lives. One tradition Julie and I borrowed from a movie was the activity of going around the table asking each family member what their high and low was for the day. This simple family tradition helped us open up and share our day. These high low stories produced some of the funniest, proudest, and saddest moments for me as a dad as it revealed my daughters' feelings about boys, teachers, mean girls, tennis coaches, and more.

After the funeral home buyout, my parents sold their house at the Lake of the Ozarks. My Mom and Dad had rented houses in Nantucket over the years. Now, they decided to buy a house in Nantucket. Our daughters, through the years, loved Nantucket, making friends and using the whole island as their own backyard.

In St. Louis, society had its own version of the New York Post of Page Six. Jerry Berger was a daily gossip columnist who could make or break a reputation. He was a very powerful man who attempted to know all the secrets about the important people. I first met Jerry when Tyler was seeing Robert Lococo, an art dealer, who was a close friend of Jerry. Soon, Jerry became a close family friend, too. He began artfully placing our names in his column about popular parties we attended or business announcements with our company. Over time, this became very helpful creating the positive perception that we were a family on the move doing good things, and distancing us from the ugly press of the early 90's. Jerry was instrumental in arranging a feature story in the *St. Louis Post Dispatch* about our new way of remembering a life with our Forever Life stories.

Tyler and I had gone back and forth on what the new name of the company would be. Tyler wanted the company named after the Egyptian god of death Osiris. I understood his thinking behind the name. Yet I was concerned that the name would present a darker feel than what we were trying to market to the general public. The name "Forever" seemed fresh and contemporary, but easier for people to understand the essence of what our company was attempting to accomplish by creating a new way of remembering a life. Thus Forever Enterprises was born.

Tyler had worked on getting the Forever Console fully installed at Bellerive Forever Cemetery. We had digitized our library of VHS interviews into the computer console accessible to the public. Now, our job was to market the new service of touch consoles to our cemetery clients. Our business plan was to first work out all the kinks at our own cemetery. We also needed to figure out the proper pricing structure for each chapter a family would buy. Our company would then attempt to contract to become a third party provider for Forever Life stories with cemeteries across the nation.

CHAPTER 22:

The NPS Way

NPS was not growing at the same rate in the late 90's. States had started making it more difficult to contact people by phone with Do Not Call lists, and other new solicitation laws. The other issue was Mike McCoy, who had become President of Marketing. He was a short, angry micromanager who had a chip on his shoulder. He did not understand what it took to inspire new managers. You know the coach who criticizes everything you do, thinking that will inspire you to prove him wrong? I had the opposite belief for building people's confidence up through achievable goal setting, so McCoy and I never saw eye to eye from the beginning.

We had bounced around the idea of having funeral directors write the preneed contracts, bypassing the need to rely predominantly on our counselors. We did not have a program in place to sell the concept to funeral directors. If we were going to enter the funeral director market, we would have to be different to compete with the size of Forethought and Homesteaders.

I was particularly interested in researching the pharmaceutical sales companies that had a predominately female sales force. The name of the game in the doctor's office was getting past the 'gatekeeper' to be able to pitch the doctor on their drugs. I believed the doctor's office was very analogous to getting past the 'gatekeeper' at the funeral home to speak to the funeral director. These sales contacts were particularly relationship-driven with funeral directors who had an aversion to change. The current marketing structure was old men making sales calls to old men.

I saw an opportunity to turn this structure on its head by hiring smart; professional women to call on Funeral Directors. The funeral industry was ripe for a new approach. One thing that I had learned in business, is that it's always easier to find something that has already worked, and then figure out how to make it fit what we needed to accomplish.

I talked to Jim Crawford about creating a new division of the company that mirrored the female sales teams in the pharmaceutical market. Crawford knew the personalities of funeral directors better than anyone in our company. He was convinced that this could be the idea that would totally upend the funeral preneed world. It wasn't long before Jim told me he found the perfect young woman to head up this new division. He had been at Lake of the Ozarks for a sales meeting. There had been a problem with the meeting room, and the food. Roxanne Schneider, the manager of the hotel, had stepped in and corrected all the issues to everyone's satisfaction. Jim said he had never seen customer service like hers. He started talking to Roxanne about a big national opportunity for her to help us start a new division of NPS. He could be very persuasive, and Roxanne became our first hire for our new way of marketing preneed funerals.

Roxanne began training in the field with Crawford. I finally met her in our home office. I walked into the conference room with Crawford, and I was immediately caught off guard because Roxanne was clearly pregnant. I thought why would Jim hire a pregnant woman from the get-go to head up a division for us? It concerned me because she was going to be a first-time mom. What would her commitment be moving forward? This was going to take someone's full focus to be successful.

I couldn't have been more wrong. I have never met a person in marketing like Roxanne. She understood exactly how we wanted to bring new marketing concepts to a tired and staid industry. She believed it was a rare opportunity to grow this idea nationally. She got excited like I did about the fun of sneaking up on the big boys in our business. She assured me that she had always wanted to be a mom, but she could never be a stay at home mom.

Every idea I brought up about how we wanted to grow, she would grab and add ideas that made the original idea more effective. NPS Advantage grew from Missouri into nineteen other states, representing 2,500 funeral homes with over 100 women in our sales force. At our peak, NPS Advantage was creating $2.5 million a week, and over $125 million a year annually. Roxanne, as our President of NPS Advantage, was a natural goal-driven leader. She inspired her sales force to strive to be a success like her.

As we began to grow the NPS Advantage division, I continually looked for ideas to improve our system to accelerate our growth. I found an article in the *St. Louis Business Journal* about Dennis Jones, who had just sold Jones Pharma for $3.4 billion. His was an inspiring story of a small town guy in Illinois who didn't go to college. His story was much like the Sam Walton of Walmart.

What caught my attention was the strong system of sales he had implemented and perfected, sometimes outselling newer drugs because of the relationships his sales team had built. As I had done before, I needed to figure out a way to speak with Dennis. I guessed that Jerry Berger, would have his number. He did, and I picked up the phone.

I told Dennis that I was building a new division that was not in the medical field, but had many of the similarities. I told him that I would love to sit down and talk to him about his systems.

"You caught me at a good time," he said. "I'm retired. Why don't you come by the house?"

Dennis and his wife had just built the biggest house in St. Louis. I called Jerry to thank him for the phone number, and told him I was going to Dennis's house to visit. Jerry said, "I want to see the inside of that beautiful home. I'll call him to see if I can tag along with you."

Dennis and his wife Judy could not have been more down to earth. They gave us the grand tour. I thought it was funny that they had a 22,000 square foot home, but they chose to smoke in a small room off the kitchen. They explained that they didn't want their new home to smell like smoke.

Dennis and I immediately fell into the discussion of the philosophy of growing a company. I was fascinated with his life story, and what he had accomplished. He was a pure salesman at heart. It felt like I was secretly getting the answers that would be on a test, and no one else knew I had discovered the test questions.

He had created an awards program for his doctors where they could earn points to purchase things for their doctor's office with a catalog. There was another catalog that allowed you to use the points for personal things like vacations, golf equipment etc. I loved this idea for our funeral directors. He brought out his three-ring binders that detailed his training systems, and levels of how salespeople were paid. The roadmap was right there before me.

"Can I take these binders back to the office to make copies?" I asked.

"Sure," he said. "I hope it can be useful for you."

CHAPTER 23:

Hollywood or Rose Hill

With our touchscreen console, Forever Enterprises, we were ready to take the next step to become the 'Library of Lives" for cemeteries across the nation. Forever Life stories created a new opportunity to reload, and sell a new memorial to cemetery operators' existing client base. We geared up to make our splash at the annual Funeral and Cemetery convention in Las Vegas.

Our Forever booth was the buzz of the convention floor. No other company was presenting a new product like our Life story consoles and we had just been featured in a lengthy, front page article in the *Wall Street Journal*. The article presented us as pioneering innovators in the business, with a bold new idea to modernize remembrance in cemeteries.

There were two big cemetery operators in particular that we wanted to pursue after the convention. One was the Buchanan family, who owned several large cemeteries in Indianapolis. We agreed that we would make a visit to Indianapolis to further discuss a possible contract to move forward. The other guy, Bruce Lazenby, represented the largest cemetery in the United States, Rose Hill Cemetery in Los Angeles. Bruce was a clean-cut guy who looked like he had just walked off the Disney set.

Buchanan, loved the idea of creating a 'Library of Lives.' He also realized this could be a new revenue generator for their operation. He asked us to come and see his cemeteries in Indianapolis.

Only four hours away from St. Louis, Indianapolis was an ideal location for us. My visit resulted in our first Forever contract representing eight large cemeteries. We immediately dispatched Randy Murray to train the salespeople how to present our new product.

When Bruce Lazenby came to St. Louis for his visit, he was sold. "Now, we have to get past the board of directors to get this approved," he said. "I am going to head back to lay the groundwork."

We had several discussions with Bruce by phone. We were set to meet the board of directors, who would not be an easy audience. Finally, the meeting was set in Los Angeles.

I was a ten on the nerve meter, but when we walked into the room and started our presentation, it went just as we had rehearsed. We had created a variety of interviews that showed the emotion packed into these profession-ally edited stories. Tyler had done an excellent job of computer rendering the touchscreen consoles to blend in with various locations throughout their cem-etery.

Several board members asked questions, mostly about film production, and the amount of time it would take to get up and running. All buying questions. When we came to the end of our presentation, the board voted unanimously in our favor, signing a letter of intent.

Tyler and I called Dad to tell him the good news. Dad congratulated us then switched gears, "Your mom and I were just watching Entertainment To-night," he said. "Their cover story featured the famous Hollywood Cemetery, home of Rudolph Valentino, Bugsy Siegel, Cecil B De Mille and others. It's fallen into bankruptcy. You guys should go and check it out if you have time."

This idea seemed completely out of left field. We had just signed a letter of intent with the largest cemetery in the United States. Our plan was not to acquire more cemeteries.

But Tyler said, "Let's go check it out, bro."

The Hollywood Cemetery could have been the perfect setting for a film noir. In fact, the sixty-two acre, 100- year-old property's southern border connected to Paramount Studios. The grass was nearly knee high. The tomb-stones were disjointed and slanted. The community mausoleum had earth-quake damage. The walls were crumbling. On the rare occasions it rained, water seeped through the cracks and leaked onto broken glass scattered all over the floors.

I took it all in, "This is going to take how much money just to get operational?" I said. "Repairs are easily in the millions."

"I know," said Tyler, "But, there would be no better place to showcase Forever Life Stories."

I felt as if we had entered the Twilight Zone. The letter of intent with Rose Hill was sitting in the car, not even two hours old. There was clearly no doubt that Hollywood Cemetery would be in competition with Rose Hill.

Tyler said, "Why don't you fly back. I'm going to figure out what is going on with the bankruptcy."

"Are you serious?" I said.

He was dead serious. I flew back that night wondering what had just had happened, and how we were going to resolve this if Tyler wanted to buy the Hollywood Cemetery? When Tyler set his mind on something, he usually made it happen.

I met with Mom and Dad the next day. Mom had a long conversation with Tyler who told her that he planned to attend the hearing, and was planning to make the $375,000 bid to buy Hollywood out of bankruptcy.

"This is something that he really wants to do," said Mom. "And he knows he will have to move out there to make it work. Brent, you've had so many projects that you've been able to operate, and he deserves to have something that he feels passionate about."

I had many concerns. We were still working out the business plan of having a touchscreen console in every cemetery in the United States. Buying Hollywood cemetery would put us on a totally different path requiring ownership of the cemetery. Then there was the issue of the money it would take to get the place up and operational.

Mom said, "Your dad and I talked about that. Your dad said the only way that we can agree to do this as a family is to get a partner in the development." Dad had already discussed the partnership idea with Tyler. There was no changing anyone's mind. Tyler was going to buy Hollywood Cemetery.

I was playing golf with my fraternity brother Dan Nester, and told him about the Hollywood Cemetery deal. "We need a partner to make this deal work," I said.

Dan was getting ready to strike the ball, and paused, "I know a guy in real estate, Rick Zimmerman. Rick's old roommate's uncle owns cemeteries in Chile. They have all types of investments, such as Lan Chile Airlines. We're talking huge wealth."

We finished playing our round of golf, and Dan got on the line to Rick and put us on speaker phone. I pitched Hollywood as a unique opportunity for the Cueto family to enter the cemetery business in the United States. I told Rick about our Forever Life Story product that would be featured in this famous cemetery. It would garner tons of free press.

"I like the idea," said Rick. "Let me run it past Javier (his friend and nephew of the Uncle who owned the Chilean cemeteries), and see if I can set up a meeting."

Rick called Dan back and said Javier, who lived in Miami, would come to St. Louis. We met at Bellerive so I could show Javier the type of cemetery operator we were. He thought the idea had legs, and that he had enough information to bring to his uncle. I told Dan and Rick if we could make it happen, our family would cut them in on equity as a finder's fee.

Rick phoned me a few days later. Javier's uncle would be in New York the following week and wanted to meet us to discuss the project.

Rick, Javier, and I headed to New York. The uncle was seated at a table in the Oak Room at the Plaza Hotel. He stood to shake our hands. He was a tall man with a mustache and salt and pepper hair, radiating old money wealth. One thing that Rick and Javier forgot to share with me was that the uncle did not speak any English.

Rick and Javier were fluent in Spanish. I had six years of Spanish classes, so I could understand bits and pieces, but there was no way I could carry on a conversation. Everything I said would have to be translated. I pitched the property, sharing its history and a list of celebrities buried there. The Cueto family would enter the U.S. with a trophy property that would get a lot of favorable press, increasing the property value. I thought there could be a possibility of offering tours to people who had finished their Paramount Studio tour. I described our Forever Life Stories Company, and how that would add value and glitz to the overall investment.

Javier appeared to be doing a good job of translating, because his uncle was nodding and smiling. We had a few more drinks, and the Uncle asked me questions about competitors in the Los Angeles market. I could not get a solid feel for how all of this was going with the language barrier. Finally, the uncle made a long statement that I did not understand, and he looked at me like it was a question.

"My uncle is intrigued with the idea," said Javier. "He wants all of us to visit the cemetery."

"Okay," I said.

Javier said, "Tomorrow."

We arrived at Hollywood Cemetery the following afternoon. Tyler was waiting. He showed the mausoleums, and how there was room to add thousands of new mausoleum crypts to create new sales. I was sure to point out that we planned on licensing the property as a funeral home location. We would use the old chapel as the venue for our funeral services. SCI had a large funeral home directly across the street from our main entrance. I knew that if we could provide the funeral service and cemetery as a combo property with our price advertising, SCI could not compete with us.

We had stopped by Cecil B. DeMille's monument overlooking the Hollywood lake. The uncle had not said much. He nodded his head like he was taking it all in and spoke to Javier. Finally, Javier translated, "My uncle can see the tremendous opportunity this property has. He believes this could be a good investment for both families. We should take the next step to see if we can reach an agreement, so we can remake this property into something that the community can once again be proud of."

A partnership was born.

Tyler immediately went to work on renovation plans to get the cemetery operational. One of the greatest assets that was born out of the Cueto-Cassity partnership was hiring Yogu Kanthiah, who has a brilliant mind for business and can out-negotiate anyone in any business.

Numerous publications followed our progress. Tyler had done an incredible job tying Hollywood Forever back into the fabric of the Los Angeles community. He had become somewhat of a local celebrity himself.

It didn't take long until Entertainment Tonight, who had recently done a segment about the Cassity brothers from the Midwest who were taking the cemetery out of bankruptcy, to do a follow-up story. Only this time, we were the cover story as the new owners, showing the nation our new technology of Forever Life Stories that would create a 'Library of Lives' for the community.

As Tyler had predicted, Hollywood Forever was the perfect platform to expose our ideas for revolutionizing the death care industry. HBO came calling. This scared me, but excited Tyler. He was right again, and agreed that HBO should do a feature length documentary. 'The Young and the Dead,' featured a young company twenty, thirty-somethings who were breathing new life and technology into the old fashioned death care business.

That documentary caught the attention of Academy Award Winner Alan Ball who was looking for an idea for a new TV series for HBO. No one had normalized death for a TV series before, and Ball's idea was to loosely base the show on the Cassity family. Thus, 'Six Feet Under' was born. Ball and his writers worked with Tyler who contributed storylines to keep the events and scenes believable and current.

It was interesting how they handled the character of my dad played by the actor Richard Jenkins. The character was hit and killed by a bus in the first episode, and became a recurring character, a ghost giving his sons opinions and advice throughout the next six seasons. With his droll view of life, the Jenkins character couldn't have been more different than Dad, who was optimistic and charismatic.

'Six Feet Under' ran from 2001 to 2005 to critical acclaim for its storylines and acting and is regarded as one of the greatest television series of all time. The wrap party for the final season took place at Hollywood Forever, and the scripts of the show are buried 'six feet under' next to the lake.

CHAPTER 24:

Acquisition Idea

The Cassity family had grown into our roles. Dad handled the numbers end of our business; and worked with Sutton, Tony Lumpkin, Jim Fisher, and Cliff Mitchell on all business that involved our Insurance Companies. Tyler managed the production company producing Life Stories, and managed the Hollywood Forever funeral home and cemetery. I oversaw the national sales of NPS, and managed our other funeral and cemetery properties. Mom continued to develop homes for her friends and built and sold her own homes.

The insurance guys were in the process of selling off a block of our business for $14.5 million. I didn't understand how any of this worked, but I liked the idea of generating money to fund cemetery acquisitions.

One day Dad popped his head into my office, "Hey," he said. "I'm heading to Howard's office to meet a potential buyer for our block of business. Wanna come?"

"Sure," I said.

Two men sat in the conference room in Howard's office. Larry, 60ish, and Mitch Barrington in his early 40's. Mitch's family owned the largest privately owned insurance company in the United States, located in Kansas City. Tall, athletic looking, Mitch had a twinkle in his eye as if he was about to say something funny or ingenious. Larry had been brought in to help run the company when Mitch's dad got sick ten years earlier.

As we talked, Mitch said, "I've always had a fascination with the death care business. I even bought some SCI stock in the past. Have you been following all the craziness that's going on with the Loewen Group?"

Loewen had just lost a civil case in Mississippi and was saddled with a judgement of $200 million. Their stock had fallen from $47 a share to below $2. I had followed the soap opera with intense interest, because several funeral directors had taken stock for payment of their funeral home or cemetery with Loewen. Word on the street was they were breaking up all their properties and would sell them off in big blocks.

Mitch and I left the meeting, so I could show him Bellerive Forever cemetery and our library of Life Stories on our touchscreen console. The more we talked, the more I felt like I was talking to an older brother. In ten years, I wanted to be where Mitch was.

"Why don't you fly back with me and take your Dad," he said. We'll get dinner and talk about the Loewen deal." Mitch had what I had always dreamed of, a Challenger Private Jet just like in one of my favorite movies, 'The Thomas Crown Affair.'

Talbot Barrington, Michael's Dad, was intelligent, funny, unpretentious, and a lookalike for George H.W. Bush.

Mitch said, "Why don't you see what you can find out about the Loewen situation. Maybe we could get in the business for a steal."

I loved the idea. The Barrington's took us back to their plane and we took the quick thirty-five minute flight back to St. Louis. My head was spinning with the possibilities, as I was flying back in my dream jet. The Barrington's passed on buying the insurance block of business, but Mitch was interested in something much bigger.

When I called Mitch the next day to thank him he said, "Let's partner up on a cemetery in Kansas City where my family is buried. It's fallen into disrepair much like the Hollywood Forever cemetery. You could do your magic. This will give us time to do our due diligence on Loewen and get you up to Kansas City on a regular basis."

I had never met a guy in business whom I liked or respected more. He told me that like me, he had never been an insurance guy, preferring real estate and investments. He said the smartest thing he ever did was to find the smartest guy in the insurance world and hired him "That freed me up to do what I like doing. That is what you should do, Brent, with your insurance company. It doesn't appear that you really have a solid insurance guy at your company."

I told Mitch that Dad managed that part of the business.

Mitch said, "The reason we didn't do a deal with your insurance company was because Larry said your policy loans of $13.5 million are too high."

I didn't fully understand how policy loans worked, but when I got back in town I asked Randy Sutton what would be the easiest way to wipe them out. He told me that about $80 million in preneed annual volume would do it. Since, I knew that we would probably grow through that number by the following year I never revisited that issue with Sutton, again. That oversight would change my life beyond anything I could have imagined.

Mitch and I bought Mt. Washington cemetery for virtually nothing because of the terrible disrepair it had fallen into. We renamed it Mt. Washington Forever. Forever Life Stories were an immediate hit. The *Kansas City Star* did a feature about how our company had brought the once proud cemetery back to life. Feature cover stories followed on all three networks in the Kansas City area.

In the meantime, we had submitted a bid for the western properties of Loewen's, encompassing 250 funeral homes and cemeteries in California, Nevada, New Mexico, and Arizona. We knew we were going to have to accept some real dogs, but there were some diamonds in the rough. Barrington called and told me that he was afraid that we might not have enough time to get our deal done. He said that the word on the street was that Loewen would be forced into bankruptcy. I was crushed. It would have put us on the map with our preneed marketing experience, operational knowhow, and a new Forever innovative technology to expose to the masses. I knew I had to refocus my efforts on growing NPS Advantage. SCI was beginning to have its own troubles with their mountain of debt and declining stock price. Maybe there would be another opportunity down the road.

CHAPTER 25:

Positive Press

Tyler and I were gearing up for our second cover story on 'Entertainment Tonight.' Their producer called, and said they wanted to do a follow-up story about the makeover of the cemetery. This feature not only allowed us to show off all the positive renovation work underway, but Leonard Maltin (ET Reporter) wanted us to demonstrate how the touchscreen Forever Console operated.

Tyler had read a story about Hattie McDaniel, the first black woman to win an Academy Award as Mamie in *Gone with the Wind,* who had wanted to be buried in Hollywood cemetery. At the time, Hollywood didn't allow African-Americans. This was not only unjust and emotionally frustrating, but it became a permanent sadness for Hattie's family considering she had been a pioneer breaking color barriers. We had the ability to right this wrong. Tyler spoke to Hattie's nephew.

The family decided to leave Hattie at her current resting place, but we created a beautiful memorial commemorating Hattie's accomplishments in film with a prominent place overlooking Hollywood lake.

Our team organized a dedication ceremony, which was well-attended by visitors and the media, and was featured by The Today Show. Her memorial is featured alongside several other actors of her time.

I had taken Julie and the girls with me on my trip to Los Angeles. When we returned from a day of sight-seeing, I had a voice message from a John Cloud at TIME Magazine. I thought it was a prank, but returned the call. Cloud answered and told me the magazine was doing a story about innovative companies in the Midwest. He asked me when we could set up a time for him to come to St. Louis to see our operation at Bellerive Cemetery.

John came to Bellerive with his photographers. Cloud's article caught the essence of our concept, and included interviews of our clients who had produced their Life Stories. Dad, of course had been telling all his friends that the boys were going to be in TIME magazine, possibly the cover. That was so Dad to take great news and pump it even bigger.

In later articles with Forbes, Fortune, and on CNN, Tyler and I were featured as rebels of our death care industry innovating change. I liked that!

CHAPTER 26:

Julie's Stroke

Julie and I had the home we loved. Our kids were in a good school. We loved watching our kids perform at the Thursday morning assemblies. My business was going well. We had a close, fun group of friends.

At 32, Julie's goal was to run a marathon, so she began going to the gym and working with a trainer to prepare for the St. Louis Marathon. She also wanted to get her body in the professional range, so she began researching fat burning energy boosters. I found a popular one called Thermo-Burn, made with natural ingredients, but provided an energy level that made you feel like you could run forever.

Julie and I began using Thermo- Burn. After months of training, Julie stood at the starting line for the St. Louis Marathon. It was a cold and drizzly day, but I thought that might be better than hot and humid. When the girls and I met Julie at the end of the race, she was surprisingly energetic. She had run at an 8 minute 32 second average clip per mile. This put her in the top five for her age group and qualified her to run in the Boston Marathon.

On Monday, I was at my office in a meeting when I got a panicked phone call from Julie's trainer. Julie had gone out for a run and then come back to finish her workout. She put a squat bar on her shoulders, and had collapsed. The gym had called an ambulance.

When I got to the gym, they had already loaded Julie in the ambulance. They told me to follow them to the hospital. They didn't even bother to turn on the ambulance lights. Their thought was probably the same as mine. Julie was simply dehydrated. It couldn't be anything serious.

The doctors started running an IV. Hours passed, and Julie kept complaining of a numbness in her left arm, and she said she was nauseous with a terrible headache. Even with everything that Julie was describing the doctors never ran an MRI. It was now around 5pm, and doctors released Julie. This doesn't seem right, I thought, for someone who is only dehydrated. We got home and I put Julie to bed. Almost immediately, Julie said, "We have to go back to the hospital. I feel like someone is sticking a knife in my head."

Now, we had a new crew on a new shift who immediately sent Julie upstairs for an MRI. Dr. Lee, the Neurosurgeon, shared the results. Dr. Lee explained that Julie had torn the artery in her neck that connected to her cerebellum, the part of the brain that gives you your balance. Julie had been complaining about having a creak in her neck. He said the artery had been repairing itself, and when Julie put a squat bar on her shoulders, it pushed the repairing clot to her brain.

Julie's mom fell into my arms sobbing.

I felt numb. I asked the doctor, "Is she going to be okay?"

He said the next few hours would tell us what, if any deficits she would have.

It was now morning, and I had to relieve the neighbor from watching the girls and drive them to school. I told them that mommy was sick, but the doctors figured out what was wrong with her and she was going to be okay. They said they wanted to go see her. I told them we would go see her tonight. After I'd dropped off the girls, I called Mom and Dad who were out of town visiting friends. When they answered, I completely broke down. They told me they would be on the next plane out.

I went back to the hospital, and Julie said we needed to try to keep it as normal as possible for the girls. She told me Carly had a birthday party after school, and I needed to go and get a birthday gift so she would have one to give at the party. Dr. Lee came into the room. Julie's balance had been impaired. He believed her balance was equivalent to having 8 -9 alcoholic drinks. He also believed that her balance would improve over time with physical therapy.

He said the numbness that she felt in her left-hand fingertips could last for years. Making things more difficult, Julie is left-handed.

Julie and I looked in each other's eyes in disbelief. I said, "The girls desperately want to see you. Are you up for that?"

She said, "Let's plan on doing that tonight."

I brought the girls back to the hospital, and Julie had fixed herself up, and had put some make-up on to look more like herself. The girls were 8, 6, and 3 years old. We walked into the room, and the girls ran to the bed. Julie gave them a long-extended hug and held it all together. I was the one who was about to lose it. We explained that mommy would be okay. It would take a little time to get back to doing all her mommy things. That was good enough for the girls. They were just so happy to see her.

Julie was determined to get back into some type of normal routine, but I knew she was struggling. The doctor had said that it was normal when someone goes through a traumatic physical experience like a heart attack or stroke that you can drift into a form of depression. You do not trust your body, and fear something else is going to happen unexpectedly.

We went to our first physical therapy appointment, and the room was filled with amputees and stroke victims. It seemed like some horrible dream. There were good days and bad days as we went to the physical therapy over the next three months. We would celebrate any new accomplishment like Julie had just won an Olympic gold medal.

As Julie began to grow physically stronger, she struggled mentally trying to reach out of the depression and fear of having another stroke. We found a series on tape with a lady who had gone through a similar experience to be helpful.

Julie latched on to one thing that her therapist told her. She analogized that you would never go back and watch a bad movie repeatedly if you didn't like it, but we tend to do that with our own life experiences. We have to eject the bad movie from our minds and put the good movie in your memory bank. Along with talk therapy, that made sense to Julie and me.

Julie had the numbness in the tips of her fingers on her left hand for years, but she mostly recovered her balance. I have noticed that through the years she tends to use her right hand more, even though she is left-handed. We will never really know what caused the tear in Julie's neck artery, but I have always thought it could have been from the Thermo-burn. There were other stories of runners who had taken this supplement or something similar and had suffered a stroke. Or, it could have been that Julie just had a weak artery, and it was a complete fluke. I have loved Julie since we were kids, but her courage made me fall in love with her all over again.

CHAPTER 27:

NPS Internal Divorce

The new division of NPS, named NPS Advantage, was now producing over 80% of total sales volume for NPS. We were the talk of the national funeral and state conventions. Roxanne had the brilliant idea for the conventions. She had all her sales reps dressed exactly alike, giving the impression that our sales reps were everywhere. Marketing at its finest, and the NPS Advantage team was a force to be reckoned with in the Funeral Industry.

This created jealousy within the company. I was at the office late one night and received a call from Mike McCoy. Mike was in charge of the original NPS counselor division. He made his pitch that we could no longer have a two-headed monster at the top of NPS. He believed that Roxanne should be reporting to him so there was no confusion in the field with the counselors and the funeral directors.

I told Mike that since Roxanne produced over 80% of the company volume, it made no sense for her report to someone from another division. Mike continued to push the issue as an ultimatum. I told if him if he couldn't live with my decision then we would have to shake hands and move on our separate ways. I offered to have him fly in from Texas to meet in the home office with Jim Crawford and me, which he accepted.

When Mike arrived, Jim and I sat down with him in the office. Mike was steadfast that Roxanne must report to him.

Jim said, "Then, Mike, we wish you the best of luck, but we've hit a roadblock."

We stood up and shook hands. Mike left the room. But, I knew that was not going to be the last word from him.

The following week, Mike served NPS with a lawsuit for gender discrimination because he was a man. There was no hiding the fact that we had a female sales force with NPS Advantage, with two male reps out of the more than 80 total sales reps. The division that Mike managed employed more than 50% being male salesmen. This was a crazy, frivolous lawsuit that we had to defend with depositions and attorney fees.

With McCoy leaving, it finally put an end to all the internal bickering and kingdom building between the two divisions. That kind of stuff eats up so much good energy and time when you are growing a company.

We eventually settled out of court. One by one, several of Mike's loyalists left the company. Mark Monia, who had been close with Mike followed him to Homesteaders, a competing preneed company. They teamed up to do anything in their power to bring harm to our company as we moved forward.

Mike's departure freed Roxanne to shift into another gear. Using her talents, she continued to expand our national growth.

CHAPTER 28:

New Company, New Success

Julie, the girls, and I traveled to Nantucket to meet Mom and Dad for our annual summer vacation. I was able to stay plugged in to my conference calls and reports with my Nantucket home office.

My parents had begun the renovations with their new home on Cliff Road. They had dreamed of buying this home for years. The design and renovations my mom was doing with this house was her masterpiece, showcasing all her decorating talents.

One night before dinner, Dad and I were having a few drinks at Straight Wharf when he said, "I've have been thinking about something that could be far less risky than acquiring new cemeteries, but could give us a much bigger return on our investment." He continued, "Back in the 70's I created the Medical Defense Associates, a medical malpractice company. It grew to represent almost 50% of the doctors in Missouri. I created a system that drastically cut legal expenses and had the highest percentage of dismissed claims. I lost the company when I had all my troubles, but I think the market is ripe again. I've been researching shell insurance companies available to purchase. We could use my system with Howard Wittner's law firm and your ability to help manage the sales by contracting with insurance agencies to sell our policies. I've talked to Tyler and he's not hot on the idea, but I think it is a solid opportunity."

I said, "I like the idea."

Dad told me that they finally had an insurance company under contract named Professional Liability Insurance Company of America (PLICA).

Dad's system became an instant success. We were able to undercut providers with our premiums by keeping our expenses low, and producing incredible results for our doctors. We led the state with claim dismissals, and early low cost out of court settlements. This was the type of company that doctors were looking for, and word got around quickly. Within two years, we were writing premiums of $35 to $40 million a year. The medical malpractice business had a far greater margin of profit than anything we had ever been involved with.

We had hit our stride as a company. Our funeral homes and cemeteries were making headlines and revolutionizing the industry, NPS Advantage continued to expand into new states, and PLICA had become a successful malpractice insurance company.

CHAPTER 29:

New In-House Counsel Hired

I was getting frustrated with the amount of time it was taking for us to get approval to write business in our new states for NPS. Howard Wittner and his law firm was becoming more focused with his work for PLICA. NPS and our Insurance Company had also received a bad annual audit from Texas, mostly sloppy mistakes, but Tyler and I felt it was time for us to hire an in-house attorney who solely focused on state audits, new state approvals, and acquisitions.

Jim Crawford said he might have the right candidate for us after talking to Elizabeth Callahan. Elizabeth was the recent ex-wife of the current U.S. Attorney, Richard Callahan, of the Eastern District. Richard Callahan would end up playing a big role in my life.

We had hired Elizabeth as our lobbyist for Forever Enterprises in Jefferson City. We had recently been awarded a state contract to interview World War II veterans, and had a touchscreen console installed in the statehouse so visitors could view the war hero's interviews. These interviews could also be viewed online to assist teachers when their students studied WWII.

Elizabeth said her best friend was looking for this type of work with a company. Elizabeth had graduated law school with Kati Scannell, and said she was smart and tough.

Tyler and I set up the interview. Kati was everything Elizabeth had advertised. In her 30's, smart, and engaging. We had found our in-house attorney.

I broke the news to Howard, and he could not have been more put off. He saw the hire as an invasion on his legal turf.

Kati, however, immediately made a positive impact. The next Texas audit we had received the highest score an insurance company could receive. What had taken four to five months to get approval to enter a new state with NPS, was now down to just over a month.

Even though Howard was our Trustee for RBT Trust, Tyler had never trusted Howard. We agreed that we had made the right decision to bring Kati into the company. I am confident that Howard never forgave us for hiring her.

CHAPTER 30:

2007 – The Beginning of a Nightmare

This is where my life takes a terrible turn. I made mistakes that if given the opportunity, I would go back and change. I will share events as they happened, so you can decide what you would have done if you were in the same situation as me.

The year, 2007, was a milestone. I had just turned 40, and Julie had organized an unforgettable surprise party, a perfect exclamation point for a decade of feeling happy and accomplished.

We had a wonderful home we loved that was a gathering place for our daughters and their friends. I could not be prouder of my three beautiful daughters who were making a difference in everything they set their mind to do. All three had become accomplished tennis players. I lived to be in the stands to watch them play. I would wait for one of them to have a big moment. They would glance up at me, so I could give them the proud Dad fist pump. We were living the life we'd always dreamed of having.

May, 2007 – Kati had been doing a remarkable job with insurance and banking audits for the states in which we were licensed to do business. One day, she told me she had been contacted by the Texas Department of Insurance requesting a meeting with our Lincoln Insurance Executives regarding concerns from their recent audit. At the meeting, the Lincoln Executives were told by the Department of Insurance that they wanted the company to commit to not taking any more policy loans. Kati reported that we had received a good score on our most recent audit, so she didn't seem overly concerned about the request. She felt the meeting went well with the Department.

A few years earlier, my partner in Kansas City, who had a large insurance company, had brought up the issue of policy loans to me when he was looking to buy our book of business. Whenever policy loans were discussed, I was told they were legal, but were not looked upon favorably by the industry. I should have known more about what all of this meant. We owned an insurance company. I always hated math in school and my college major, political science, magically did not require math courses. I stubbornly looked at the insurance operation as a necessary safeguard to fund our preneed sales contracts. That was dad's side of the company.

Still, after the meeting I had an unsettling feeling that I was not getting all the information about what was really going on with our insurance operations. Dad currently had two men in charge whom I did not know very well. Cliff Mitchell seemed smart, but selfishly power hungry. Tony Lumpkin, our chief operations officer, was an odd man, a former marine standing no taller than 5'5". When I saw him, I got a strange vibe from him, and the gossip was that he socialized and was close friends with NPS's arch nemesis, Mike McCoy, former president of NPS Marketing.

I met with Jim Crawford to discuss my uneasiness. We agreed that we needed someone in charge whom the company could trust to give the straight scoop of what was going on. Texas was about networking and politics, and we filled neither category at the top of our executive chart. We needed someone who had political experience to meet and talk to the right people.

Randy Singer, who was working for NPS, had formally been appointed by the Governor as Director of Professional Registration in Missouri. Crawford was close to Randy and trusted him. Crawford and I agreed he could be the perfect man to appoint President of our insurance company. I needed to sell this idea to Dad, and I didn't know how he would take the suggestion. I had never strayed into dad's side of the company.

Surprisingly, Dad thought Randy Singer was a great idea, and could be effective dealing with the other bureaucrats in the Texas Insurance Department.

Soon after Randy moved to Texas, Crawford and I went down to meet with him. He reported that we had bigger problems brewing than the Texas

Department of Insurance. He said we were spending millions of dollars in arbitration with our reinsurer Hannover. It was beginning to stress our capital and surplus in our insurance company. Our insurance company had a reinsurance agreement with Hannover RE, headquartered in Germany, the largest insurance company in the world.

Simply put: A re-insurance company takes on a company's insurance risk. in exchange, Hanover would pay our company a commission upfront for the business we booked, earning us somewhat less than we would have earned over time if we had kept the business in house.

Re-Insurance with an A+ rated insurance company like Hannover helped NPS build our credibility when we were marketing our product to funeral directors.

From time to time, our insurance company would enter an arbitration proceeding if there were disagreements with the agreed contract. Howard told me that we had negotiated an incredibly profitable reinsurance agreement with Hannover. Hannover RE had been unlucky with some positions they had taken in the stock market when 9/11 occurred. They had come back to our Insurance Company to attempt to renegotiate the terms of our reinsurance agreement. They wanted to lower the commissions they were paying us.

Dad and Howard, without any discussion with Mom, Tyler, and me, refused to renegotiate the terms of the deal. When negotiations came to a standstill, Hannover began withholding our monthly commissions. Dad and Howard, in turn, canceled and reissued all our policies with another company. They had just started a David and Goliath war.

Dad kept all this information from me. I would later learn that he had also told Kati that I didn't need to be burdened with all of the Hannover issues.

Why? Because Dad needed me to be growing the weekly sales of NPS that was already exceeding $2.5 million a week. He made the unilateral decision that he could not afford to have me distracted.

Singer was now sharing information directly with me. From my perspective, it felt like storm clouds were gathering.

CHAPTER 31:

The Thunder of the Crisis

With three dogs and our girls in tow, Julie and I embarked on our cross-country drive to Nantucket. Julie would not allow our dogs to be put on a plane. We had stopped for gas in Ohio. I was filling the tank when I felt my phone ring. I fumbled the phone out of my pocket to answer. It was Randy Singer.

"I just received the strangest phone call from a lady named Liz in the Ohio Investigative Division," he said. "She said she has information that will bring our company down, and that she would be in touch."

Fear flashed through my body. What had Dad not told me? I was no longer a child watching him fight an investigation. I was 40 years old and entangled with him in a complicated web that had potential, horrific consequences.

The Ohio Department of Insurance leaked gossip to our competitors that we were being investigated. It didn't take long for our Ohio NPS Reps to receive an avalanche of phone calls from our funeral directors wanting to know what was going on. Next, Singer received a faxed letter from the state of Ohio demanding a face-to-face meeting. A few days later, Ohio sent a subpoena requesting documents from our insurance company and NPS.

While all of this was taking place, our annual audits had begun with Texas and Illinois. Our staff was stretched to the breaking point.

A letter from the Ohio fraud and enforcement division arrived in the mailboxes of all our funeral homes in Ohio requesting contracts and paperwork with NPS and Lincoln Insurance company. We had yet to have the requested face to face meeting with anyone.

As the management team rushed to send out a response letter to our funeral directors, we were hit with a letter from Nebraska, wanting questions answered for a market conduct report.

I received another ominous phone call from Singer. Someone was leaking documents from our office and Singer suspected who it was. He feared the sealed documents of our arbitration with Hanover was among them.

There was no time to sit and play victim. NPS had just finished the week with the biggest sales volume in company history. I should have been celebrating. As I finished my congratulatory calls to the sales managers in the various states, I knew my next task was to jump back into responding to the crisis that was unfolding. I was receiving information like I was drinking from a firehose, but I was still believing we could manage our way out of this mess.

Dad and Mom were on an African safari trip with limited phone coverage. Attorney Howard Wittner, the trustee of RBT Trust, called to ask if Dad understood how serious the situation was.

When we finally reached Dad, he and Howard told me that they wanted me to go to the meeting in Ohio. The thought of sitting in a room of insurance regulators was intimidating. Furthermore, I didn't carry an official title in either the Lincoln Insurance Company or NPS, but I was the President of our Holding Company, and CEO of Forever Network that owned our cemeteries, funeral homes, casket company, and film Production Company.

Our insurance company was the company I had always kept my distance from, now I was going to be our main representative. I thought if I could be prepped by Kati and Howard, maybe I could pull off this meeting. I also wanted to make Dad proud, even though he didn't seem to be totally committed to this battle. That thought scared me.

The conference room held enough chairs for fifty plus people. As the grim-faced bureaucrats began to file in, every chair filled, but four. Finally, a stern, elderly, tall white-haired man entered the room. Frank Larson, the head of the Department sat at the head of the table next to Liz Sutton, who had made the ominous phone call to Randy. At his other side sat the lead investigator Bill Suitor.

Mr. Larson didn't waste any time. Their department had received a copy of the sealed arbitration with Hannover that alleged fraud and breach of contract. Singer had been right about the office leaker. This immediately put us on defense with something that we had not planned on discussing. Frank Larson told us if we lost this arbitration our insurance company could potentially become insolvent. He also said he did not like how this action was damaging our capital and surplus with our insurance company. He said he had a notion to execute a no new business order until this was resolved.

Kati shared our case against Hannover. I talked about our thirty-year history of paying over $500 million in death claims, never missing a payment with hundreds of letters from satisfied clients. I discussed our solid relationships with our 2500 funeral directors nationally.

It didn't matter what we said. They had made up their minds. There was something wrong with our company, and they were going to get to the bottom of it. When we took a break, I called Dad who had returned from Africa.

"This is some serious shit going down in Ohio," I said. "I have a room full of regulators sitting on this meeting wanting to eat our company alive. And, on top of that, we have a mole in our Austin office. They have the Hannover documents from the sealed arbitration."

Dad was still under the impression that if we gave them all the information they needed, we would be okay. He didn't feel the heat I was feeling in that conference room. These people had taken the strong position of guilty until proven innocent.

I arrived home and got off the plane so tired I felt like a walking zombie. It seemed that everything I had worked so hard to build was crumbling. I looked down at my phone, to see a message from my Mom. Grandpa Ralph had been rushed to the hospital. They didn't know if he would make it through the night.

I called my Mom back and told her to tell grandpa I was on my way.

I ran to my car thinking how could all of this bad stuff be happening all at once. Memories of my grandpa rushed through my mind as I drove. I was his oldest grandson, and he had always been so proud of me. I would give anything right now to go to the lake and have one last ride with him on his boat.

I got out of the car and ran through the lobby doors asking the nurse where Ralph Rollers room was. I got to the room and my mom, my uncles J.R and Dick were around the bed. Grandpa appeared to be unconscious. Mom said, "He has been waiting for you." I grabbed his hand and said, "Grandpa I made it. I am here. Squeeze my hand if you can hear me."

He squeezed my hand. I told him how much I loved him, and what an incredible grandpa he had been to me all my life. He squeezed my hand hard one last time, and he was gone.

I gave the eulogy, the last of a generation of real-life cowboys. As I walked away from the crowd feeling so sad, I knew there would be no time to grieve. Tomorrow I would be right back in the war zone.

I was having a meeting with Dad in his office, when Kati knocked on the door and came in. When Katie was nervous or stressed, hives would break out on her neck. She had hives.

"We have a problem with our Ohio paperwork," she said.

I knew that all of our contracts and forms were approved by each state we operate. How could we have a paperwork problem?

She explained that there had been a white out problem on our policies.

"What?" I said.

It appeared to be laziness in the department that was managed by Tony Lumpkin.

Kati explained that in the state of Ohio all the rights and benefits were assigned to NPS because NPS was the responsible party to pay for the funeral at the time of need. There was a line on the contract for the beneficiary of the policy. That line was supposed to be filled out by the funeral director to be NPS, and sometimes they put the funeral home name by mistake. Our staff's job was to correct the mistake by adding an addendum sheet attached to the policy. Instead, the staff had used white out to make the correction.

I was furious. It was a self-inflicted wound at the exact moment we needed the trust of our Ohio Funeral Directors. Dad told Kati we were going to send a letter to the funeral directors explaining exactly what happened. No matter what, using white out on policies sounded horrible.

In September, the Ohio Department of Insurance issued a no new business order, effective immediately. Our capital and surplus did not meet the requirements to operate in the state.

It was time for good news, and we received some incredibly good news. The Texas Banking Department had finished their audit and gave our company the second highest score you can receive.

Next, Dad got a call from Larry Brandes, our New York Attorney handling the Hannover Arbitration, "I hope you are sitting down Doug," he said. "I just uncovered a hidden email from Hannover between their executives. This email exposes their scheme to try to put us out of business by bleeding us dry while they scream fraud to the arbitration panel."

The email said, "There was no FRAUD, it's just a bad deal. We keep making the same mistakes. Now we are $19 million in the hole."

Brandes said he was forwarding the email to the arbitration panel. He was confident it would result with a dismissal of Hannover's fourteen allegations of fraud.

Even so, we needed cash to continue operations. I thought we should sell our medical malpractice insurance company PLICA, a thriving company that had over $18 million dollars in reserves and over $28 million in capital and surplus. It was licensed in thirty-five states and was writing over $40 million a year in premiums. Even in a fire sale, it could be sold for $75 million. This would shore up our capital and surplus in Lincoln, and give us needed operating capital to survive.

I shared my idea with Dad and Howard. Neither one of them saw the urgency I did. They knew PLICA was our most valuable asset and were not in immediate agreement with me.

Regulators are not risk takers and they will run for the door if they smell smoke. The annual National Conference for Insurance Regulators was in session, and Frank Larson from Ohio had made copies of the leaked Hannover Arbitration documents to hand out to other state regulators. Davey Sanchez, head of the Texas Department of Insurance, phoned Kati from the conference and said he was trying to hold the other states together while we worked on a new business plan they could approve. Sanchez worried how long he could hold the other states at bay.

As we worked on the new business plan, one of the main issues that concerned regulators was that we were paying too high of a commission on people who were 80 and older. This was creating a cash drain on the company. Why didn't our insurance actuaries catch this? Was Cliff Mitchell asleep at the wheel? Was Dad aware of this?

I believed we could survive the commission changes to the funeral directors. We were not only their preneed company, but we had become much more involved in their businesses. We owned a Chinese casket company that was selling over 5,000 caskets a year. This helped increase the profit margin for the funeral home. Additionally, we created print advertising for our clients and video tributes for their funeral services. Our NPS Advantage Reps were doing an outstanding job when it came to customer service.

I was once again regularly on planes flying from one meeting to the next. I had just flown to Iowa to meet with their regulators, who were getting more aggressive with their list of demands. I had gotten them to agree to give us more time to meet their requests.

My phone rang as I was walking to my car. It was Dad asking me to swing by our local watering hole for a drink with Howard.

When I arrived, they were well into their third or fourth drink. "Doug, can you believe we could have prevented all of this if we just would have settled with Hannover back in the beginning," slurred Howard. "We probably could have settled for less than $2million."

I was furious, "Do you mean to tell me that we could have avoided all of this shit, but for the two of you, ego-driven bastards with a chip on your shoulders showing the big boy law firms that you were smarter than them?" I glared at Howard, "You are my Trustee. You had a duty to tell me the mess we were in with Hannover. Your beneficiaries of the Trust are my mom, Tyler and me."

I found it hard to look at my dad, but I turned to him, "You chose to keep all of this from me? Now you have me running into a burning house to clean up your mess. Shame on you both. You might have cost us everything we have worked so hard to build because of your arrogance."

I got up, pushed my chair into the table, and left.

As disappointed as I was with Howard and Dad, I had spent months flying around the country meeting with state regulators who were reviewing every business practice of the company. I was beginning to believe that we could make the changes and still survive. We had been sloppy, but if they gave us a reprieve, we would be a stronger, better company.

I had just arrived at the office. We were just a couple weeks away from Thanksgiving. My phone rang. It was Howard.

"Brent," he said. "I have a company that is interested in buying PLICA."

I told Howard that if we could get a Letter of Intent, it would buy us much needed time and confidence with Davey Sanchez in Texas who was helping us hold the other states together.

CHAPTER 32:

The Ugly Holiday Season

The Missouri Attorney General was running for governor. This had helped our company stay out of the fray of the Missouri regulators. I believe the Attorney General did not want to be pulled into the drama of having to defend his 1994 negotiated consent agreement with NPS. That didn't mean that lower ranked people in the office weren't putting pressure on their boss to do something. The Attorney General's office decided to send the original monitor, Bob Lock, back to our home for another look at the Missouri bank trust he had monitored for six years.

Howard Wittner would be able to calm the waters with the new AG attorneys about how the consent agreement worked. Unfortunately, I received an urgent phone call from my Dad. Howard had been rushed to the hospital with a massive heart attack and was in a coma.

Howard survived, but the severe trauma to his body had severely affected his short and long term memory. Kati would have to dive into old litigation and be brought up to speed.

I met NPS Advantage reps the week before Christmas to explain the changes that were being made with our paperwork and commissions in the different states. Our reps had been through months of hell handling the concerns of their funeral directors. I tried as best as I could to put a positive face on how we were going to move forward in the New Year, but I could see in their eyes they were scared.

I felt the weight of the world on my shoulders with their worry about their jobs and the company's future, but I never gave up hope that we were going to find a way to survive.

Of course, Dad kept up his show of bravado and had rented a yacht in St. Bart's for the family for the Christmas holiday. I was sure Dad had planned the last hurrah for the family before everything crashed and burned. The trust I once had in the man I had idolized above all others, had dwindled down to a nagging question, "What else was he hiding?"

As we cruised the turquoise waters, I was on constant crisis calls. My mom still didn't know how serious everything was, but I had kept Julie in the loop with each step. I not only needed her as a sounding board, but we had always been fully open with each other. It was obscene to be on a yacht living like the kings and queens, while Julie, the girls and I knew our company was holding on by a thread.

I also knew that the people at our company would be pissed off by how inconsiderate it was that we were living it up, while they worried about the future of the company and their jobs. I was the leader of my salespeople. There was no way round it. We had made a big mistake.

When we returned, Larry Brandes, our New York Attorney for the arbitration, called to tell us that Hannover had abandoned all of their fraud claims. The arbitration panel, unhappy with Hannover, officially dismissed all fourteen allegations of fraud. Hannover's claims had cost us millions of dollars, putting our company in the eye of the storm with every state we operated in.

Brandes believed our odds were good to win damages from the panel. The company was stretched and fragile. Could we make it to the finish line for their final ruling that was scheduled in four months? That seemed like an eternity of time.

CHAPTER 33:

Misinformation Snafu

We had spent more than three months creating a new business plan to meet the Texas Regulators' approval. Our weekly status conference calls usually had the same players on both ends of the line. This call was different. There was a new attendee, Emma Fulton, attorney for the insurance department. From the first words she spoke, it was clear that she was not at this meeting to find a solution.

She began throwing around the idea that she would like our insurance company to pay our premiums within 30 days, even though we had 90 days by statute. We'd been working with Davey Sanchez, who believed there was a light at the end of this tunnel after we restructured the way we did business. Davey and I had created a decent working relationship.

I thought it would be a good idea to set-up a one-on-one meeting with Davey to make sure we were on the same page moving forward the next 90 days. He agreed, and we set a date to meet in his office. We had recently hired a new Texas Attorney, Hector Deleon, who had close ties to the Texas Insurance Department. Hector was close to Davey. He told me it was a good thing that Davey had cleared his schedule to meet with me.

The day I was scheduled to meet with Davey, St. Louis had a severe ice storm and the airport shut down. As fast as everything was moving with requests from all the other states, I knew I couldn't wait another week. I called the guy from whom we had chartered private jets in the past and told him I needed to get out of St. Louis in the worst way for a very important meeting.

"Get here in the next forty-five minutes" he said, "And I'll do it. It is not going to be a fun ride."

When I got there, they had the plane warmed up and sitting on the tarmac. I jumped onboard and buckled into my seat. I was thinking this is crazy nuts. This is what you read about when private planes crash.

The last few months I had been getting panic attacks where my heart would start racing, I would start sweating, and I would feel as though I needed to flee the room. I had only talked to Julie about them. While, I didn't have an attack on my very turbulent flight, when I walked into Davey's office, my heart started racing. Sweat rolled down my neck, and my eyes narrowed with a strange tunnel vision.

Davey said, "Are you okay?"

I was honest with Davey. I told him it would pass after a few minutes. Davey was kind and understanding, telling me he had to believe I had been under a lot of stress. He told me to take a moment and handed me tissues to wipe off my face.

I was embarrassed, and sensed that Davey felt bad for me. Years later, I read Davey's FBI interview. In it, he said I was profusely sweating at the beginning of our meeting. It clearly meant I was guilty.

After my panic attack, the meeting seemed to go well. I told Davey I needed his help, that we were working around the clock trying to respond to all the requests from the different state regulatory departments. Since our insurance company is domiciled in Texas, could Texas be a clearing house for these requests? Then we wouldn't double and triple our efforts. I also needed time to get to the final ruling of the Hannover arbitration, along with enough time to sell PLICA.

I also told him that I believed that Mitch Barrington could put me with the right buyer for PLICA. Davey said he was willing to give us time. He said he may need to have a signed pocket order with us that would put the other states at ease. He believed this would give the proper appearance that Texas was monitoring the company, while we continued to cooperate with the restructuring. If we did not continue to cooperate, he would have an order to put the company in liquidation. He believed this would give us the 90 to 180 days we needed to get our new business plan in place, sell PLICA, and get a final ruling with our Hannover arbitration.

He asked me, "Do you know of anything that has been done fraudulently."

"No," I said. "But things have been done sloppily, and there has been mismanagement in some areas that have been corrected going forward."

He said, "It does me no good to move prematurely while you're working to right the ship. You're asking me to trust you, and I'm telling you that you need to trust me."

We shook hands, and I walked out of the meeting believing that the meeting could not have gone any better. Davey and I had an old fashioned handshake agreement.

Meanwhile, Dan Ottman, the deputy Attorney General for Missouri, who negotiated with Howard Wittner the terms of the 1994 Consent Agreement, was now the head of the Missouri Department of Insurance. He was now conducting an audit of NPS/Lincoln.

Just a few days after the meeting with Davey Sanchez, Emma Fulton, got a call from Dale Keller with the Missouri Attorney General. He told her that it appeared there were millions of dollars missing from our Missouri trust. Keller was unfamiliar with how the trust worked. Trust money either paid premiums on old policies or bought new policies. At the end of the month there was very little money left, because the value of the trust was the face amount of the insurance policies.

Fulton immediately went to Davey and told him we were a bunch of crooks. She went on to say NPS had stolen millions of dollars from the Missouri Bank Trust. Now, Davey believed that I had met with him and lied directly to his face. This was the turning point where Emma took control out of Davey's hands. She now felt liberated to move against our company.

Davey contacted Kati and told her about the bad call from Missouri. Katie immediately went into damage control and contacted Bob Lock to help her clear up the misinformation that had been given to Texas. He laid out in a detailed email exactly how he monitored the trust.

We had been following these procedures for fourteen years, mandated by the negotiated 1994 Consent Agreement with the Missouri Attorney General's office. Kati forwarded all this information to Fulton and Sanchez. Emma didn't want to hear it. Davey's tone with me went from friendly and understanding to harsh and unforgiving. He reiterated that he could put the company down at any moment with a stroke of the pen.

At the same time, the Missouri Deputy Attorney General called Texas saying that his office needed assurances that Texas was not going to put our company in liquidation. This begged the question, if the Missouri Attorney General's office discovered that our company had stolen millions of dollars out of a Missouri Bank Trust, why would they want reassurances from Texas that we stay in business?

The answer to my question didn't matter. Fulton was intent on shutting our company down. I had to do something and make a move to build back up some credibility with the Texas Department. I couldn't do it alone. What I needed was someone a hell of a lot bigger than our company. Someone who carried respect. I picked up the phone and made a call.

CHAPTER 34:

A Game and a Prayer

Mitch Barrington immediately answered with his cool, easy-going demeanor.

"I need to see you", I said. "It is important."

"Okay," he said. "Do you want to go drive up and go to the Kansas basketball game tonight? I'll make you a hotel reservation. We can talk on the way up and back from Lawrence."

I got on the road and drove up to Kansas City. Mitch arrived at the hotel, and I got into his car. Mitch said, "Man, Brent, you must be in one hell of a jam."

On our drive to Lawrence, I don't think I left out a detail of my six-month odyssey.

When I finished, Mitch said, "I'm going to help you. The first thing I am going to do is have Bill Davidson, our Texas guy who is close with Davey, call and tell Davey you are a good man, and we are here to help. We need time to put things in place." He added, "You have an incredibly successful trained sales team. I think I can purchase Lincoln for the amount that is in your capital and surplus. NPS can then write business for my insurance company. This will remove your headache of dealing with an insurance company, and leverages your talents allowing you to build a strong national sales force. I can't imagine how Texas couldn't be satisfied with that plan. Don't worry we will work this out. I do wish you would have come to me sooner."

I looked at Mitch like I couldn't believe what he had just told me. It was the first time in months I was able to take a deep breath and exhale. I called my

Dad and Kati at halftime and told them the news. I walked back in the arena after the call, thinking to myself I had finally saved our company.

Bill Davidson called Davey, but he didn't get the positive response everyone was anticipating. This was not what Emma Fulton wanted to hear. Barrington's people were warned that if they jumped in the pit with us, they too could get burned.

Kati had sent Larry Morton, Barrington's top man, all our correspondence with the department, along with our new business plan and audit reports. Larry was a lot more conservative than Mitch. He was paid to be the safety valve for Barrington's deals. Larry was not ready to jump in with both feet if it could damage their company. I did not like this, but I understood how powerful government regulatory departments could be for anyone.

I called Mitch and told him that Emma Fulton was now demanding that we put $4 million of Cassity personal funds in the company, and create an escrow account for all our assets. If we didn't do this, she would move to execute the pocket order that would be our death knell. Mitch told me to do whatever they asked because it was better to survive weakened than be shut down.

"There are always options once you get past this," he said.

Hector Deleon, our Texas Attorney, called Fulton to set up a meeting with the Texas Insurance Department players, and the Cassity family (Dad, Mom, Tyler, and Brent.) The family met first with Hector.

"Emma can be very nasty," Hector said. "I don't want anyone losing their cool. I'll handle most of the needed communication."

The meeting room was cold and drab. We took a seat across the table from Emma, who glared at us. Hector had prepared a list of all our assets with values attached. Everything we had worked for was in those folders.

Fulton said, "I don't think Doug Cassity can be at this meeting because he is a convicted felon."

Hector said, "You said you wanted to meet with the family. Doug is part of this family."

I was sure she said that for shock value. We went through all the assets in her folder. After, she said, "I'm ready to enter a liquidation order today if your clients are not willing to put in $4 million dollars of personal funds."

I looked at my mom. She was in shock. The meeting ended with a dead-line to put the money in the company, and the attorneys agreed to work on an escrow agreement.

I had set aside my million dollars after the SCI buyout to pay for my girl's college educations, weddings, and anything else they might need. I would be giving this money away now with a hope and prayer that it would be put to good use.

Mom, Dad, Doug and Rhonda Cassit

Tyler, Doug, and Brent

Julie and Brent at Leavenworth

Starting from left: Carly, Connor, Brent, Courtney, and Julie

CHAPTER 35:

Death by Perception

Various states were sending out letters to our funeral directors that they were conducting an investigative audit on our company. Those letters then created more news stories in the funeral industry media, scaring funeral directors. All the while our company had never not paid a claim, commission, or premium for over 25 years.

This was not a storm created by customers or funeral directors. This was about regulators who did not like our current business plan, and who had been convinced of the Hannover misinformation. We even had some state auditors opine that our company was underfunded, because if everyone died on one day there would not be enough funds to pay off all the funerals. Well, of course not. Think of your own insurance policies. That's why you have actuaries in insurance companies. They base their calculations on age, sex, medical history, etc. For that matter, if everyone went to withdraw their money from the bank in one day it would not be possible. The banks are only allowed to keep a certain amount of funds at each location.

When my family returned from the Texas meeting, Kati walked into my office to inform me that she received a call from our old nemesis reporter Miles Olsen, from NBC Channel 5. Olsen had been waiting in the shadows for 12 years hoping to have another opportunity to finally slay our company. This was not good news that he had caught the scent of our troubles.

When Emma Fulton received the $4 million wire, she contacted Hector and accused us of not sending personal family funds. She said we would need to prove the funds were personal. Someone in our office had made this accusation to her. We later discovered that Tony Lumpkin, Chief Operating Officer with Lincoln, had been consistently giving bogus information to the department to specifically hurt us. Tony had secretly teamed up with Mike McCoy with a company called Texas Memorial Life. They believed if they could run our company out of business, they would then be the recipient of the windfall of our company's business in Texas.

Larry Brandes, our New York attorney, emailed Fulton a case summary of the arbitration showing how the arbitration panel was leaning strongly in our favor. This was the final paragraph of his email to Fuller:

'Hannover would still be making its claims of fraud against Lincoln knowing full well that these claims, and every element of them, was completely false." The smoking gun email was found at the 11th hour after denying Lincoln for 2 years the proper document discovery. He continued, *"Indeed, Lincoln strongly suspects that Hannover and its agents have defamed Lincoln and others by repeating these knowingly false charges to others, possibly including several State insurance departments. Lincoln intends to pursue these matters at the Hearing. It will seek an award of many millions of dollars of fees, expenses, and lost executive time that it has been forced to incur to defend itself against now provable exceedingly vicious, but utterly baseless charges; it will seek compensatory damages in an amount to be determined but is believed to exceed $50 million for the crippling damage to its business and its franchise resulting from Hannover's unconscionable dissembling; and we will seek punitive damages in an amount equal to Hannover's entire surplus because no reinsurer as dishonest as Hannover should be allowed to continue in business." Hannover knows its chances of prevailing in the arbitration are slim, and it has followed a calculated strategy of trying to drive Lincoln into liquidation before the case can be heard. Personally, I feel it would be a shame if that strategy were to succeed, particularly as we are so close to a resolution of the arbitration.'*

Brandes told Fulton that he was no longer charging our company for legal fees because of our weakened position, and that he and his firm believed we would prevail. Fuller was now working against the clock. If our company succeeded in our arbitration, we would be awarded damages worth millions of dollars. This email was Fulton's trigger to act before it was too late.

I sent Davey an email reminding him of all the progress the company had made the last four months with his assistance. I also told him that I had been a man of my word with all our agreements. I pressed the fact that it was very damaging to our relationship to have someone from our office give his department damaging misinformation. I pleaded with Sanchez to stay the course. We had thousands of customers and hundreds of employees who would be affected, but he was now on the side of Fulton who needed our company to be as weak as we could be for the final hearing of the arbitration panel.

The best way to do that was to issue a no new business order. No one received a heads up. Our attorney was livid. Our act of cooperation was supposed to buy us time and calm the waters. It bought us seven days.

On March 17, Fulton issued a no new business order. We decided to go ahead and with our meeting with the Texas Department of Insurance on the 20th. I told Dad he should attend the meeting with Hector and me. I thought maybe he could talk sense into someone with his knowledge of the financial side of our business. When we arrived, Fulton again said she believed that a convicted felon couldn't be at the meeting. It was agreed Dad could stay.

Larry Brandes gave his summary of the Hannover case. Davey asked if I would be willing to appoint a manager to our company with the financial experience to implement the new business plan. I said I would welcome anyone who could help. He had someone in mind, and dialed Dale Williams number. He was a very accomplished man from Kansas who would later be nominated by President Barack Obama as a U.S Attorney. Dan requested that he be allowed to hire his attorney, David Smith. I also accepted his request.

I met Dale Williams and David Smith in person at our home office the following Monday. Dale was a tall slender man who appeared to have a gentle nature. David was a white haired, middle aged, intelligent looking man who could be cast in a role as a corporate attorney. They spent days in the office across the hall from mine looking over everything from top to bottom with our company numbers.

This action by Texas caused an explosion of media coverage in several states bombarding our offices with interview requests. We also received a call from our bank that they were very nervous about the recent news reports. Forever Enterprises had a $9 million- dollar loan with Southwest Bank.

It started to feel like all the bad news was coordinated. The Missouri Department of Insurance sent the report of their recent audit, which completely ignored the 1994 Missouri Consent Agreement. The most important agreement from those negotiations was that our insurance policies would be valued at their face amount not cash value. It was déjà vu 14 years later. Meanwhile, the closing arguments were being made before the arbitration panel. It would take at least 30 days to receive their final ruling.

Dale Williams and David Smith had a conference call with the Texas Department of Insurance to report their findings and opinions of Lincoln and NPS. They both had attended the closing arguments at the arbitration hearing, and they agreed that there was a very good chance that Lincoln would be awarded a favorable outcome. Our attorney told us that Williams reported that they did not uncover any fraudulent activity or criminal business plan on our part. They told them that, yes, there were sloppy procedures and commission adjustments that needed to be made for the older ages, but ours was a company that could rehabilitate, survive, and grow. Fulton fired Williams and Smith four days after their conference call.

She then moved to put our company in formal receivership rehabilitation. Immediately our St. Louis home office was swarmed with Texas regulators. Fuller appointed her brother, Charles, as lead counsel for our company Receivership. Formerly, Charles had been working out of his house making $50,000 a year. His new position, as reported in public court documents, would pay him over $780,000 a year. Charles Fulton's first official act was to immediately stay the arbitration ruling and have the court seal the final ruling.

When the final ruling was sealed, the Fulton's had successfully locked the door to our company's rehabilitation and thrown away the key. To this day that ruling is sealed. Were there millions awarded to our company? No one knows.

CHAPTER 36:

What Was Left to Survive?

One of the toughest, saddest days of my life was telling our loyal company employees it was over. They had been fighting the whole way through, putting in long hours, hoping for the company's survival. I had attended every regulatory meeting with those lives constantly on my mind. I thought I had the ability to create a different outcome for everyone. I will never shake that feeling of all those lives affected by the closing of our company. It will no doubt haunt the dark places of my mind forever.

The family had a meeting at Howard Wittner's law office with Kati, Mom, Dad, Tyler, Julie and me. The local newspaper had called and said they were preparing a Sunday story. Howard said, "Everyone is going to be fine. It will just be a couple of weeks of bad press."

Kati spoke up, "I'm going to obtain a criminal defense attorney. I have a much different opinion of how this is all going to play out. These people are out for blood. If you're smart, you'll get representation, too."

I looked at Kati, "I've not done anything criminal. Why would I need a criminal attorney? What did the company do criminally wrong?"

"It doesn't work that way," she said. "The government can take down anyone if they choose to target you."

I stared at the floor. I knew Katie was right, and the thought froze me down to my bones.

There was no hiding from a collapse. It isn't like you hang a sign on the door, "We are out of business." It was all so public. We got our friends together for dinner the night before the big article. I shared what was going on, and that there was going to be a nasty article in the paper the next day. "It is not a big deal," said our friend Joe. "We'll be wrapping our garbage with the page's tomorrow."

The St. Louis Post Dispatch came out that Sunday blazing an above the fold picture of my brother and me taken for our TIME Magazine article with the bold headline, *"Big Dreams Buried by Big Questions."*

I had lived my life striving to be a role model to my daughters. There would be no way to properly respond with our story under the full weight and force of the media and the government narrative.

The Sunday article led with… *"if the funeral industry has celebrities, they are the Cassity's of St. Louis… With an HBO Documentary. It is said the family inspired the HBO Series SIX FEET UNDER. The parents received press a couple of years ago when they sold their house on Nantucket for $16 million to Google's CEO. The Cassity men – Doug and his two sons, Brent and Tyler – even look like movie stars: handsome in an All-American way with chiseled features and perfect hair. Ambitious, they set out to revolution-ize everything from prepaid funerals to how Americans memorialize the dead. The father – a man who worked behind the scenes – built an empire, prov-ing second acts in life are possible. His sons branched out with innovations, garnering acclaim. The family made millions. But now, the family's empire appears pushed to the breaking point.*

Last month, regulators took control of three companies that make up the heart of the Cassity holdings. Government agencies in at least 10 states are trying to sort out what happened. Their attention is focused on one unsexy, but lucrative part of their sprawling firm – prepaid funerals. This was Forever's financial engine, spin-ning off cash and powering promises of change.

Regulators are trying to determine if enough money remains to honor the pre-paid funerals of perhaps 100,000 people. "Everything is just falling apart", said Ron Hast publisher of Mortuary Management and Funeral Monitor magazines. It is just ricocheting across the United States."

This article went on to fill up a newspaper page describing the history of our business, and the confusion over what had happened.

Everything was right out in the open and examined. The regulators created a self-fulfilling prophecy. Their theory was that our business was not sustainable. Then they began taking the arms and legs off the business model, and said, "See, I told you it wasn't sustainable."

Dale Williams and others knew we would have been able to sell our way out of the crisis. Proof was that the company had to refund $1.5 million of that week's preneed sales to our loyal funeral homes. This article was the kickoff of five years of unmerciful one-sided press reports.

Oddly, life went on. I was in charge of running the St. Louis Children's Hospital golf tournament the Monday after the Sunday article. This tournament hosted celebrities, and all the business who's who in St. Louis. This was the last place I wanted to be. Mike Shanahan Jr., a longtime friend, called to give me a pep talk. He and his Dad had just recently been through a very similar nightmare.

"My Dad always told me," he said. "In times like these you have to suit up, show up, and shut-up. You can't hide, so show strength. No one wants to hear the sad story. Just be yourself. People will say, "I saw him, and he seems to be doing fine. Maybe there is more to the story."

As hard as it was, I took Mike's advice to heart. I learned that if this was going to be a long battle in my hometown there would be no hiding out. I was going to be the same Brent Cassity everyone had always known.

After the golf tournament, it was time to figure out what I had left to work with in order for the business to survive. We still had PLICA Insurance Company. I was going to need to meet with my insurance brokers to calm any fears they, no doubt, would have had from the press reports. We still had our cemetery and funeral homes. I would have to dig deep to make sure we could continue to make our loan payments to the bank. Surely, they would be looking for any reason to call in our loan. Howard had told my Dad that we should put more assets up for collateral to the bank. We included my house and my parent's house in St. Louis. These new assets added value of our collateral to $14.5 million for the $9 million loan.

It was determined it would be better for the company to handle our debt with the bank breaking off Hollywood Forever from Forever Enterprises with an internal sale. This created extra monthly cash to pay the loan payment to the bank. The bank president, with whom I had been friendly over the years, pulled me aside and said, "I can hold everything together while you try to unravel from this mess. But, Brent if you get indicted, the bank will call the note. It will be out of my hands."

Every night I came home, Julie and I would huddle up for our nightly ritual to try and figure out our next step. Our girls were in private schools and the tuition was very expensive. I was going to try to do everything I could to keep them there.

Dad and Howard had signed off on a new lease for office space for PLICA. The office was only a couple of blocks away from our corporate headquarters where we had occupied 90% of the seven story building the last 25 years. Our new home was a bland nondescript building in a small low-profile office. I also created a personal office for myself at Bellerive cemetery.

I felt like I was living two lives for a while. The new life that was fighting for survival through the dark unknown, and my old life with my friends at the country club playing golf, going to dinners and parties, and putting on a positive front for my girls.

Ryan Manczuk, one of the owners of the gym where I worked out weekly had become a close friend. He'd been through some difficult times in his life and we shared most everything with each other. No matter what battle I was tackling that week, Ryan would keep things in perspective. It was helpful to talk to someone who wasn't directly involved in the crisis.

CHAPTER 37:

The PLICA Disaster

Dad and I met with Howard Wittner at the University Club bar to discuss how PLICA would operate going forward. Howard had survived his near-death experience five months earlier, but his memory had been dramatically altered. Donna, his secretary, took notes for him because he could not remember long or short term details. His personality was noticeably different. He had lost his self-confident demeanor, and seemed fragile.

Kirk, Howard's youngest son, who had joined his dad's law firm, was increasingly becoming someone Howard relied on when making decisions. There was something about Kirk that didn't seem quite right. He had the personality of an oversized, offensive brute who could possibly be employed by a crime boss.

Dad and Howard had been like brothers as long as I could remember. They had a deep trust in one another, but something began to splinter after Howard's health crisis, and Kirk had become involved with Howard's daily decision making. It was the first time in my life that I realized my Dad was questioning Howard's loyalty and trust. Dad knew that if he and Howard did not walk through this crisis together hand and hand, only bad things would happen.

I was moving straight ahead to find a suitor for PLICA. The only way we would have anywhere close to the money we needed to defend ourselves was to sell it. A newer friend of mine, Don Davis, had recently cashed in on a large bank sale. He was actively looking for acquisition opportunities. The best way to way to describe Don is a fun-loving guy with a big heart, and an incredible eye for putting together deals. That is a talent not taught in school.

One day on the golf course, I told Don, if I won the next hole he owed me the chance to tell him about our company, PLICA. I won the hole. I told him it was licensed in 35 states, it wrote over $45 million in premiums a year, with $18 million in reserves, and over $27 million in capital and surplus. Don said he had an investor who might be interested. Once Don got into the due diligence on the company things started to move along at a quick pace.

Strange things started to occur internally. I received a disturbing call from Kirk Wittner, saying that he did not want Dad or me working around anything that had to do with PLICA. He told me that you Cassity's are like poison and will kill anything you touch.

I reminded him that we owned PLICA, not him; and that I had been working to keep the company's top producers on board with us. "They are growing our business," I said. "Don't forget we're on the same team."

In a cold voice, he said, "Go fuck yourself, Brent. And stay out of my way." My only response was, Kirk you must be out of your mind."

I found out from an attorney who was working in Wittner's firm that the Wittner's were trying to put together a deal with a buyer that would assure themselves equity in the deal, and would cut the Cassity's out of the company going forward. On top of that, the deal was to pay out over a number of years without any buyout money upfront. Howard was the Trustee of our family trust, and was making moves against us without notifying Tyler, Mom, or me.

I met with my dad and told him what I had learned. He decided to have a face-to-face meeting with Howard who denied everything. Dad left the meeting knowing that Howard was lying and could no longer be trusted.

Dad had already been talking to a Danielle DeBenedictis who owned her own law firm out of Boston. They had become friends on Nantucket Island. She was interested in being the Trustee of RBT Trust. She also saw a big upside for herself and her law firm to handle the medical malpractice business if we sold the company to Don Davis. Dad and I phoned Danielle, the attorney, and told her about our predicament with Howard. She was in complete agreement that Howard could not be the Trustee if he was working against the beneficiaries of our trust. Tyler and Mom were more than ready to make a change with Howard.

The family moved forward to remove Howard as our Trustee, and we appointed Danielle as the new Trustee. I then signed a stock purchase agreement for PLICA with Davis. But, the Wittner's were not going down without a fight. They had come to see PLICA as their company. Howard immediately filed a lawsuit, which I believe was the first of its kind. He sued the beneficiaries of the Trust for removing him as our Trustee. Howard had a fiduciary responsibility to protect the beneficiaries.

When he became aware that we had submitted a stock purchase agreement to the New York Department of Insurance, he did the unthinkable. He went to the state of Illinois and filed a motion to put PLICA in Rehabilitation.

PLICA was not insolvent by any stretch of the means. He had found a statute that could place a company in Rehabilitation for management chaos. If he could not steal the company, he wanted it taken over by the regulators. He used all the information in the press about Lincoln and NPS to make his argument to the judge. The judge granted his motion. The company's domiciled state of New York automatically recognized the action until there was a hearing in New York. My New York attorney, John Higgins, whose firm represented the likes of AIG, said he had never seen a company put in Rehabilitation without being insolvent or having some form of cash struggles. Howard had shot the company in the head, and effectively killed my $70 million stock purchase agreement. The crazy thing was that dad had given Howard 10% equity in PLICA. He ruined his own opportunity to cash in on the sale. He had lost his mind.

I began working with a lady out of the New York Department of Insurance, named Frankie. She told me this was the craziest situation she had ever been a part of in her tenure. She wanted to keep the profitable company moving forward because it was a solid company with a strong client base. She encouraged me to meet with the brokers and assure them that this would all be worked out. I again met with our brokers. They were sticking with the company as long as we could still provide the same type of product and services.

I was at my oldest daughter Courtney's high school graduation day. Our family had found our seats to get ready for the ceremony. I looked down and saw an incoming call on my phone from Frankie. I excused myself and walked out of the auditorium. Frankie said, "Brent, this is all above my pay grade, but the Federal government agencies must all be working together to see to it that you have no way out. The New York Department is taking over the PLICA offices and issuing a no new business order." She said, "I am sorry. This is all out of my hands. I just don't understand why they would take this action."

The U.S. Attorney did not want us to have any means of real income to be able to fight them with what would lie ahead. I came back into the auditorium to Courtney's graduation ceremony, and realized, just like that, that I had just lost my company, and my main source of income. There was my beautiful daughter graduating with honors, and I was so proud of her. I was not going to do anything to bring down the happiness of my family today.

CHAPTER 38:

Parents Marriage Woes

Mom hadn't fully trusted Dad since his imprisonment thirty years before. Now, he didn't think he could fight with her and the government at the same time, so he kept pushing her farther away. Confidentially, he told me he was sure she would leave him if he wasn't able to provide for her. This was dad's insecure thinking. Dad's drinking had gotten much worse with each passing day. I understood that part. Since I, too, was drinking more than I should to dull this nightmare. When I thought about my parents, I knew they fought a lot, but they had grown up conquering the world together.

But, this time, their arguments were different, and much uglier, and I was put right in the middle of their feuds. I got calls in the middle of the night to break up their arguments. It didn't occur to them how much extra stress they were putting on me by forcing me to act as referee.

One night I got a call from Mom. Dad had locked the door to the room above the garage. When I arrived, mom had taken a broom and smashed out the window on the door. There was glass everywhere. They were like two crazed animals who had lost their minds. This particular argument had been started because Mom had taken Dad's name off all their checking accounts. What they were saying and doing to each other was not retrievable.

It just kept getting worse. I got a call from my mom. She said, "Brent, I hate to put more on you but I have just been to see the doctor. They have told me my cancer has returned in my other breast." I felt like I stopped breathing while she was talking. She had been cancer free for over 25 years. Mom was convinced that the cancer had returned because of all the stress. I could not argue with her about that.

Julie jumped right in and started helping my mom. She wanted to find the best doctor. Julie was great at researching these types of things, and she had been through her own crisis with her stroke. Mom needed her support. We had a good friend who was a respected surgeon, who got mom in right away to see her. It turned out that it was exactly the same type of cancer she had before. It was not a cancer that was spreading. It was encapsulated in her breast. The doctor assured her that after the surgery she would be cancer free. They had caught it early.

She would not need to have chemo treatments. This was good news. Dad and Mom were not speaking to each other at the time. Dad did show up the day of the surgery and sat in the waiting room with us. It seemed when he walked into the room that my mom was happy to see him. I was hoping that things could begin to thaw between the two of them. I felt like that was all I was doing nowadays…hoping. We brought my mom back to our house to recover. She was my mom, but Julie was like a daughter to her, taking care of her while she recovered. There were so many emotions we were all dealing with, but we were lucky to have caught this cancer early. Every day was such a battle on so many different fronts, but we were all still fighting through it in our way.

CHAPTER 39:

So I am Indicted?

The actions the government had taken left me nearly broke. Now, NPS and our insurance companies had been seized, and I knew I was going to need to get a good attorney. The U.S. Attorney, Callahan, was only getting started.

My friend, Mike Shanahan, had just gone through a father-son investigation with the same Assistant U.S. Attorney who was investigating my family. I picked up the phone and called him to get his opinion about who I should hire for an attorney. Mike told me that he thought that Barry Short was the best around. Barry was exactly what I was looking for. He was an accomplished and respected criminal defense attorney. Most importantly, he gave me a confident feeling that he believed in me. Barry agreed to take me on as a client, but I was running out of money.

My mom still had some money after selling the house in Nantucket. I could not believe I had worked all my life to build a successful business, and I was now asking my mom for money for my criminal defense. I had grown the company from $30 million a year in sales to over $125 annually. I never diversified by buying other assets. All my wealth had been taken by the government. Here I was with virtually nothing left to show for what I had created over the last 20 years.

Barry went right to work on the case. He said it was clear from all the emails and company documents over the years that I was not involved in the financial side of our business. My thought was that once everyone recognized this fact I would not be a target in their investigation. The U.S. Attorney's theory was that the bank trust was underfunded by not recognizing the face amount of the insurance policies in Trust, therefore, every transaction loan or acquisition the company made was deemed to be illegal. But even if this was their stance, finance was never my role.

"Don't they need to show criminal intent on my part to be charged with a crime?" I asked.

Barry said, "The Federal Government can indict anyone on any day if they decide to do so. We have to make sure we point out the relevant information about your role, or lack thereof, early and often."

From 2007 to 2013, the years of investigation, I was never given the opportunity to talk to or sit down with the FBI or U.S. Attorney's office. It was different for Dad. Scott Rosenblum, the nephew of Howard Wittner, was Dad's attorney. Scott and Howard had a falling out 10 years before. Scott left the firm and became one of the best-known criminal defense attorneys in the Midwest. Dad and Scott did have a sit-down meeting with the assistant U.S. Attorney investigating our case. Jeff Jensen, was a tall handsome man right out of central casting, and was later promoted to be U.S. Attorney of the Eastern District. Jensen told Dad that he was the guy they wanted. He would cut his family loose from all of this if he would plead and agree to a 10-year sentence. Dad told them to go fuck themselves, and that he and his family would be vindicated in court. Scott later told me that there was a deal that involved pleading and the sons would be spared. They were using us as leverage.

It crushed me when I was told this story. I loved and idolized Dad. I had spent my life trying to make him proud. I had run into a burning building to meet with the regulators when he asked me to protect our family and company. He had gone through this before with the federal government. I was now a father of three daughters. Was he that confident he would win going to trial? It seared a hole in my heart that will never leave me.

I finally got the call I had been dreading since this all had started. I had ridden my bike out to our family's favorite beach in Nantucket. The sun was starting to set on the ocean with the waves crashing onto the beach. Barry Short's name popped up on my phone. I answered. "Brent," he said. "It's it is not good news. They have decided they are going to indict you. It is a travesty, and I have done all I can do. They are traveling down this path for their own reasons, and you are the unlucky one who has been swept up in this mess."

I knew the statistics that 97% of the individuals charged or indicted plea. Meaning once you are indicted 97% are convicted. It is damn near like a conviction when you get indicted. Barry said, "Evan and I have talked, and we think we could get you a much better plea deal if you do it right away." I told Barry I was not ready to throw in the towel.

I still wanted my date in Court. I sat down on the cliff looking down on the ocean waves crashing down on the beautiful beach. I had lived such an incredible life with Julie and the girls. How could it all have come to this? I had tried to avoid anything like this happening since I was 15 years old going to visit my dad in prison. Now I was going to be indicted.

I rode my bike back to the house, knowing that I was going to have to share this scary news with Julie and the girls. I knew I had to appear strong; that I was still fighting. We would get through this because of the strength of our family. When I told the family, the girls just accepted the news as it is. "Okay Dad, you will beat them." Julie knew the news was a lot more ominous, but she played along with the girl's spirit of fighting and winning. I still believed I wanted to go to trial and win too.

The girls handled the indictment news like the dreaded news of me recently telling Carly and the Baby that they were going to need to transfer to the Clayton Public Schools. They knew I could no longer afford the tuition at MICDS. They did not want to make me feel bad. The Cassity girls had made a huge impact at MICDS. The Baby had just won the coveted Elliot award that was voted on by the faculty and students as the most outstanding student. Carly had just won a tennis state championship with her older sister Courtney. They said they understood, and it might be fun going to a public school. Carly and the Baby, were outstanding students and athletes at Clayton High School. They gave me one of my proudest days as a Dad. I was at the Missouri State Tennis finals. On one court was Carly playing as a State Finalist for singles, and the Baby was on the other court as a State Finalist for doubles. My other proud Dad moment was Courtney gritting through the State tournament in

38 -degree weather playing with a broken wrist wrapped almost like a cast. Courtney later applied and received an academic scholarship from SMU. I am so proud and love my girls so much. I am so impressed with their strength and courage through all of this. As much as I tried to shield them through the nightmare, they were always there standing tall. They just kept excelling at whatever they went to accomplish, regardless of the storm surrounding them. They created their own chapter of profiles in courage.

CHAPTER 40:

Get a Job

Julie and I huddled together for our ritual, nightly catch up. "You'll need to find another job after losing PLICA.," she said.

"I know," I said.

I still had the two cemeteries in St. Louis. I had never taken a paycheck from any of our funeral or cemetery operations. I had earned my income by building the national sales volume at NPS, and taking a percentage of the monthly premiums from PLICA. I was now making nothing.

Julie and I decided that I could teach her how to run the cemetery. Jodi, Julie's sister, could help. Jodi had worked at NPS and PLICA for years. That would free me up to get another source of income.

Don Davis and I had become close friends while we were working on the PLICA deal. He had an interest in buying a golf course. He told me if I worked with him on securing Winghaven Country Club, that I could run the club for his investment group. I went to work on the deal and we bought the club for a good price.

I was hopeful about the new opportunity. Barry, my attorney, made me feel like he was engaged and smart in how he was moving forward representing me. But his wife who had been very sick with cancer, had recently died and he was grieving.

He had become hard to track down and after making several calls with no response, I called his assistant Evan. "Things are not good with Barry," he said. "He's gone through a deep depression since his wife died and I'm afraid he is not going to be working for a while."

Finally, one of the partners called. Barry was not going to be able to go forward with my case. The timing could not have been worse. I had paid Barry a large amount of money to take my defense through trial. Evan informed me that there were not any funds left.

I told them I felt terrible for Barry, but this clearly was not fair to me. It was bad enough that I was in the process of being indicted, but to lose my attorney and my defense dollars was devastating. The law partners relented and cut me a check minus $25,000 of the original amount. I didn't have time to sit and sulk. I had to focus on finding a new attorney who would have to catch up on months of research.

Dad's attorney recommended a lawyer who was good at writing briefs and had won a case in the United States Supreme Court. When Julie and I met Rick at his office, he appeared to look like a bruiser. He was stocky and square-jawed, dressed nicely but not completely polished. He had somewhat of a quirky personality and would say things to get a laugh. He assured Julie and me that he had been keeping up with our case with the other attorneys who were already on the case. We decided to go with Rick because of his experience. I also believed he could work well with the other attorneys. We never had the personal chemistry that Barry and I had over the last several months. I missed that connection as the case rolled forward, but there was nothing I could do about that.

The indictments finally came in the news across all media platforms. The government had indicted six people in the criminal case. They were my Dad, Randy Sutton (President and CFO of NPS), Nicki Province (Vice President and Executive Assistant to Dad), Dave Wulf (NPS Investment Advisor), Howard Wittner (RBT Trustee and Company Attorney), and me. As strange as life was, my day of arraignment was also my first day on the job at Winghaven Country Club. I went down to the Eagleton Federal Courthouse with Rick that morning. When we entered the courtroom the judge read off the charges. I was being indicted for mail fraud, wire fraud, money laundering, and allowing a felon to work in the business of insurance.

The government's trick is to take those charges and stack them with multiple charges, such as, over 25 years, counting every time you mailed something or every time you executed a bank wire. Each of these charges carried five to twenty years. Once my charges were added up, I was looking at over 900 years in prison if I was convicted on all counts.

There's nothing like the gut-punch you get when you see the United States of America versus your name. I read through the document and thought, this is someone else, not me. I had no idea about the statute of not allowing a felon to work in the business of insurance, a federal statute passed by Congress in 1994 that I had only recently become familiar with through my attorneys.

Because we were charged with running an illegal criminal enterprise, every contract the company sent in the mail was deemed illegal. Anything the company ever bought was money laundering because it was from "ill-gotten gains." There was never any criminal intent of mine to break any law, but none of that mattered. All funerals for every client had been paid. We had paid over $500 million of death claims, and all premiums and commissions to funeral directors. Everything our company did was audited every year by the state of Texas, where our insurance company was domiciled.

Another curious point was that the State of Missouri amended the 436 Preneed Statute in 2009, a year after NPS had been shut down. The new statute made our old business practices illegal, but we were being prosecuted under the old statute, another crucial point to make in a courtroom.

Our civil lawsuit was filed by the plaintiffs in the Eastern District Federal Court before Judge Webber. Larry Pozner, a highly respected attorney from Colorado representing the Special Deputy Receiver, filed a motion to freeze all our assets in July of 2010. Judge Webber made his ruling March 23^r, 2011. He stated in his ruling, *"He was not persuaded that the plaintiffs in the case had a "fair chance" of succeeding on the merits on their equitable claims, which are based on the allegations that the defendants unjustly enriched themselves by misappropriating pre-need trust funds."*

I often wonder, if Judge Webber had ruled months earlier, would it have made the U.S Attorney's office stop to take pause before they indicted me in November of 2010? It definitely showed that when both sides presented evidence to a Federal Judge, there was a fair argument to be made that the government's theory could be plagued with gaping holes.

I met Rick Sindel in the lobby of the Eagleton Federal Building. He assured me this would not take long. We both entered the courtroom, and there stood the men who had made my life a living hell, Assistant U.S. Attorneys Burlington and Morrison. Burlington looked like a young fit surgeon with a premature receding hairline and wire frame glasses. He had his teeth deep into this case and was not going to let go until he won.

Morrison looked like a career government employee. I never had the opportunity to speak to either of them over the last three years. I decided I would walk over and introduce myself, so I could look both of them in the eye. I wanted them to know I was a real person, not just a name on a piece of paper.

After I pleaded not guilty to the charges, I was led downstairs to a jail a few floors down. I was fingerprinted, photographed, and released on pre-trial bail. I would have a pre-trial probation officer whom I would now report to, requiring home visits. It also required me to call the probation officer every Wednesday, and to also notify them and gain permission if I would be traveling outside the Eastern district of Missouri. The probation also required random drug tests.

I had been having dreams that I was in a dark room and I was struggling to find the door. Every time I got close, I would get hit by something or someone. In many ways, the dream had come true.

Once I was back to my car, I had to pump myself back up. It was now time to drive to my new job at Winghaven Country Club. Nothing like having a news story like this follow you to your first day of work. But, I was excited to focus on a new job.

CHAPTER 41:

Winghaven Safe Haven

November of 2010, I was starting a new job after spending the last twenty years of my life working for a company I owned. It was invigorating to jump into something new. Wing Haven was its own suburban community outside of St. Louis County. Our goal was to bring at least 100 new members to the club. I would need to put on my marketing hat, but I had already been thinking about how to do it.

I called a meeting with the staff and shared with them our goals for the club. This was the stuff I really enjoyed doing when we bought new funeral homes. I have always believed it is so important to create excitement and buy in with big goal, to sell the dream of being part of a team, of being something bigger than themselves.

I shared that we would add at least 100 new members within the next year. We were going to create a new upstairs bar and restaurant. We would build a new covered 1,500 square foot deck overlooking the 18th green, and connecting to the new upstairs bar and restaurant. We would also paint the ugly brick on the building creating an overnight makeover. I wanted to introduce a new classy logo for the club to replace the current awful one. This new classy logo would also be displayed on the new stone and black granite entry sign to the club, to replace the flimsy cheap looking plastic one. We would fix the drainage on the greenside bunkers. All of this would be featured with renderings for the club members, and new prospective members. We would also be including these renderings with our welcome back letters to all the club members who had resigned over the years promoting all the new changes.

I told the group that I wanted to include them in the membership drive. I told them for every member they brought to the club as a new member, they would get paid the equivalent of the first month's dues. This got everyone excited. Nathan Charnes, the golf pro, who had been at Winghaven for eight years had never brought in a new member. With the new incentive, Nathan brought in 38 new members.

I told Don that I wanted him to host a membership meeting where all the members were invited. We would share with them all the new great changes displayed with our renderings. I wanted to include the members in our membership drive, so we told the members to bring their friends and neighbors back to the club. The members would get two months free dues for every member they brought to the club as new members. This meeting shot a lightning bolt of new energy and enthusiasm through the Winghaven membership.

The last piece that would drive a lot of revenue was the need for corporate golf outings, and weddings. We did not have anyone focused on doing this big job. I researched the area and found a girl called Adria who was killing it with weddings and golf outings at the Missouri Bluffs, just up the road from us. I walked into Adria's office, and asked if she could give me a tour of the facilities. Adria was an intelligent attractive girl, with a great friendly smile. When we were done with the tour, I said, "Adria I want to hire you for Winghaven Country Club." I shared with her all the things we were doing that she could promote. I told her I would give her 10% of everything she brought to the club. Adria was sold. She was an outstanding addition to everything that we had planned. My favorite golf outing that we snagged was the Annual Mizzou Alumni golf outing. It had been at another club for the last 20 years.

Winghaven added 142 new members the first year of our operation. Adria had the place booked up with new golf outings and weddings. The new membership was loving the club with all the new improvements. Our new logo improved our pro shop sales by over 38% because everyone wanted to be outfitted with the cool new club logo on everything. I loved hanging out and playing golf with these members. They mostly lived in the Winghaven community and soaked up all the new opportunities to socialize at the club. Our food and beverage revenues dramatically spiked with these fun-loving members.

Winghaven became a safe haven for me with its unpretentious, friendly community. Setting new goals with a plan, and seeing my ideas come to life and succeeding with the club brought me hope.

CHAPTER 42:

Bank Calls Our Loan

I knew the other shoe was going to drop with the bank in regards to our bank loan after my indictment. The bank had previously told me that they would call our loan if I were to get indicted, regardless of the fact that we had recently, and dramatically over collateralized the loan. They called the loan in a couple of months after my indictment. I received a certified letter in the mail that the bank was foreclosing on my house. Now this mess had come to my home's doorstep. Julie and my girls were going to be directly affected by this nightmare, losing the place my daughters had called home their whole lives. How was I going to battle against this not happening to my family? I picked up the phone and called the bank. They agreed to a meeting to discuss the situation.

I called Jack Spooner, who had been involved with representing our company over the years. I asked him if he would go to this meeting with me. I knew the bank would have their high-powered attorney there. Jack agreed to go with me.

This turned out to be a very ugly meeting. The Bank's attorney, Sara Melly, spent most of the meeting making all kinds of threats in various different ways. I felt like she must have been related to Emma Fulton the Texas Insurance Attorney. She had read, studied, and highlighted the book of 'mean.' The meeting ended with the bank giving me a lifeline. The bank was giving me six months to sell the bank note to another party or investor. My drop-dead date would be December 24th. Yes, Christmas eve. Either I found a buyer for the note, or my family was out of our home on Christmas Eve. I had always thought I was a good salesman, but being an indicted man trying to sell a $7.2 million bank note in six months was going to be some heavy lifting.

When Jack and I left the law offices, Jack said, "Brent, do you have any way to pull something like this off?" I told him I had some ideas, but it was going to be tough considering the situation I was in with the government, but I was definitely not giving up.

The next day I had a meeting at Don's office with Don, Harry Freeman, and Mike Hopson. This was the group of guys that Don had as minority investors with WingHaven Country Club and Purus Vodka, Freeman Homes, along with some other commercial real estate deals. Harry Freeman and I had gone to DeSmet High School together. If you looked up Country Club looking guy in the dictionary…Harry's picture would pop up. He was perpetually tan, and friends often joked that Harry just looked wealthy. His wife Julie and my Julie were very close friends. Our kids had grown up together. Harry and I had been golf partners with the two-man golf tournament at our club for years. Harry's Julie had been incredibly supportive helping to get Julie decorating jobs with our friend group. I didn't know Mike as well, but he was also a member at our Country Club. Don liked to include Mike on deals to help with due diligence on investment opportunities.

We all huddled around the table, and I let them know the whole story of what was going on with this bank loan. I let the guys know how we had over collateralized the loan with additional assets when things had started to go south. I laid down all the assets that were included in this loan. Bellerive Cemetery had an old appraisal valued at $8.4 million. This was before we had built the first and second phase of the beautiful Georgia white marble community mausoleum. The value of Bellerive would have been at least $10 million. The Oak Hill Cemetery was valued at $2 million, my parents knockdown house had a value of $1 million, and my house had a value of at least $1.5 million. The loan had $14.5 of collateral for a $7.2 million- dollar loan. This deal was in Don's wheelhouse. He had been in the banking business his whole life, and had a talent for buying discounted notes. Don said he thought he could get the note bought for under $5 million.

Don said this could be a friendly deal that would be good for everyone. The new company would continue to have the Cassity's run the successful cemeteries, and Harry and Don could use Freeman homes to develop the valuable home lot in the envied location in Old Town Clayton. Don said this would be an opportunity where my Mom could work with Freeman homes on future projects. I would be able to keep my house from being foreclosed on. We all agreed that this could be a solid deal that our group would start pursuing.

Julie had been waiting on pins and needles to hear how this meeting had gone. I got home that night, and we huddled up in our home's bar room with our dogs to go over the meeting. I told Julie we had a long way to go, but I really believed the bank would eventually come to an agreement with the guys. The real positive was that the bank really wanted to be as far away from this loan as possible. The last thing the bank wanted was the daunting task of dealing with trying to unload two cemeteries. Banks are very unfamiliar with valuing and selling cemeteries. They used the fear of foreclosing on my house to make me go to work on getting this note sold for them.

I began to work with the group to help them with all the due diligence to help get a good bank interested in a financing deal. Mike Hopson was able to get real familiar with all the numbers in the deal. The more he looked at everything, the more he thought this was an incredible opportunity. This was a friendly deal. I was helping give tours of the cemetery to the prospective banks. I was able to show how we had created revenue opportunities year after year, and how the future plans would continue to make Bellerive the most sought-after cemetery in the St. Louis area.

As the clock was ticking on my deal with the bank, Don was beginning to have his own financial difficulties. He was one of the majority stock holders with a local bank. He was attempting to take control of that bank, but at the last minute the owner of the bank reneged on the deal. Don had his shares of the bank up as collateral with his other deals across town. The bank collapsed, which caused a domino effect with the other banks demanding that Don put up new collateral or cash.

Don was the majority partner on several deals including Winghaven Country Club and Purus Vodka. His minority partners began having cash calls that would eventually start to diminish his status as the majority partner in his partnerships.

Don was eventually able to successfully negotiate terms with the bank for buying my note before the Christmas Eve deadline. I had barely survived a disastrous foreclosure from the bank. The investment group for the Cassity Bank Note needed an additional investor because of Don's financial situation. The group decided to bring in a guy that had just cashed out as a high-ranking marketing executive with Anheuser Busch. Evan Athanas happened to be a guy that I knew and liked, andthat was a fellow Old Warson Country Club member. I had the job of selling Evan on the opportunity of what an incredible investment this would be for him. Evan and I met and toured Bellerive. Evan was a guy in his late 30's who was pressed and put together, very cautious, without a hair out of place. I went over the numbers with him, and we toured the luxurious grounds of the cemetery. I was able to show him how I had continually created marketing opportunities for our families over the years. Evan was a marketing guy, so he was impressed how I took a no name cemetery and converted it to the most sought after place in St. Louis to be buried. Evan was sold on the opportunity. He asked me if I had a problem continuing to develop and manage the cemetery going forward without being the owner. I told Evan that I welcomed the opportunity to be part of the new ownership group doing what I loved doing.

Every time I avoided a catastrophe the government would pop up to create a new barrier for me. Burlington, the Assistant U.S. attorney was monitoring everything that I was doing. I am sure he was surprised that I escaped foreclosure in December. Now it was time for him to stick his nose in the new investment group. He called and demanded to have a meeting with Harry Freeman and Evan Athanas. Burlington told the guys that it would not be wise to have Don or myself as part of any deal that goes forward. He pulled out two three ring binders marked Don Davis and Brent Cassity. He told Harry and Evan that they could create these binders on whomever they chose, so it would be smart to follow their advice. This meeting scared the hell out of Harry and Evan, as it should have. The Government is ruthless, and they can destroy whomever they choose, when they choose.

Our friendly deal that we had structured took a drastic turn. If the deal went through I would not be any part of managing Bellerive going forward. The immediate question was if Evan would be scared out of the deal. Evan and Harry had a talk with Don effectively cutting him out of the deal that he had put together. It was such a good investment opportunity Evan was persuaded to stay in the deal. My part of the deal was to get my house untangled as collateral from the new note, and the new group would issue us a satisfaction of judgement to me. That meant that the Cassity family would be released from any debt obligations from the old bank loan. Evan laid this out in an email to me, and he said that the deal could not have happened without all my efforts. This was going to be a much better option than having the bank foreclose on the loan on Christmas Eve, and my losing everything. I had worked hard on getting the deal to this point, and I felt like everything should be okay.

CHAPTER 43:

National Sales Manager of PURUS Vodka

I was spending hours a day trying to respond to my attorney about issues for my defense in my indictment. I had put together a timeline of all the events leading up to the NPS fiasco that was supplemented with corresponding emails and documents. This took me over two months to compile for my attorney. I never felt like Rick Sindel was wanting to put in the time necessary to get into the meat of my defense to prove that I was not involved with the things I was being charged with. He was happy to have his name associated with this big case that served as a marketing tool to get even more clients. That was definitely the feeling that I had.

I never got over the fact that I had lost Barry Short as my attorney. Barry was all about trying to figure out a way to show the prosecutors who I was, and how I fit into this overall case. My frustration was continually mounting with Rick, and it was creating a bitterness that I did not like seeing in myself. I had always been a guy that was very good about compartmentalizing and focusing on the things I could control. Dealing with the government was putting that way of thinking to the test. You start feeling like you don't have much control over anything. Working on new things was the one thing that was keeping me sane.

When Don and his investment group acquired Winghaven Country Club they also acquired Purus Vodka. Purus Vodka was an Italian Organic wheat vodka that had been created by Anheuser Busch. The company that acquired

Anheuser Busch did away with the vodka and tequila divisions to focus solely on their beer brands. Purus had a very cool bottle, and the vodka had won some medals in taste competitions. It was a very smooth tasting vodka, and organic items were a hot trend for marketing purposes. Don had decided to hire the marketing guys from A-B that had worked on the brand. This seemed like a good idea since none of the investors had any experience in the spirits market. Don's investor group was also able to secure a $3.5 million line of credit to help grow the new company.

I had been working at Winghaven, but I had also had an interest in seeing what it would be like to market a liquor. The guys from A-B did not want me to be a part of anything they were doing. They did not like the fact that I was indicted, and they thought it would hurt the brand. I was thinking that a good story in the liquor business is one place where a wild story could help market and sell the brand.

It did not take long for the A-B guys to run through the line of credit. I think they thought they were still at A-B. They had not created any significant distribution for the product. Purus was sitting on 25,000 cases of vodka that needed to find a way to be distributed. Once the money ran out they left too.

Don called a meeting with Harry Freeman, Mike Hopson, and me. He said, "Brent, you are going to get your wish if you want it. We need someone to try and sell this vodka without hardly any money to promote it." I told the group that I would like to try. Mike Hopson would be the new President, and I would be the new National Sales Manager. I had known Mike at the country club as the little gambling golfer who loved good restaurants. He had a lot of energy, was personable, and was good with numbers. I wasn't starting this project without any knowledge. I had kept up with what was going on the last two years.

My whole life I have looked at similar models and borrowed ideas to create and grow companies. Vodka companies had a ton of models out there. We could not afford to have the celebrity endorsement like many brands do. I had researched start-ups and what might fit our plan. The story and plan of action I liked best was Tito's Vodka. Tito had started small without much money in

Texas. His plan was to become the best-known vodka in Texas, and then he began expanding nationally. He leveraged his local contacts with a homegrown entrepreneurial story that Texans always love. He also priced his vodka at a price for the masses at $15.95.

I told the guys the first thing we needed to do was get out of our distribution agreements with the A-B beer distributors. Beer distributors take orders; they don't hand sell an Italian Organic Wheat vodka. They are not trained that way. These agreements were in place only because A-B created the vodka and planned to use their own distributors to push the new product. We did not have any leverage with these distributors, and they had proved they could not move the product. We needed a strong credible Liquor Distributor to partner with, and then try to become big in our home market. I also knew we needed our own unique marketing niche at popular bars. I came up with the idea of infusion vodka recipes, and the big infusion jar would sit on the bar counter with our Purus vodka logo. Vodka infusions were becoming popular, and we would just ride that wave. We would supply the bartenders the big glass jars. The bartenders liked this concept, because it gave them something unique to make that was easy to pour and serve. The bar needed at least a case of vodka to make the infusion, instead of selling a bottle a time on the shelf. This was a big hit in the St. Louis bar scene. We would promote infusion party nights with our Purus girls going around serving the customers shots and posting all of these fun party pics to our social media sites. Our cases per month began to pick up. Now it was time to go tell our story to a Liquor Distributor.

Mike Hopson found a friend of a friend who had played baseball at Vanderbilt with the son of the Company President of Glazer's that was the second largest liquor distributor nationally. He was able to secure us a meeting with the head of marketing at their Dallas headquarters.

Mike and I flew down to Dallas for the meeting. I had prepared a cool looking marketing newsletter that showed all of our different Purus parties with groups of people drinking Purus. I tried to make the pictures look like the whole city of St. Louis was drinking Purus. We had some fun pictures of all the bartenders pouring from the big infusion jars on the bar tops. I then listed the big grocery store chains, and liquor stores that stocked Purus. We needed someone to take this hot new brand to the next level.

The marketing executive was about an hour late to the meeting. He finally entered the room, and I remember the guy looked like Matt Laur's twin. He apologized for being late. He said he had just got out of a meeting with a company from Belize that had a two-hour PowerPoint presentation with subtitles. I was thinking, 'um we don't have a PowerPoint presentation.' I didn't know if that was bad or good. He told us he was in a rush because he had to make it over to the Red River Tailgate party that was between the Oklahoma Sooners, and the Texas Football teams. It was an annual thing that was a big deal for Glazer's. He said I only had a few minutes.

I knew it was go time. I quickly went through the history of the Italian Organic Wheat vodka, which was one of a kind. There was no vodka on the market with this much marketability, along with the taste test awards. I then pushed forward our bottle that was on the table. I said there is not a sexier, cooler, teardrop vodka bottle on the shelf of any bar, and our infusion marketing concept not only sells more cases, but is something fun the bartenders enjoy. I said would you be interested at looking at our newsletter? He said, "Of Course." He didn't say anything for an uncomfortable period of time. At first I wasn't sure if we were getting ready to be kicked out of the office, but my gut told me he liked the newsletter that showed our passion for marketing the product in our local bars. He said, "You guys are in the Schnucks and Dierbergs grocery stores? That is impressive." Again, he just sat there reading the newsletter. I didn't know what to do, so I let him continue to read without interrupting him.

Finally, he said, "You guys have elephant size balls to walk in here without a fancy PowerPoint presentation with just your story, a newsletter, and a bottle, but I gotta tell you I like your style. The old school way. That is the way liquor is sold by hand selling the bottle with your story. That is the passion we are looking for to partner to move a brand." He picked up his cell phone and called the Glazer's President in Missouri, and said, "Scott we are going to give Purus a shot in Missouri."

Just like that Purus had the second largest Liquor Distributor in the nation agreeing to buy and promote our product. He said, "Guys, I have to run to the party, but I will be talking about this presentation to the guys at the tailgate. You always want to be memorable in marketing, and you did that today." We shook hands, and off he went. Mike and I just stared at each other in disbelief at what had just happened. Mike said "I know one thing for sure, we need to get out of here and find a bar to do some real partying. This is big!"

It was big, but I had personally agreed to take a pay cut to make this work with Purus. Harry, Mike, and Don told me the company didn't have the funds to pay me like they should, so they paid me half of my salary, and booked the other half to pay me back as we grew the revenues. I was also in agreement to do this because we were still working on closing the bank note with Southwest Bank. I felt like we were all in this together.

CHAPTER 44:

Messy Friend Deal

As the deal was getting closer to a closing with Harry, Evan, and Mike buying the bank note from Southwest Bank, things were getting tenser between the group and me. The feel-good feeling for the deal had dissolved since Don had been removed from the investment group. I was in a strange position because I was working for Harry and Mike with Purus.

For the new owners to legally be able to own and operate Bellerive Cemetery, they needed Tyler and me to sign over the Cemetery Trust to them. This was the only leverage I had to make sure we were released from the debt, and that I would get the title back to my house. I did not know Evan and Mike as well, but Harry and I had a long friendship. Our wives were great friends, and we traveled with our families on family trips. I felt like Harry would make sure that all the promises that were made would be followed through to the end. I also thought that I had been more than a team player having half of my salary booked. I was owed over $50,000 of booked income while we were negotiating the final pieces of the bank note closing. I had also worked diligently with their new loaning bank to get them comfortable with the historical cemetery numbers and the overall opportunity.

My biggest mistake was not to see the official satisfaction of judgement document before we ever went to closing. I obviously needed an attorney looking over everything to protect our interests.

When Harry and I talked, I felt like he was holding back and pushing away from me. He was acting like I had some disease that he would catch if he stayed in the room with me too long. I now understand that he was getting pressure from someone that all of the promises were not going to be kept. I think this made Harry uncomfortable trying to act like all was good with us. I naively trusted Harry that if something was unfair, he would stand in my corner.

When Julie and I arrived at the title company for the closing, Harry did not attend. Mike Hopson and Evan Athanas were there to close the deal with their attorney. There was a mountain of papers to sign. I did not have the money to have an attorney with me. Once we signed all the closing documents, Mike and Evan said, "Why don't we meet at Bricktops to have a few drinks to celebrate this transaction?" I told them that I would meet them there. While I was driving over to Bricktops, I was going back in my mind over all the documents that we signed. I could not remember signing the satisfaction of judgment release for our family. When I got there, Harry, Mike Hopson, and Evan Athanas were already at the bar. Evan ordered me a drink, and we all toasted to finally getting the deal done. I told the guys I was concerned that we did not sign our release for the satisfaction of judgment. Evan said, "No, I am sure we did, and if we didn't, we can clear that up with the title company." That was the famous last words. This ended up being the beginning of an ugly protracted battle.

I contacted the title company the next day, and there was no unsigned document for the Cassity's satisfaction of judgment. This meant we were still on the hook for the total amount of the $7.2 million loan. Just to review… the friends bought the mortgage at a discount for $4.7 million dollars. They were getting Bellerive Cemetery appraised over $10 million dollars. This also included the Oak Hill cemetery that I had signed over the current lease we were receiving from the operator for $10,000 a month. The value of that cemetery was at least $2 million, which they sold after the transaction. Finally, they had my parent's property with a $1 million value that they also later sold. My house was released back to me, and I sold our house immediately after the closing to a friend. The friends had gotten one hell of a deal. In return they promised to release us from the debt with the satisfaction of judgment and return the deed to my house.

When I talked again to Evan, he said he did not understand why the satisfaction of judgment was not signed. I called Harry to talk about trying to get this done, and he told me Evan was handling this. My Dad had contacted an attorney that he had researched that was supposed to be an expert with this type of situation. The guy seemed like a renegade that didn't seem like he covered all the bases. My Dad was still living in the teardown house. Dad believed that the teardown house was not supposed to be in the transaction as collateral because of some legal reason that was stated in the bank loan papers. The new attorney also believed that Dad was correct. This issue began causing issues with the friend group. All of this was cruising down the wrong lane in the wrong direction.

I was still working for Mike Hopson and Harry Freeman. This all was getting very uncomfortable, and they were still booking half of my income that I desperately needed. Harry was no longer accepting my phone calls, so I decided to send him an email. I laid out what we had all agreed to with the emails between all of us backing up what I was saying. I pled with Harry that we just need to sit down and work this out. I told him with us being friends there was no reason why this couldn't be solved. I told him I really needed his help to resolve this situation. Harry never responded to my email.

Dale Wiley, the new attorney, said we had no choice but to file a lawsuit to force the action to be taken with the satisfaction of judgment. I knew things had finally unraveled with no options. I met with Wiley and my Dad. I said, "I understand this is our last option, but I am going to have to find a new job." It was not a great time for me to be looking for a new job.

Don Davis had been pushed out of everything he had except his dealership that he had bought a few years back. He was now trying to make a go of it with Gateway Buick GMC. Don said, "Brent, I could really use your help in the dealership with your sales, marketing, and operations background. Why don't you just come to work with me at the dealership?" I said, "Don that would be a great opportunity for me. I really appreciate it!" I called Julie to tell her I found a job working at the dealership with Don. She was thrilled. Julie had also found a new job working for Joy Tribout, who had help decorate our home over the years. She had become a good friend of Julie's.

Dale Wiley filed the lawsuit against the friend group. My hopes were that this could be immediately settled, so everyone could avoid the hassle of legal fees and go their separate ways. This lawsuit ended up dragging on for years with incredible heartache for my family. I still to this day do not understand why the friend group refused to follow through with what was promised to me. They got the deal of a lifetime because I was in a desperate situation. Harry was a friend who had known all along what I was going through with the government. Athanas was where his bread was buttered, and this was an ugly end to our friendship.

CHAPTER 45:

The Car Business

Before I started my new job in the car business, my brother in-law Grant and sister in-law Jodi surprised Julie and me with a trip to Rosemary Beach in Florida. They paid for our flight and the condo where we all stayed. Grant is a big 6'4" guy who looks like Will Ferrell's brother, and has the same humor. He and I had become really close over the years. Jodi was like a sister I never had. We always had a blast hanging out with them wherever we were. Grant had spent years in the car business, so it was an opportune time for me to pick his brain about the business. This was a great fun getaway for Julie and me.

When I started my new job, I also knew the clock was ticking on my government case. It was May of 2013, and the Judge had set our court date for the middle of August. I was spending long hours going through documents and emails that my attorney would send me, and I knew I had to make a difference with the new job. I never had enough hours in the day. I hit the new job with gusto. I tried to read all the books and articles about successful people in the car business.

I ran across an interesting article about Everett Buick GMC that was located in Little Rock Arkansas. They had bought their dealership back in 2007 and had grown the business from 70 car sales a month to selling over 500 new cars a month. I knew there had to a story there. This is what I had done all my life. I needed to find a system that worked, and then go talk to the person. I picked up the phone and called the sales manager. I finally got Chad on the phone. He happened to be the son-in-law of the owner. I told him that we were new to the car business, and we were looking for people who were making it work. I told him how impressed I was with their story. We really hit it off on the phone. He was a basketball player that had played Division II. We both talked the same language. I asked him if he could carve out some time next week to meet if I drove down. He said to come on down, and he would show me around. I told Don it was time for us to take a road trip. I filled him in on the Everett story, and my conversation I'd had with Chad.

The next week Don and I arrived at the Everett Dealership. It was impressive. They had outgrown their parking lot. A sea of cars was parked in the grass field next to the dealership. All of the employees were busy, and were all dressed with the same colored Everett shirts. I was thinking how ironic this was that I had set-up my company so many years with the systems from the Carl Sewell book, 'Customers for Life.' Things had really come full circle.

Chad came out to the showroom to meet Don and me. He was a younger, athletic looking guy in his 30's that oozed confidence and charisma. He toured us around. His showroom only had room for two cars. Our showroom was the largest showroom in St. Louis that could park twenty cars. We went back to Chad's office, and he began to share their success story. He told us when they started they got the seventeen salesmen huddled up in the conference room. Chad told them that they were going to sit down with everyone individually and do some goal setting. He told the group that they would have a daily sales meeting that started at 9am sharp. He told the group that they would need to have their day planned with at least three appointments for the day. He also told the group that they would be taught how to prospect for their leads. They would have one day a week of training on how to do it the Everett way. Chad said, "The next day I showed up to the 9am meeting, and there were only two salesmen left." Chad said that was okay with him. He now knew what he had to work with to build the system he wanted. He said he had stayed close with his high school coach, and he usually had a summer basketball camp, but his wife had been sick. He had stopped by the dealership that summer because he had free time. Chad said, "Coach you should come work for me. You would be an incredible salesman, and everyone knows you." The Coach agreed to the opportunity. He was an immediate success and mentor to the new hires. The coach now sells over thirty cars a month, and Chad now has forty salesmen working his system like a well-oiled machine.

This sales system was music to my ears. It was our old NPS way, only in the car business. Chad also shared with us his compensation system that kept the guys pushing to reach their goals, along with how he priced his cars. This was an incredible road trip for Don and me. I couldn't wait to get back to start getting all the new stuff implemented. Our dealership was at the same sales per month that Everett was before they became GMC's national number 1 dealership in sales. We had a goal, we just needed to implement the plan. The government clock was still ticking in my head. I was going to need to work six days a week, and all hours to get this engine started. The only thing I added from the Everett plan was I created a monthly company newsletter. This helped us recognize the people doing it right with positive stories, and the company scoreboard for all to see. It is always smart for a company to produce their own propaganda machine, so people can read and feel what you expect as a business.

The other advantage we had was Moe Hunn, who was our General Manager. Moe had been at the dealership in the old glory days when the dealership had been the top selling store in the Midwest. Moe, was a 60 year- old who stood about 5'8", and had boundless energy to spare. He was the fun guy that would energize any party, and who could strike up a conversation with anyone. Sometimes you might catch him doing a Fred Astaire dance slide across the show room floor because he liked the music that was playing. He was a wealth of knowledge for me on things that worked, and didn't work over the years.

CHAPTER 46:

Hanging by a Thread

In the middle of June, Rick Sindel called and told me he wanted to sit down and talk about my options with the case. I knew Rick did not want to go to a trial that was slated to last four months. Until you get involved with a criminal case, you don't realize that rarely do any cases go to trial…97% of the cases are resolved in a plea bargain that works the best deal for the client. I felt Rick's advice was tainted because he did not want to do the hours of work it would take to defend me in a real trial.

Rick said he had gotten a phone call from Assistant U.S. Attorney Burlington to discuss the plea bargain. After six years, I still wasn't ready to give up the fight. I wanted my day in court, so everyone could hear my side of this story.

Rick said, "The prosecutors are admitting that you are the least culpable. They want you to plead guilty to mail fraud, wire fraud, money laundering, and willfully allowing a known felon to work in the business of insurance. They'll offer 0 to 5 years in prison. There's no guarantee that the judge would not max out your sentence to 5 years."

"I've never had criminal intent to do anything wrong," I said. "Don't you have to have criminal intent to commit a crime?" I said.

Then we got into a discussion about proof of *mens rea* – a guilty mind. Traditionally the criminal statutes required to punish someone for a crime, because intentional wrongdoing is more morally culpable than accidental wrongdoing. Our justice system has usually been content to evaluate accidents that injure others to civil wrongs, but criminal punishment has been reserved for people who do a bad act on purpose.

The Federalist Society wrote an article, "Morally Innocent, Legally Guilty: The Case for Mens Rea Reform." In the article they give the example in 1997, of three time Indy 500 winner, Bobby Unser, who was convicted of a federal crime that exposed him to a $5,000 fine and a six month prison sentence. He and his friend were riding a snowmobile and got caught in a horrific blizzard in the woods. They abandoned the snowmobile and sought shelter, becoming trapped for two days and two nights, and nearly died from hypothermia. What was Unser's crime? He had abandoned his snowmobile in a federal wilderness area, which is a crime. Unser had not known that was a crime, and certainly had no intention of violating a federal law. Nevertheless, the justice system found him guilty of a federal offense.

The change in our justice system has come about as the orientation of the criminal justice system has evolved. In addition to seeking to punish those who act out of willfulness or malice, the system now seeks to punish those who do things that result in some harm that we do not like, regardless of any intentionality or malice on their part. Absent sufficient mens rea standards, prosecuting malum in se offenses – acts that are bad simply because the law prohibits them, can result in unwitting individuals being labeled as criminals and incarcerated for committing acts that are not inherently immoral, and that a reasonable person might not realize could subject them to criminal liability. Today, the United States Code and the Code of Federal Regulations contain an estimated 5,000 statutes, and more than 300,000 regulations that carry criminal penalties for violations.

I had grown up believing that someone needs to have a willful criminal intent to break the law. I was struggling with the fact that I had been so proud of my business, and with our accomplishments as a company. I never once got up in the morning and said, "Well, it is time to create a criminal enterprise with a scheme to break the law."

If I chose to give in and accept a plea, I would admit that is exactly what I did. My family and friends had supported me through the whole process. I told everyone I was going to fight this to the end. How could I live my life going forward knowing I voluntarily pled guilty? I was not only letting myself down, but everyone who had been supporting me.

I told Rick the only thing I would feel comfortable pleading to would be allowing my Dad to work in the business of insurance. This was a law that was passed by Congress in 1994. I was never made aware of this law by any of our attorneys, but it was a law that had been violated. This charge carried a maximum five-year prison term. I said, "Rick, go back to Birmingham and see if he would agree to that one charge."

I returned to the house we were now renting in the same neighborhood where our girls had grown up. Our youngest, Baby, had just gotten her driver's license and would soon be home.

Julie and I had kept the girls informed, so they wouldn't be surprised by news from one of their friends where they had incredible support. When Baby arrived, we gathered in the family room. "I met with my attorney today," I said. "The government is offering a plea bargain for me so I won't have to go to trial. They want me to plead guilty to four counts. They said the offer would be from 0 – 5 years of prison time. I can tell you that there is nothing I like about pleading. I want to fight so I can vindicate our good name."

Carly said, "You've been dragged through this whole mess, and it has all been so unfair. What makes you think that you can suddenly change everything by going to trial?" Baby added, "Dad, if you lose, we will lose you for God knows how many years. You can't go to trial. It is just too big of a risk."

Courtney said, "You can't be selfish. You have to plead for us. This just isn't only about you."

"Girls," I said. "For the rest of your life you'll have to live with a dad who is branded a convicted felon. If we fight, we have the possibility to avoid that lifelong branding."

They said they would always be proud knowing how I had fought the good fight, and that I should plead because of my family. My girls were 21, 19, and 16, and they had real opinions. We had raised some strong girls.

Julie just let them talk, because we had already talked through all of these possibilities over the last few weeks. Julie ultimately wanted me to become comfortable with whatever I had to do to be able to live with myself, but she knew she wanted me to plea. A trial scared her that only a bad result would happen.

Finally, Carly said, "Dad I would have a hard time forgiving you if you went to trial, and you were taken away from us for 20 years when you could have pled. We can do this even if it is the maximum of 5 years." They were adamant about what I should do. I had to let all of this sink in. I did not realize that they were going to be so adamant about me taking a plea.

Rick called me back the next day and told me Burlington was not going to go for the one count. He wanted more counts. I told Rick that was the deal. Rick began calling and emailing Julie, telling her that she had to convince me to plead. This made me furious. Rick didn't need to put more pressure on her.

I drifted into a dark place in my mind. I began to think the girls and Julie would be better off without me. They didn't deserve this. If I wasn't around any longer, Julie and the girls could get a fresh start without this black cloud following them. I didn't know if I could live the rest of my life as a convicted felon. It would be the first thing everyone would think when I entered the room. I had fought all the way to the end, and I had folded.

It was time for our family to head to Nantucket for July. The last two years we had rented our house out while we were not there, so we would have enough money for the family to be there this summer. I had a few days left until the Burlington plea offer expired. Julie said she wanted to wait until the plea date. I told her I definitely wanted her to go. I would only be a few days behind. I began sinking into a darker place mentally.

I called Mike Shanahan for lunch the next day. "Well, Cass," he said. "Things have to be crazy for you with the trial looming in a couple of months. I'm sure they're hounding you to work out a deal."

"That is exactly what is happening," I said. I unloaded the whole situation on him.

He looked at me. "Cass, don't make a deal now. Wait until you're on the courthouse steps, and they're picking their jury. You have your maximum leverage right before the trial starts. That's when my dad and I made our best deal."

I knew he was right.

When I got back to my car, Rick Sindel called. He had the full court press on me. I again told him that I was not comfortable pleading to the other three charges. It is all a complete farce. I told Rick, "You've not gotten one concession for me the whole time you have been on this case. I would have loved the opportunity to plead my case. They've looked through all the documents. They know exactly what my role was with our companies. I don't even recognize the person they describe. Burlington is calling me the finance guy. What a joke! You should get ready for the trial," I added. "Because I don't like their offer."

I hung up the phone in anger. I had had it with Rick. I had had it with everything.

Rick later called back and said he had talked to Burlington who said he would knock off the money laundering if I would agree to 0 to 7 years on the plea.

I said, "That is how you negotiate? Good God." I hung up and mindlessly drove my car through the dark St. Louis streets.

My mind drifted back to our company's destruction. I am not saying that our company was not sloppy and made mistakes that needed to be corrected. I also believed if Dale Williams would have been allowed to make the needed changes to our business plan, the company could have survived and thrived. The destruction of so many lives could have been avoided. None of this mattered. It had all really happened, and I was now dealing with what I was going to do with my fight against the Justice Department. I struggled with my pride, my refusal to give up. How was I going to come to terms with myself to move forward? Dad called me, and said we should get together and talk things through. He came over to my house. I told him about the conversation I had had with Julie and my girls, how they were adamant about me pleading. "They feel that nothing good could come from going to trial."

"I understand why they feel that way," said Dad. "They've lived through five years of hell, and at every turn it has been something worse than before. I should be the one to carry on and go to trial. I can speak to our defense better than anyone. It would be my way to vindicate you and your family."

We only had less than 48 hours left before the U.S. Attorney's deadline would expire for the plea bargains. Dad put in a call to Scott, his attorney. He told him that he was not going to accept the plea. Scott told him that he should think more about his decision, but he would call Burlington to tell him that he was leaning against the plea. Dad and I continued to drink and talk well into the night about the good times and the bad until we both couldn't talk any longer…we both knew there was nothing good that was staring us in the face as we drifted off to sleep on the couch.

The next day was a flurry of phone calls between the defense attorneys and the U.S. Attorney's office. Scott, called Dad to tell them they were willing to deal on some assets for the family, if he would plead. Burlington told Scott that he was willing to set aside Hollywood Forever, my parents' Naples condo, and my mom's artwork and jewelry. This could be a way for the family to survive financially. In turn, this would avoid a long drawn-out trial for both sides.

That night we had a family conference call with Julie, Mom, Dad, Tyler, and me. Dad laid out the deal that Burlington was proposing. It was a way for the family to move forward to try and survive. Tyler and Mom both adamantly agreed that they would be there to help the family. Tyler had already been helping with the girl's college tuitions and expenses. He had been a great uncle giving the girls what they needed in their world. Mom had covered my legal expenses. Dad said that he would be willing to give up going to trial if everyone thought this was the right plan to move forward. It was done. We would accept the government's deal. There would be no Cassity's going to trial to defend and tell our side of the story.

As I look back, it is hard for me to recognize the person I was that night when I got off the phone with my family. I had convinced myself that Julie and the girls were going to be taken care of, and that they didn't need me staining the family as a convicted felon in their lives. The girls and Julie would have a way to be taken care of with what we decided tonight. I did not believe I could go into that courtroom and say that I willfully and knowingly committed illegal acts.

I had been drinking heavily. Dad had fallen asleep on the couch. I now had my solution. I would end my life. I went into the dining room with my pen and paper to write out my suicide letter. I explained why this was the best way forward. I tried to explain to Julie and the girls why I had decided that this was the best way forward. I gave them advice on how to move forward in their lives. I explained to them how proud I was of them, and how courageous and strong they were. I could not be prouder or love them more as a dad. I told Julie that I loved her, and that she had been a true warrior for me all of my life. I wanted her to have a clean slate, and I wanted her to find someone with whom she wouldn't have to deal with all this baggage. I then went through all my friends and how they had helped and supported me. I ended the letter by stating this was the only way to not give in to the government.

In the garage, I got in the car and started the engine. The more I thought about what I was doing, the more I realized I was a fighter, and a survivor. I had way too much to live for with Julie and the girls. This was crazy. I would look like the ultimate quitter to everyone who had supported and loved me. It would be the worst way to be remembered. I decided right then and there in the car that I was going to live and continue to walk through this nightmare to get to the other side. I had hit the rock bottom of the barrel of my life, and thank God that I came to my senses. I wanted to live and do the best I could to make those around me see me as a survivor and not a victim.

I turned off the engine of the car. I felt different. I had finally come to terms with what I was going to do. I thank God that I did not pass out in that car that night. I kept my letter for months to remind myself to never let myself get into the ugly fog of horrible thoughts of ending it all.

There is always a way to take another step forward, regardless if the thing you are stepping forward to scares the hell out of you. You have to know that having the courage to take another step will be better than standing still or falling back. The only way to have success in life again was to keep stepping forward. Tomorrow was going to be an awful, dreadful day in the courtroom, but another step forward.

CHAPTER 47:

Finally Giving Up... The Plea

I woke up the next morning to a text from Julie saying that she was jumping on a plane back to St. Louis to be with me. Somehow in my drunken stupor, I had texted Julie in the wee hours of the morning telling her I had pulled myself off the cliff from ending it all.

Everything that morning seemed to move in slow motion. I stood at the bathroom mirror, shaving like I did every morning. It had been six long years of fighting the fight. I kept thinking how I got to this point in my life. I had lived my life to avoid what I had seen my dad go through. Now, I was taking the exact same steps he did over twenty years before. It was strange to be home in the house without Julie and the girls. My court appearance was set for 11:00, and my Dad was to plead later in the afternoon. Rick called to make sure I would be there.

I picked out my pin-striped suit and a gray tie. Okay, I thought, here I go. I am really doing this. There is no other way to write this story. It will always read that I voluntarily pled guilty to ugly charges. I drove downtown, parked my car, and headed up the steps to the Eagleton Federal Building. Rick Sindel met me in the lobby and told me the judge would make me admit guilt. "You have to confess that you knowingly and willfully did criminal acts," he said. "She'll tell you to say it aloud in open court."

Rick and I entered the courtroom to see Burlington and Morrison. They handed Rick the plea agreement to look over before the judge entered the room. The document stated that I was the president of NPS. I said this is wrong. I do not carry that title. I think that needs to be corrected. Rick said he agreed.

When Judge Hamilton entered the courtroom, Rick and the other attorneys approached the bench to speak to the judge about the correction. Burlington crossed out the title, and I initialed the change. Judge Hamilton then took over. She read the counts. She said, "Mr. Cassity, do you understand them?"

"Yes," I said.

She then read all the rights I was giving up by making a plea agreement including the right to an appeal. "Do you understand?"

"Yes," I replied.

She then asked me to state that I willfully and knowingly created and participated in these criminal acts. I couldn't get the words out of my mouth. I knew that I had never had any criminal intent to do any harm to anyone. I had been broken all the way down to this moment in court. I was now going to be forced to lie to a federal judge to be able to accept this plea.

The St. Louis Post Dispatch reported it this way, *"Brent Cassity appeared reluctant to take the plea deal, pausing several times when asked by U.S District Judge Jean Hamilton whether he agreed with what was contained in the plea agreement."*

My mind was racing. I came so close to turning to Rick, and saying, "I can't do this." I had not even waited to the day of the trial like my friend Shanahan had advised me to do. I was stunned back into reality by the Judge's voice, "Mr. Cassity, you can choose not to accept this plea. Do you need time to speak with your attorney?"

I stared at Rick and slowly turned back to the judge. "No, Your Honor, I am ready to proceed." I strained to get the ugly words out of my mouth agreeing to the court that I was a criminal, and agreeing to a plea bargain giving up my rights to a trial and any option for an appeal.

It was over. Judge Hamilton told me that I would need to return to her Court November 14th for sentencing.

On July 3rd 2013, I drove home to change clothes, and then I headed to the airport to pick up Julie. When Julie got into the car, I gave her a long tight hug. I didn't want her to fly all the way back, but it felt so good to have her with me. She said, "Honey how are you doing? I said, Babe it has been a whirlwind 24 hours, but I am at peace with everything. I have been knocked down to the darkest place I have ever been, and thank God I got back up. We will just keep taking another step forward, and get through to the end of all of this together." The real rock of strength through all of this was Julie.

The next day was the 4th of July. Julie and I got up and went for a long walk through the neighborhood. We were both in our own daze, but together. She knew me better than anyone, and she knew what it had taken out of me to get through that experience. She was also confident that we had made the right decision. Tomorrow we would fly to Nantucket to be with our girls.

Every day counted now more than it ever had in my life. When we arrived in Nantucket, there were our girls waiting for us. I hugged each one of them like I hadn't in a long time. I had almost made the worst decision in my life 48 hours ago. I had told myself on the flight that I was not going to mope around for everyone to feel sorry for me. It was time for me to be the same easy-going dad and husband that they had always known.

CHAPTER 48:

Waiting for Sentencing

There is not a good analogy to describe where your mind goes before you are sentenced to go to prison. But, my senses were heightened to everything around me. I didn't want to miss any moments with Julie and the girls. I wanted my friends to know how much I appreciated them. The big thing for me was to try and stay busy to keep my mind occupied. I was working six days a week at the car dealership where I had taken a job in management. I wanted to prove my worth and make a difference, so I had something to come back to when I left prison. Shanahan had just become an investor in the car dealership with Don Davis. We were starting to see some steady gains in our car sales from the changes we had implemented. Although we still needed to implement some more changes to the service department to get the results we needed. But I liked the fast-paced environment of the car business.

Towards the end of the summer, my life long childhood friends from Springfield (Hunter, Belk, and King) called me up and said, "You need some Springbilly time down on Table Rock Lake." We used to think we were funny calling Springfield Springbilly. Hunter said, "Cassity all you have to do is get in the car and get down here and stay at my lake house. I will take care of all the rest." It was good medicine for me to get down there for a weekend with my boys on the lake I grew up loving. We moved all my troubles to the side, and we just enjoyed being together like old times. It felt like that weekend was in a time capsule… nothing had changed, we had just gotten older. I was reflecting looking out over the lake on our sunset boat ride with the Eagles music playing in the background, and knew this would be a memory I would plug into my mind when serving my time. How good it is to appreciate times like these. We had someone snap a picture of the four of us on the boat that day. I kept that picture, along with the pictures of Julie and the girls on the inside of my prison locker. It was a constant reminder to me how many good moments I had to look forward to when I got out.

As fall approached, I was sitting in Don's office going over a few things when Don interrupted and said, "Brent, Shanahan and I have been talking. We are going to take care of Julie and the girls with your income while you are away. We don't want you to have to worry about them while you are getting through your stuff. Julie could even work here if she would like."

This caught me completely by surprise. My eyes immediately welled up with tears. I told Don it was the best news I'd heard in years. There was no way I could express how much it meant to me and my family. Don and Shanahan, good men both, had become incredible friends and had been in my corner through everything. We gave each other a big guy half hug, and just stared at each other with teary eyes.

I couldn't wait to tell Julie. This would be our lifeline for however long I would be gone. As bad as things looked, I was so thankful for how strong my friends had been for me.

Julie and I went out to dinner that night. I shared with her the conversation I had with Don. I think she first couldn't believe it was real, then her eyes welled up with tears, and she said, "Brent, we are going to be able to get through this." How could I have known that this 13 year-old girl I met in the neighborhood so many years ago could be so strong and courageous through our darkest hours? There could not have been a better role model for our girls to witness real courage in action.

My pre-trial probation officer, Susan Hendrickson, called saying we would soon start the process of completing my pre-sentence report, commonly known as your PSR. This report is compiled and sent to the judge to review before sentencing. Susan, who had been great to me and my family the last three years of pre-trial probation, assured me not to worry about the report. "Just be yourself," she said.

Ryan Wilke called me later that day. He seemed to be a friendly guy on the phone, and we set up a time for me to meet him at his office at the Eagleton Federal Building. Ryan came to greet me in the probation office lobby. Ryan was a guy in his late 30's to early 40's with a personable disposition. We entered his office, and he explained how the presentence report worked. I had been researching programs offered in prison that could shave time off someone's prison sentence. There did not appear to be any, except one program. It was called the Residential Drug Abuse Program known as RDAP. If someone is accepted into this nine- month program you could get a year reduced from your sentence.

I did not have a drug addiction issue, but my research showed that someone could be admitted to the program if they abused alcohol. Ryan began by asking about my early childhood, school, my parents, my brother, my work history, and about Julie and my girls. He also asked me questions about our case, and how I had handled the stress of being investigated. This was a long interview. He then asked me, "Brent, do you drink? Do you drink daily? Do you drink to relieve the stress that you are under?" I answered, "Yes."

Ryan told me that he was going to recommend in his report that I be accepted into the RDAP program. I was willing to do any program that could get me home sooner. When we finished, Ryan said he would need to meet with Julie and the girls without me. We shook hands, and that was it. I hated putting Julie and my girls under this kind of stress.

I called Julie to tell her about the interview and that I liked Ryan as a person. I thought the interview went well. I also told her that Ryan would recommend me for the RDAP program. In our strange world, this was good news.

Ryan called me after he met with Julie and the girls, and said, "You should be very proud. I can see that you have a very loving supportive family." He added. "Brent, this is going to be a hard thing for you and your family to get through, but I think you are some of the rare people who will be okay once you get this behind you."

Oddly, after being investigated for six years, Ryan Wilke and Susan Hendrickson were the only Federal Officers that I had any interaction with. I never was interviewed by an FBI agent or any of the assistant U.S. Attorneys. I would have thought that they would want to speak to the person they were investigating.

In October, I was able to travel with my oldest daughter Courtney out to Tucson Arizona to see Carly, my middle daughter, play in her first fall warm-up Division 1 tennis tournament. We were so proud of Carly to be competing out on the court as an Arizona Wildcat. In typical Carly fashion she got down in her first match 2-5, and grinded her way back to win the match against her Colorado opponent. She finished the tournament with two wins and one loss. I could not have been prouder of her. The bonus was that Courtney and I got to watch Mizzou beat the Georgia Bulldogs on the road, between Carly's matches. We took pictures with the three of us, and it was another day I was savoring as an incredible memory, as I knew my days were closing in on my days of freedom.

When I got back, I had an appointment to meet with Rick about preparing for the sentencing. I needed to compile a list of family and friends who would be able to write a letter to the Judge on my behalf. He gave me a prepared document that had the address and contact information of where to send the letters. Rick said the more specific they can speak to your character and the type of person you are, the better. He said they should avoid stating what they think about the case, or if you are innocent.

After a few days, copies of the letters sent to the judge began coming to me. It is almost analogous to being conscious at your own funeral with the ability to hear what people have to say about our friendships and specific things they thought were important to mention about my life. I will forever be so appreciative of all the friends and family that took the time to sit down and write a letter on my behalf. Attorneys say that the judges read the letters. I have become so cynical after going through this process. I want to believe the good judges do, to honor the time someone spent to write such a letter. I would later have Julie mail me all of these letters while I was in prison to lift me up on my down days.

The last issue were the losses incurred when we shut down the companies. Burlington wanted this number to be jaw-dropping to create the most sensational headlines.

Our company had paid into state guaranty funds tens of millions of dollars over the years. Every funeral was paid to every funeral home. The only thing that was not paid was the additional growth commission the funeral director would receive at the time of the service. No one lost money. They simply didn't make as much money as they would have if we were still in business paying growth.

The U.S Attorney was interviewed by the St. Louis Post Dispatch on June 28, 2013. He was asked about NPS losses and had an interesting answer. '*Callahan said, "There are no losses to date, but as more people who bought plans die, losses will pile up."* The article goes on to mention, *"the company stopped selling funeral policies in 2008 after Missouri and other states began scrutinizing its business practices, and Texas forced the company's liquidation later that year."*

The point is that five years had passed with no losses to date, quoting Callahan. I know there were losses to shutting down the business, but we wanted to argue the loss amount. It would be the amount of restitution we would carry around our neck to pay the rest of our lives. When our attorneys told Burlington that we disputed the loss number, and even pointing out U.S. Attorney Callahan's quote to the press, Burlington said that he would remove our two points of cooperation in our plea agreements, and would ask the judge to remand us immediately to county jail after sentencing.

All of the defense attorneys called up the defendants, and we all meekly put down our swords. At this point, we were like abused dogs who kept getting kicked in the corner. I regret that we did not have the courage to dispute this issue.

CHAPTER 49:

The Day of Sentencing

November 14ᵗ, 2013

The day before, I reread the Pre-Sentencing report. Rick told me he didn't think the judge would give me probation, but a year would be possible. He also said, the judge could stretch it to a three-year max. It seemed so strange to casually be discussing years of my life in prison.

Mom flew in from Florida the night before, and stayed at our house. Carly was at school in Arizona. Julie, Courtney, and the Baby were upstairs getting ready. I was dressed and ready downstairs with my mom. My Mom said, "Brent, I have a good feeling that this Judge is going to give you probation."

I said, "Mom, I hope you are right, but I cannot plan on that with how I am approaching this day. I don't want to get my hopes up. I just have to be ready to accept whatever is handed down."

When we reached the court house, my mind flashed back to my 14-year-old self, scared and sad on my Dad's sentencing day. I was relieved that we were not hounded by reporters when we entered the courthouse. We all eventually made it through the security and rode the elevator to Judge Hamilton's courtroom. The place was packed with family, friends, attorneys, reporters, and general spectators. We met up with Julie's parents Larry and June, and my brother-in-law and sister-in-law, Grant and Jodi.

Judge Hamilton would be sentencing Nicki Province (Executive Assistant), Howard Wittner (RBT Trustee and Company Attorney), Randy Sutton (President NPS), Doug Cassity (Company Founder), Dave Wulf (Company Investment Advisor), and me. It felt like a scene at the end of my favorite movie Braveheart. Everyone had come to view the spectacle in the town square.

The Judge opened, called the case number to order, and asked if any aggrieved wished to speak. Two funeral directors rose. Dad was the first defendant. The Judge read through the plea agreement and the special conditions that were set forth with the supervised probation after prison. Scott Rosenblum spoke on my Dad's behalf for leniency. The Judge then asked if my dad would like to make a statement.

I sat up in my chair. I did not expect Dad to make a case for his innocence, but I hoped he would make an impassioned defense of me, his son.

"No, your Honor. I have no statement."

It was like someone had just sucked all the air out of my body. It was my knockout blow to the head. I had flown around the country defending his financial model he had constructed from regulator to regulator. The man I had grown up believing was a real-life superhero; stood there as the shell of the man I had admired. The true loss of the finality of this day had been the last six years of a gradual torturous tearing apart limb by limb of a special relationship we once shared as father and son. When I had needed him most, I was left searching for the Dad who had always been there for me. Where did that man go? I wasn't mad at him. I was just completely crushed knowing our relationship could never be the same. The Judge then returned back to reading from her voluminous three-ring binder, and sentenced my dad to the maximum of 10 years in prison.

She turned to Randy Sutton and sentenced him to the maximum of 7 years in prison. Howard Wittner was next. His attorneys went into a lengthy defense for his leniency. Several friends stood up and spoke. He also had a medical report that spoke to his failing health. I turned and looked at Rick. I had friends and old business associates who had told me they wanted to speak on my behalf, but Rick didn't think it would be a good move. But, now I knew. I should have gone with my gut.

Judge Hamilton gave him a 36-month prison sentence. He would be released after 8 months on compassionate release.

Susan Kisker, Rick Sindel's assistant, patted me on the back. It was her acknowledgement that Howard's sentence was a good sign for me. The Judge called the next defendant, Brent Cassity.

I took a deep breath and stood at the podium with Rick, who had prepared brief remarks about my character. He referenced some of the heartfelt comments written in the letters sent to the judge. Rick said, "I believe Brent is here today because he volunteered to run into a burning house in an attempt to save this company."

The Judge asked me if I would like to make a comment. I started with how difficult this process had been, and that I truly appreciated the help along the way of the strong support of my family and friends. I turned around, thanked those who were in the courtroom and proceeded with my statement, "My goal in life was to always make a positive difference in whatever endeavor I chose to undertake. As a Dad, I have tried to instill this belief with my three daughters, but by standing before you today, I have failed in my own personal lifelong goal. I want to apologize to anyone who was directly or indirectly negatively affected by what has happened with our case."

Judge Hamilton opened her three-ring binder and began to read each count, "Mr. Cassity," she said. "I am sentencing you to a term of 60 months, 5 years."

I let out a breath that it was audible to all that were in the courtroom. And just like that, it was over.

I went numb. I turned to leave the courtroom with Rick and my family. We got outside the courtroom. Julie and the girls were shaken and crying.

Rick stopped me, and said, "Brent, I am really sorry. I feel like I have failed you. You should not be going away for five years." I told Rick there is nothing we could do about it now. I would gear up and get it over with.

Reporters and cameras were everywhere. One rude reporter followed us down the sidewalk shouting questions at me, and sticking the microphone in my face. I finally said, "I do not have any comment. I just want to be with my family right now, thank you."

The next day the St. Louis Post Dispatch had a huge picture above the fold of my family and me walking out of the courthouse. I hated that for my girls and Julie. Out of six defendants in the case our family picture was the one they chose to run with…the stoic tear- filled pain pictured on the Baby's, Courtney's, and Julie's faces broke my heart.

CHAPTER 50:

Preparing for Prison

I was running against time. I still didn't know where I would serve my term when a letter finally arrived. A short paragraph designated me to the Federal Prison Camp of Leavenworth Kansas. Leavenworth, four and one-half hours from St. Louis. I had heard of Leavenworth, mostly from movies. I immediately got on Google earth. An image showed an old, rundown building. Next to the camp was the United States Penitentiary, built in 1879, looking like the prison in the movie, *Shawshank Redemption.*

As strange as life is, I had a friend at the car dealership who had recently served time at the Leavenworth prison camp. Ed Levinson was a well-known homebuilder who fell on hard times with the financial crash of 2008. We sat down one day in my office, and he drew me a map where everything was in the prison. Oddly, this exercise helped put my mind at some ease. At least I would know what I was walking into, and some helpful advice on what to expect, and the way I should act when I arrived.

Julie and I were under the gun to find a place to live. Our lease was running out at the end of December. We wanted to find a place and move before I had to report. There was no way I wanted Julie to make this move without my help. Julie's Mom, June, was a real estate agent. Julie really preferred to find somewhere close to where her mom and dad lived.

Our biggest obstacle was that through six years of fighting the Unites States Department of Justice, I was flat broke. I had no money to put down for buying a house. The money that we received from selling our house, we lived on the past year. I will always be so grateful to Julie's parents being supportive throughout my entire ordeal, but they stepped up in such a big way when we needed help for a house. They never shamed me for the position I found myself in. They just steadfastly stepped in and said they would buy a house, so Julie and the girls would have a place to live. There is no way to put into words what this meant to our family. The final step was finding a house.

After looking at several houses, we finally found a house that Julie's parents were able to buy with a quick closing date, so I could help with the move before I went to prison. The house was nearby where Julie had grown up, but way outside the area of the High School that the Baby was attending. My brother stepped up again and said he would cover the out of district cost for the Baby to be able to stay at her high school. Our Baby never complained about having to get up extra early to drive 45 minutes in the traffic to get to her school. Everyone was stepping up to make things work in a very painfully strange situation.

Sadness crept into daily life. It pained me that each of us was dealing with our own sadness and sense of loss. We managed to rally through holidays, the internal clicking of the clock beating inside each one of us.

I decided my last day at work would be a week before I left. I packed up my office and said my final good-byes. Moe helped me put the last piece in the car, and said, "Don't worry, Don and I will look after Julie and the girls."

The night before I was to leave, Dad called and asked if we could have a drink at the neighborhood bar. Dad was to report a week after to Marion Prison Camp, the same prison he served his time in over 30 years ago. We had communicated back and forth after the sentencing about my feelings on how things went down in the courtroom. I told him I was crushed. He knew I was hurt. He said that Scott, his attorney, had told him that it would not be smart for him to make a statement. I'm sure Scott would have felt differently if Dad had told him that he wanted to defend his son.

We sat at the bar, two beaten up boxers after a 12-round match, and talked about all the things we had been through the last six years. There was this empty feeling between us of so much loss. Oddly, we didn't discuss prison. I thought my Dad might have had some thoughts to share with me about prison. We finished our drinks and hugged in the parking lot.

"You know I love you, son," said Dad. But it seemed so sadly empty.

"I love you, too, Dad," I said, and I drove home.

The morning had finally arrived and it was time to leave. I loaded the car, hugged my girls and told them how much I loved them. I said goodbye to our dogs, Lucy, Wayne and Tucker.

It is such a strange phenomenon to voluntarily drive yourself to prison. I had asked my Mom and Tyler to ride with Julie and me. Tyler had reserved some rooms for us on the Plaza in Kansas City. We stopped along the way in Columbia at my favorite pizza place, Shakespeare's. Julie and I reminisced about our college days as we drove through the Mizzou campus. That night we went out to eat at my favorite Kansas City restaurant Jack Stack. We always ate there with the girls when they had their tennis tournaments on the Plaza. That night I was nostalgic about everything. It was like I had a movie reel of fond memories rotating in my mind. It was all happening too fast as the minutes were ticking away. No one really wanted to talk about the big event that was happening tomorrow.

Julie and I dropped off my mom and Tyler after dinner. We wanted some more alone time, and thought we should drive to Leavenworth to see what we could see. When we arrived, we could see white security trucks circling the main medium security prison with a yellow light flashing on top of the truck. There were 30 feet old brick walls with additional double fencing, with enough barbed wire on the top and bottom of the fences to look very menacing. We turned on the street off the main road to the prison camp. We immediately saw two signs on each side of the road stating in bold letters "FEDERAL PRISON CAMP! NO UNAUTHORIZED PERSONNEL BEYOND THIS POINT! UNAUTHORIZED PEOPLE WILL BE FEDERALLY PROSECUTED! That scared Julie to death, and I have to admit it was unsettling to me. I immediately backed up the car. The prison camp was lit up with outside spot lights. It was hard to get a good look at what the prison camp building looked like. It was a rundown, red brick, two storey structure that looked like an old building. The backyard of the place looked like it had a baseball field, and a sidewalk that ran along the menacing looking tall barbed wire fences. Julie and I both agreed that it really didn't make us feel any better seeing all of this. I kept thinking I am going to be in that building behind that fence tomorrow night. Julie and I drove back to our hotel, knowing that the clock was ticking for us. We both just felt such a weight of sadness that was indescribable.

That night as I laid in this nice comfortable hotel bed with Julie, I was thinking tomorrow night I am going to be lying in bed in a prison with no one I know around me. Julie and I won't be together like this for another five years. I knew I was just going to have to walk right through this incredible fear of the big unknown. I was ready to do it because my mind was worn-out thinking about all the fearful unknowns.

CHAPTER 51:

Prison: Day One

We drove to Leavenworth early to check out the prison in the daylight. Oddly, there were buffalo roaming in the field in front of the prison behind the barbed wire fence.

At a nearby ATM, I withdrew $200. I had read that I could take money with me to put in my prison commissary fund. My next stop was McDonalds for a Big Mac. I was fearful I did not know when I would eat again, and I knew my next meal wouldn't be as good as a Big Mac. I wanted my last meal of freedom to be one that I really liked! I scarfed down the Big Mac. I could tell that Julie was stressing about our time, so we drove to the front of the prison and parked to wait until 1pm. God knows I did not want to go in this scary looking place early.

And then it was time. I hugged my Mom, and I turned and hugged Julie one last time. I felt sick leaving her to handle the outside world alone when we had done everything together. We kissed and looked into each other's eyes knowing that we were both getting ready to head into two separate unknown worlds. Julie and my mom stayed in the car, but Tyler got out with me. "Bro," he said. "I'll walk with you."

We went up a mountain of steps to the front door and Tyler hugged me goodbye. I opened it to see a man in uniform. "I am here to voluntarily surrender," I said.

"Not here you won't. Go down by the dumpster. There's a security gate there. Wait until the gate buzzes. Someone will be on the other side of the gate to get you."

The January Kansas winter wind whipped through me. I had taken off my coat and given it to Julie because I didn't want the prison to have it. And now I couldn't stop shivering. A few minutes went by and Julie jumped out of the car running my coat to me. I said, "No Julie, I will be okay. I love you!" Frustrated, she turned and headed back to the car.

Finally, a guard came to the gate, and buzzed me in through two tall razor wire- lined fences. The gates slammed shut. I was leaving my world of freedom. I was heading into the Big House. My immediate thought, as I was walking up the sidewalk, was I hope they know I am supposed to be at the camp.

I entered the prison into a fenced cage. They ask me over the intercom for my name, then buzzed me out. I was now in the basement of an enormous prison building. At a counter, a man told me to empty my pockets. He would put my cash into my inmate account.

I followed the guard down a hallway of prison cells. He opened one up, told me to enter, and said someone would be with me later. There were concrete benches on both sides of the cell and a metal toilet on the center of the wall. Lack of information is the first thing I immediately became aware of. I had no idea how long I would be there.

I did push-ups just to try to stave off my nervous energy. Over an hour had passed when the cell door opened. Another guy walked in. He was tall, clean-cut and slender with a country accent. He immediately introduced himself as Jay Jones. "You must be doing the same fucking thing I am doing today, fucking checking into prison."

Jay was a likeable guy from Jerseyville Illinois, just outside of St. Louis. I told him I was from St. Louis. He looked at me sideways, and said, "Hey, you that funeral guy from TV? Boy, did they do a number on your family. They should owe you money helping them sell their ad time."

"Yeah," said. "I'm that funeral guy."

Another hour passed and the cell door opened. Jay and I were led into a room with a big dumpster and clothes in piles. The guard told me to strip down and throw my clothes in the middle of the room. I bent over. He told me to spread my cheeks and to cough. He then handed me khaki boxers, khaki pants with an elastic waist band, socks, and a t-shirt that had a large blood stain down the front. Next, came the funny-looking, slip-on, blue tennis shoes. I was officially prisonized in temporary prison garb.

In a small office, nearby, a doctor asked if I was suicidal. I had learned that even if you were, you said "No," so you wouldn't end up in the dreaded hole for days. Finally, in a room with several metal desks and no windows, a woman with long stringy dirty hair, big glasses, smelling of cigarettes and wearing an oversized navy-blue, dirty Leavenworth windbreaker, told the guard she would take it from there. She wanted me to know immediately that I was the inmate, and not to ask her any questions. She pulled out a big file that was all about me. It turned out that she was really just verifying that I was Brent Cassity, and I was thinking I wish I could have had the option of having another Brent Cassity doing this for me.

Jay arrived in the cell shortly after I did. "Shit, Brent, he said. "I hope they don't keep us up here. Finally, the guard returned. A white minivan idled in the driveway. We got in and drove to the prison camp hemmed in by thick, mean, barbed-wire scrolling across the top and bottom of a 10-foot chain link fence. Leavenworth was one of only three Federal Prison Camps that had a fence.

All the inmates were gathered in the hallway watching us. We were told to wait at the glassed-in area where the guards sat. It was called the 'bubble'.

Finally, an inmate named Watson, with a buzz cut and built like a linebacker asked us to follow him. He was covered in tattoos from his neck down. Watson opened a door to a basement stairway that was so narrow you had to walk in a single file line. The basement was dark and damp with a low ceiling that made me feel immediately claustrophobic. A couple of black guys sat in plastic chairs watching a TV. There was also a glassed off barbershop with two barber chairs. We walked to the back and arrived at an area cordoned off by a chain link fence from the floor to the ceiling. The sign on the door said, "Keep out." This was where the uniforms and bedding were stored.

Watson told Jay and me that he only had one uniform for each of us. We would get two more uniforms in a few days. He gave us three pairs of socks, three pairs of underwear, and two white t-shirts, along with black, steel-toed boots and a winter coat. Finally, he gave us our bedding with two towels and two wash clothes. He added, "We don't have any pillows right now. Good luck locating one. All right guys, let's take you to your bunks in A2. It's called the Ghetto and is a pretty funky place to live. Maybe if you get lucky, you can move to the suburbs in B1 or C1."

The Ghetto housed fifty guys in a room with metal bunkbeds squeezed in close together. Everything went quiet as Jay and I walked to our bunks. I peeked inside the restroom where a group huddled up in the chill air smoking by the three toilets. There were also three showers, three urinals, and six sinks. My top bunk was located just beyond the restroom entrance. Jay was two bunks down from me. Watson gave us a list of rules. I would later find out that while these rules were important, what really mattered, were the Inmate Rules.

A short Hispanic, well-built guy approached me, and said, "I'm Romo. You must be my new bunky. I can tell by the looks of you that you have never been here before. Let me show you how to make your bed. It has to be made military style."

When we finished making the bed, Romo said, "Cassity I need to introduce you to Clark. He is one of your kind." He walked me over to the corner of the room, and introduced me to Jim Clark, a clean cut, white guy eight years older than me. As we talked we learned that we both grew up in St. Louis, had gone to DeSmet High School, and played basketball. I could not believe that we had this small world connection. Clark had already been there for over a year. I told him I had read that I could make a phone call in the counselor's office to let my family know I was okay. Clark volunteered to walk me down to the counselor's office to meet Mr. Goodwin.

When we got to Goodwin's door, two guys waited in the hallway. I told Clark he could go on, and I would wait.

"So you are the new guy?" said one of the inmates.

"Yeah," I said.

"We have been watching you on the Kansas City local news," he said, and gave me a curious smile, and then said, "we were wondering if you would make it here." I hoped he and the other inmates hadn't formed opinions about me before they had a chance to know me.

Goodwin had a friendly disposition. "Come on in new guy," he smiled. "I've seen your paperwork, but I swear you look like a Ray Romano."

I laughed because Grandpa Ralph used to say the same thing.

Goodwin handed me the phone, and Julie picked up. My emotions threatened to take over, but I pushed them back down. I said, "Julie, I have made it in, and I have already met some nice guys that have helped me get set-up. My bunky Romo has been a big help, and he introduced me to a good guy Clark who actually went to DeSmet. The new guy I came in with is also a good family guy. I want you to know I am going to be okay. I've got this. I don't want you to worry." Julie said, "It is just so good to hear your voice. We just got home, and we so desperately wanted to talk to you. I am so happy that you have already met some nice people." She put me on the speaker phone with the girls, Tyler, and my mom. I said, "Everybody, I love you so much! I am going to be just fine. I will get everything figured out. I've got this! I don't want anyone to worry." Everyone said they loved each other, and it was time to end the call. I told Julie I would get the visitor forms approved and figure out how to work the inmate phones tomorrow. I said, "I love you guys!" Just like that the phone call was over.

Goodwin said, "It sounds like you have a great family. That's not common for most inmates in here." I told Goodwin that I appreciated him letting me make the phone call. It meant a lot to me to assure them that I was okay.

Goodwin said, "Welcome to Leavenworth Cassity. I'm your counselor. You will thank me over and over that your counselor is not Swanson."

I had already heard the name Swanson, and that he loved to mess with inmates. Goodwin continued, "We will get to know each other over the next few years."

The next few years sounded really depressing. If I was going to live in a rundown building for the next few years, I needed to write down some goals, just like I had every time I started something new.

When I got back to my bunk, I found three diet Pepsis, three bags of chips, and a candy bar in my locker. A note from Clark said, "This is your official

DeSmet Spartan welcome kit. Don't worry, I will show you the ropes. I will help you find a prison job tomorrow."

I went over to thank Clark for the house warming gifts. He told me that I needed to go to the Chapel at 9 pm, and the inmates would give me some toiletries to use until I was able to go to commissary. I went back and sat down in my plastic prison chair next to my six-shelf locker. Welcome home, I thought.

In the bed next to me, a huge, building of a man looked at me, and said, "You ain't ever seen a black man this big, or is it you ain't ever seen a black man? I noticed you ain't got no shower shoes. You can't go in that nasty shower without shower shoes. I have an extra pair, I'll let you use them until you get yours at the commissary."

"Wow, that's a really nice offer," I said. "I don't know what I would have done."

"No one wants a stinky side bunkmate. I'm the black Watson. You already met the white Watson, and I am much nicer."

"Good to know," I said.

I told Jay about the Chapel deal with the free toiletries, so we both went down to get a clear toiletry bag holding a toothbrush, soap, toothpaste, and shampoo. An inmate led us in a prayer, and told us that everything was donated by other inmates. "The prison doesn't give you any of this stuff," he said. "We're on our own. After you're here awhile, you can donate something, too."

On our way back, we stopped by the gym to watch a group playing basketball. In an upstairs mezzanine guys sat on plastic chairs watching four TV's alongside two worn out pool tables. In the hall, a nurse handed out pills as people waited in line. Just beyond was a bank of phones on the wall. There, where two hallways came to a point, was the bubble with its bored-looking guards.

There was no sound in the cafeteria. This was also where people watched TV at night. It was also the only room that was air-conditioned in the summer and everyone had radios with earphones tuned into the channel for each TV. Down the other hallway that led to our dorm, a bank of computer screens sat on gray desks with dividers. This was called trulinks where you could email people for five cents a minute. This hallway also contained the counselor's office, and three case manager offices. At the very end of the hallway double doors led to the commissary. That was it. The rest of the building held the dorms of A block, B block, C block, and D block, housing 425 inmates.

Jay and I returned to find Romo waiting.

"Okay," he said. "I need to tell you about count time. Standing count time is at 4 pm and 10 pm. There's an additional standing count at 10 am on the weekends. You need to stand at the end of your bunk. They'll come by and count you like cattle. Don't move or talk. Never be late. That can be counted as being out of bounds. It's serious and will earn you time in the hole. They also shine a flashlight at you at midnight, 3 am, and 5 am."

I heard keys clanking as two guards headed up the stairs. Because they didn't carry guns, the long chains with the jangling keys created enough intimidation on their own. It became a familiar, jarring sound to every inmate over time.

"Count!" the guard yelled.

We stood at the end of our bunks. The guards walked through and counted us like livestock. As they exited the dorm, they turned off the lights. I had just stood for my first of hundreds of counts to come.

Book lights went on. A light in the bathroom went on. The smokers had arrived for their last smoke of the night.

Romo and I talked into the night. From the little I knew, I could tell Romo was a good man who would help me. I would later learn that Romo was a very influential man at Leavenworth. He was the 'shot caller' for the Hispanic gang, Texas Homeboys, who were more powerful than the Hispanic gang, Pisces. He was also the commissioner of all inmate sports. Romo was a good friend to have on your side, and he had taken me under his wing.

When Romo fell asleep, I got out paper and pen. By the light of the bathroom I began my goal list:

1. Find a good prison job to keep me busy and hopefully learn a new skill. Secondly.

2. Learn the inmate rules.

3. Learn how to make phone calls and figure out how to use the trulinks system to communicate with the outside world.

4. Find out how to get accepted into the RDAP program to earn a year off my sentence.

5. Read as many books as possible to keep my mind active and give me a mental escape from my surroundings.

6. Remain strong, positive, and upbeat to my family, so they wouldn't worry about me. Finally, I was going to get in the best shape I had ever been in my life.

I would tackle prison just like I had with all new challenges in my life. I would write goals, plan, and take it one step at a time.

I wondered if I would sleep. I was using my winter coat as my pillow, and was still dressed in my t-shirt and khaki pants with my socks on. I looked out the window to see the big penitentiary up the hill all lit up. What a day it had been. After a six-year fight, I was lying in bed in prison. It was still hard to believe I was inside the fence at Leavenworth prison.

Exhausted, I drifted off to sleep.

CHAPTER 52:

Adapting

At 7 am, I heard my name over the prison intercom telling me to report to Ms. Alexander. I had slept in my clothes, so I popped out of bed, washed my face and wet down my hair because it was sticking straight up.

I saw Ms. Alexander through the tiny window of her door. She waved me into her office. She had forgotten to give me my prison I.D., and handed me the red and white card with my picture on it and my prison inmate number 38-224-044. I was to keep it with me at all times. I would also attend orientation in a couple of weeks and should look for my name on the call out sheet on the trulinks system.

Because I had to pay restitution to the courts, Ms. Alexander added that 50% of whatever I earned with a prison job would come out of my pay. "It looks like you're a horrible person who hurt a lot of people," she said. "Don't expect any favors from me."

I had a lot work ahead of me to get above water with my case manager.

I had a much better rapport with Mr. Goodwin, so I decided to drop by his office to make sure that Julie and the girls had been added into the system for a visit that weekend. While I was standing in line outside of the office a short rat-like man walked up to the line, his shoulder twitching. This was Mr. Swanson, the other prison counselor who had a horrible reputation. He began asking everyone in the line what we needed. None of them were there to see him.

He reached me, and I said I was waiting to meet with Mr. Goodwin to make sure my family was in the system so they could visit.

"Didn't you just get here?" he said. "You ain't getting any visits for a month or two. You have to go through orientation, and your family has to be approved after they send their visitor forms in, so get out of here."

This was not what Mr. Goodwin had told me the night before. He told me if they were in my PSR report, they would be automatically approved.

I went back upstairs to A2. I decided to take a shower to try to reset everything that had just happened. Romo had explained that I should bring your plastic chair to set outside the shower for my toiletries. "Exit the shower wearing boxers and a t-shirt," he said. "Shower shoes are a must."

I was pleasantly surprised that the shower heads had fantastic water pressure and plenty of hot water. I almost felt human again.

When I got to my locker, I told Jay Jones about Swanson, he told me to go downstairs and clear things up with Goodwin. When I got to the office, Swanson and Goodwin, whose offices were connected were both in. I would have this discussion and Swanson would hear it.

"Can you give me the names of your wife and kids?" Goodwin said, and typed their names into his computer. "Okay," he said, minutes later. "Ray it is all taken care of, and remember I am your counselor."

I knew this situation probably put me at odds with Swanson, but I got what I wanted, and I felt Goodwin was looking out for me.

Since Jay and I did not have jobs, we decided to go for a walk outside until it was time to come in for lunch. There was a sidewalk that you could walk along the perimeter of the fence. It was cold, but Jay and I decided it felt a lot better to be outside than to be in an ugly, rundown building. Jay and I talked about our counselors. Goodwin was definitely the good cop, and Swanson the traditional bad cop. Clearly, there was a power struggle between the two men on how things should be handled.

Lunch in prison is served at 10:30, and dinner is at 4:30. Senior Citizens hours. I quickly learned there were also long lines for most things: meals, phones, commissary and email terminals. No matter what meal, there were always beans. This was okay because I liked beans.

We looked for a place to sit and saw that the dining hall was loosely segregated between whites, Hispanics, and Blacks. We found an open table and sat down. The food was not that bad. I had been expecting much worse. A guy at our table said, "I just came from Marion prison. The chow is much better here."

I thought about Dad. He would be in prison long enough to celebrate his 70th birthday with bad chow.

When Jim Clark arrived, he told me he had good news. He used to work at the food warehouse, and learned that a guy had just gotten fired for stealing. He told me he would talk to Mr. Noll, the Corrections Officer who ran the warehouse to see about hiring me. It was the best job on the prison compound, besides the job he had at the Depot.

I asked Clark if he could show me how to use the Trulinks system and the phone. I had to enter my inmate number and then my PAC number, and finally I put my thumb on the thumb pad to get a green light. I could then start an email for your precious five cents a minute. The phone was the same except instead of the thumb pad I had to pre-record my name to get a dial tone. If you had a cold, the system often didn't recognize your voice. I was finally set-up to communicate with the outside world. An inmate was allotted 300 minutes a month. That meant I had 10 minutes a day to talk to my family. I immediately set up all my contacts in the Trulinks system.

That night Clark invited Jay and me to sit with his group of white collar guys in the cafeteria to watch TV. Clark had given me an extra radio with earphones. I learned very quickly the rules of the TV watching. The clicker was in the hands of the man with seniority. You watched whatever he chose. There could be vocal bitching about what was on, but you could never change a channel or you would start a fight. Everyone also had their spots. A fight could also ensue if you sat in someone's spot. Where I was sitting, I could see all four TV's. It seemed like a good location. There were certain shows that the Blacks, Whites, and Hispanics watched together on all four TV's. They were *American Idol*, *The Voice* and *Inside Edition*. It was funny to see some of the big tough, tattooed guys tear up over a good performance.

I had already started a new nighttime routine. I would walk five miles, call Julie right after my nighttime shower, then go to the cafeteria to watch TV. I would then email her goodnight before the 10pm count time. Julie would also send an email, which took an hour to get to my mailbox.

After the count, and lights were out, Romo and I caught up on our prison day. I started the routine of reading at night to fall asleep. I did not yet have a night light, but I could read well enough from the bathroom light shining on our bunkbed. This was a new routine. All my life, I had fallen asleep with the TV on.

I was having a hard time getting used to a flashlight shining in my face at midnight, 3am and 5 am.

The next day, Jay and I hit the sidewalk again. We saw some white guys sitting on milk crates by the side of the building. The guys motioned us over and said their turf was known as 'Cracker Corner.'

As we got talking to the guys, my name was called over the prison intercom to see Mr. Murouski in the cafeteria. Had I done something wrong?

Murouski, sat at a table in the office.

As he asked questions about my background, I suddenly realized that he was interviewing me. "I like you," he said. "I want you to walk out of here and through the front doors. A white van will be waiting to take you up to the food warehouse.

We drove around the backside of the big USP prison. We finally pulled up to two metal buildings with a big loading dock and parked.

"Good luck, man!" said the inmate driver.

I really liked the feeling of being away from the confines of the fenced in camp.

Inside the warehouse, pallets of food, shelved on metal racks, ran down aisles with enough room for a forklift. A short, dark-haired guy who looked like he might have some native Indian in him, jumped up from his chair and said, "You must be Cassity. I'm Matt Noll the Correctional Officer who runs the food warehouse. Jim Clark told me you're looking for a job."

212 • Nightmare Success

I still had not gotten use to the fact that correctional officers did not shake inmate's hands. In the caged office area, a Hispanic man was cooking chicken patties and French fries with a fryer. The food smelled delicious.

Noll said, "Garcia's been with me for four years. Let me show you around the place. You've run a business. I think you could be a real help to me around here because I need a warehouse clerk."

He opened the walk-in freezer, kept at a constant -6 degrees Fahrenheit. Pallets were stacked to the ceiling. "We feed about 2,000 inmates a day," Noll said. "If you accept the job, I'll show you how to enter the delivery information in a book, tag all new items with dates, and file the invoices once the food is delivered. We'll also teach you how to drive these fork lifts, and how to build an order with the pallets."

"I accept," I said.

"Good," he said. "Let's eat some lunch."

When we went back into the fenced in office I met Ralph Jackson, an ex-highway patrolman from Arkansas. He was in extremely good shape with a neatly trimmed gray beard and seemed to have a very easy manner about himself. Garcia simply stared at me.

Garcia said, "Okay, new guy, get in and get some lunch." Garcia said, "Let's hope you last longer than the other guy. He was here for one day and was fired."

I said, "Good to know. That gives me a goal to shoot for."

Garcia did not seem to think I was funny. All of a sudden, a big gray cat jumped in my lap and began to purr.

"I forgot to introduce you to Slash," smiled Noll. "He's supposed to kill the mice."

I had almost finished my chicken sandwich and French fries when we heard an 18 wheeler delivery truck backing up to the dock.

Garcia said, "Cassity, Jackson and I will unload the pallets from the truck with the forklifts. Grab a magic marker and write on the wrapped plastic who the supplier is and today's date."

Just like that I was on the job.

When we were done, Ralph showed me that there was a workout area behind the tall metal shelving racks. Ralph said, "You can do pull-ups, dips, crunches, and whatever you want with the two 25 lb. barbells. I'll show you my routine when we aren't busy." This had all happened so fast since I was standing out at 'cracker corner' just a few hours ago, but I felt like I was lucky to have gotten this job to be far away from that awful camp. I even had a good quiet place to work out. I was hoping that Garcia would eventually warm up to me.

At 3:30pm Noll said, "Cassity, you can ride the bus back to camp, or you can walk."

I decided to walk. It was about a mile from the Warehouse to the Camp. I walked in front of the big USP building, but I could see real life happening on Metropolitan Blvd that ran in front of the prison. It felt good to see the world still turning.

I was getting ready to walk to the food warehouse when I heard my name on the prison intercom to see Ms. Alexander. I knocked on the door, and she waved me in. She said, "Inmate Cassity, I said you couldn't have a prison job until you went to orientation. I could discipline you for being out of bounds and disobeying an order."

Now I was worried that not only was I getting in deeper waters with her, I wouldn't have a job, either. I walked out of her office, and saw that Mr. Goodwin was in his office. I told him what had just happened.

"Damn Cassity, for a new guy you are keeping me busy," he laughed. "Let me give Noll a call."

Ho got off the phone and said, "We'll take care of this with Ms. Alexander. Go on to work."

CHAPTER 53:

The Family Prison Visit

I had just seen Julie and the girls earlier in the week, but it seemed like a lifetime ago. I desperately wanted to make sure that I was positive and letting them feel I was adjusting. I wanted to do anything I could do to help them to stop worrying about me. I also knew how it felt to visit Dad. It was terrifying to enter a prison visiting room, and see your father in a prison uniform.

My name was called over the intercom. I walked through the doors, to see my whole world standing right there at Leavenworth prison. We all immediately embraced each other in a big Cassity group hug. The girls told me that the prison visit cop, Hudson, was really nice to them and made them feel welcome. That made me feel good. We found a table to sit around. The visitor room building was the newest structure on the premises. It reminded me of a sterile doctor's office waiting room. But, I was one of the few prison inmates who had this luxury. Of 425 inmates at the Leavenworth Prison camp, only about 30 of us received visits.

This prison visiting room became our family's new weird normal. We could eat out of the vending machines and catch up. The girls later said there were things that they noticed that bothered them on their first visit. They did not like the sign that did not allow inmates behind the red line to the vending machines. There was an inmate bathroom and a visitor bathroom, and security cameras at every corner of the room.

I told Julie and the girls about Romo, Jim Clark, and Jay Jones. I also shared with them how my Counselor Goodwin had already helped me out with run-ins with Ms. Alexander and Swanson. On top of all of that, I was able to get a good prison job at the Food Warehouse where we could cook our own food. I felt like this information put them more at ease at how their old Dad was adapting.

With no cell phones allowed, the five of us talked about everything in those three to four hours. I stayed on top of boyfriend issues, tennis, and everything going on with school or work. We had lived a very privileged lifestyle and in a flash that was all taken away. Tyler took care of the girl's tuition, but they all worked through college as bartenders. Julie was now working at Gateway Buick GMC setting service appointments. They never complained about having to take on more to get by. They all just did whatever they needed to do to make things work. I could not be prouder of each one of them.

Julie and the girls loved the nicknames of the inmates. We had Tree Licker, Two Butts, Red, Butter Bean, Go Lightly, The Commissioner, Droopy, Moon Cricket, Big Panda. I became known simply as Cass.

Julie became like a superhero road warrior for the years I was in prison. She visited every weekend, four and one-half hours each way. She would usually pick up one or all three of the girls as she passed through Mizzou, joking that the Leavenworth Express was leaving for all who wanted to hitch a ride. I believe her dedication to those visits was single-handedly the magic formula that kept our marriage and our family thriving. Julie and I refused to let ourselves think too far ahead. We would survive the day, the week, the month, the years.

One thing I never got use to was saying good-bye when the visit was over. I could feel the clock ticking down. During a visit I felt like I was sitting on a fence with one leg in the real world and one in prison. When the visit was getting close to ending you could feel yourself being sucked away from the real world. We would hug and I would watch my world walk away to the parking lot. It was the feel of real separation, as I headed back into the dingy prison.

CHAPTER 54:

The Dark Side of Prison

As the days and weeks went by, I worked myself into my prison routine. I walked the one mile to work at 7am. Noll and I had good conversations about sports and family. He had three boys and loved the Kansas City Royals and Kansas State. I loved the Cardinals and Mizzou. I had become comfortable with my job, and I became certified as a forklift driver. Since I had my driver's license, I drove the big refrigerated truck down at the camp. I had to get pretty nifty with the pallet jack to unload the pallets on the camp dock, and I was really impressed with myself learning how to back up the big truck only using my side mirrors. The big plus was my workout at the warehouse. This made it so much easier than having to work out at the camp weight pile. I also appreciated the much better lunches. Noll had us plant a garden, and in summer we ate fresh jalapenos and tomatoes.

I returned to camp at 3:30pm We would have count at 4pm, and I would walk five to six miles. I would come back in and take a shower, and make my 10- minute call to Julie. Then I went to my seat to watch TV and read the newspaper. At 9pm I emailed Julie and the girls. 10pm count and lights went out. I then read my book with my nightlight for about two hours every day week after week.

I began to get lulled into this schedule. One of the guys Jay Jones and I walked with at night was a 65-year-old man from California. He was in for growing and distributing marijuana. He had a family, and he only had a few months left of a six-year sentence. Jay and I heard that some of the guys were hassling him about being gay, pinning signs on his back and other juvenile things. He had finally gotten fed up with it, and went up to the bubble to report the abuse. This was not a good move. The CO's took him and the other two guys to the dreaded hole to investigate what had happened. It was three days later that Jay and I found out that the man had hung himself by his bedsheet in the hole.

I couldn't believe that a guy Jay and I had been walking with in the yard was now dead. I could not believe this man would have done this when he was so close to being released. You never want to die in prison. I had to tell myself that he had to have had other demons. No matter what, it felt really dark and raw.

I had also gotten pretty comfortable at work. Garcia and I were never going to be best friends, but we were co-existing. One day, we had loaded up the truck for Noll. When he was away from the warehouse he would lock it up, so we inmates had a little white shack with a space heater, and two benches along the narrow interior. Garcia, Jackson, and I were joking around, and they were teasing me about learning to use the forklift. I thought everything was all in good fun when Garcia heard Noll drive up with the truck, and said, "I was supposed to remind him to get the cat food for Slash."

He waved to Noll, who backed up. When he returned, he said "Noll must have remembered when he saw me on the dock."

"Yeah," I said, "He saw a big pussy on the dock, and must have remembered."

In a flash, Garcia got a crazy look in his eye, came after me, and started rapid-fire hitting me with his left and right. At first, I thought he was playing around, and raised my hands to cover my face. But this was for real.

Jackson pulled him off, saying, "What the hell Garcia? Cass was just joking around."

Garcia had cut his finger on my plastic watch and was bleeding. My face and forehead were a little red, but I was mostly stunned. "Are you alright? I was just kidding around."

Garcia said, "You can't call other inmates a pussy."

"I'm truly sorry," I said. I knew we couldn't call other inmates bitches, but

I didn't know joking around using the word pussy would cause this to happen. Knowing what I know now, calling someone a bitch is a throw down fight. Calling someone a pussy is definitely different, but not to Garcia that day. We shook hands and went back to work. I needed to remember that I was in prison, not at a baseball game or on the golf course with my friends.

I had not been hit in a fist fight since I was in seventh grade. I also didn't want to get a black eye. That would call attention to the guards, which would earn me a trip to the hole until they had time to investigate. This shook me into my new reality. I was living in a primitive world, and I needed to conform. Things were different on the inside.

CHAPTER 55:

Leavenworth Entertainment

My friends and family would always ask me, "What do you do for entertainment?" Well, for one thing, you never wanted to need medical attention in prison. It would take twenty-five minutes for an ambulance to be cleared to enter the prison property, even though the Fire Department was directly across the street. I ruled out playing in the softball league. Guys would break their wrist or turn their ankles. I also avoided the basketball leagues because these games were ripe for fights. Although, every Friday while the rest of the camp was having dinner, Clark and I played one-on-one, and the game 21. Clark was an unbelievable free throw shooter, but I could usually win taking him off the dribble. Both very competitive, we usually got a lot of onlookers watching two old white guys go at it.

One hot Friday night, Clark and I finished our basketball game, and headed to the showers in our A2 dorm. Music was blasting and people were already playing cards at the card table. Fans blew full blast. We walked into the bathroom. Big Watson had chicken strung out all over the sink counter. He was dropping it into oil in a plastic trash can. Two metal prongs called stingers, bootlegged from the metal shop, had heated the oil. Watson was frying chicken to sell at movie night.

Bass stood in front of the mirror by the side of the sink shaving every hair on his head and body. On the other side were the smokers. six of them in a cramped space with smoke bellowing from the bathroom. Big Watson had the showers on cold to keep the heat down from his cooking escapades. I asked him if it was okay to jump in the shower while he was cooking.

"No problem, Cass," he said.

I looked at Clark, and we both just grinned. Another Friday night at Leavenworth.

I also killed time playing an unusual game of prison tennis. Leavenworth had a worn out plastic court. Fort Leavenworth had given it to the prison because they said the court was worn out and unsafe. We had to be really careful when we started and stopped because the little plastic squares would come unhooked and would slide under our feet. We'd hook the squares back together with twisted paper clips.

I played doubles with a good group of guys on the weekends. We certainly kept the white collar stereotype going strong playing tennis. Clark and I were the kings of the court in doubles. We went undefeated the summer of 2014. All this fun came to a screeching halt when the strings broke on the rackets. We would have to wait a few months until the rackets were fixed.

The tennis court was located next to the 'weight pile' where guys worked out and lifted weights for hours while playing some really strange music. Sometimes my mind would drift back to playing tennis at Old Warson Country Club on the beautiful clay tennis courts. Times had really changed.

I had always loved playing sand volleyball. I was getting older, but I still had some good spring left in my legs to spike the ball. One spring day, I was out playing a pick-up game with some Hispanic guys. One of the guys said, "Man, that old, white guy can jump."

They ended up recruiting me to play on their league team. We were competing and having fun like we would on the outside. I think all of us felt that way.

I knew I had been in prison for a while, when the weekends actually started feeling like the weekends again. I knew Julie would come for a visit, and it was Leavenworth movie night on Friday, Saturday, and Sunday. Movie night was a big deal. They were shown on a drop down screen in the gym. Everyone would take their plastic chair with them, and sit in their personal spot. I always felt sorry for the new guys because you would see them bouncing around the gym trying to find a place to sit. You don't ever sit in someone else's spot unless you are invited. Never.

All the guys that had their "food hustle" selling their goods. Some guys would make food from things that had been stolen from the kitchen. It was incredible what could be made from a microwave. There was popcorn, candy from the commissary, oatmeal cookies, slices of pecan pie, and whatever else these guys could dream up. Everything cost two stamps or more. There was always a guy in the back of the gym with a mop bucket full of ice and soda… two stamps for a soda.

There was more than a couple of times that the movie we were watching had the line, "If you do this. If you do that, you could end up in Leavenworth." Yes, here we all were sitting in our non-air conditioned gym, sweating and whooping, "You could end up in Leavenworth."

It didn't matter if I was just walking the fence line, or playing a sport outside. Almost anything was better than being in the small rundown old building. My mindset was always to try to keep busy. Every night I would write in my calendar about something that took place that day. When I go back and review those calendar entries, I can feel the effort I was making daily to keep my mind in the present, win the day, and move on.

CHAPTER 56:

Visiting Day SNAFU

I so looked forward to seeing Julie and the kids each week. There was a crazy point system for the visits, which really discouraged families from making frequent visits. You would think the government wanted to promote the family visits as an important part of creating stability for families. There were so many broken families in prison, which only made an inmate feel more isolated and hopeless for the future.

When I first arrived, several inmates told me, "Your family may come to see you for the first few weeks or months, but they'll eventually abandon you." They would say that your family was being trained to live without you, and eventually they won't need you anymore. That was my worst nightmare, and I heard horrible stories of that happening to other guys.

The Bureau of Prisons devised the point system for visits. You were given twenty-four points per month, charged two points for each hour on Saturday and Sunday; and one point for each hour on Mondays. A prison guard sat in the visiting room with a computer and checked visitors in when they arrived. There were several rules of what a visitor was allowed to wear, such as, no holes in jeans, no open-toed shoes, no shorts, women's skirts below the knee, no exposed shoulders or halter tops. Many people were denied a visit because of their attire.

Mr. Hudson was the prison visiting guard the first six months of our visits. He was excellent. He truly enjoyed meeting and welcoming families, and he made all the visitors feel comfortable. He believed his job was to make the environment inviting, so family and friends would want to come back. He didn't care about the point system. He believed a visitor who had traveled could stay as long as they wanted. Everything changed when good old Mr. Hudson rotated out.

The new prison guard was apparently angry that she had to be there. She made a game out of being as rude as possible. She looked for any way possible to deny visits. It finally happened to my family.

The mess of that visit happened on my daughter Carly's birthday. Julie and the girls had just arrived and were filling out their visitor forms. She started typing in the information in the computer and turned to them, "There will be no visit with inmate Cassity today. He is out of visiting points."

I was sitting in the cafeteria waiting to be called, and when counselor Swanson tapped me on my shoulder, "Cassity, you've been hit! I just sent your family home."

I looked at him in shock and said, "What do you mean I have been hit? Why would you send my family home?"

He grinned slyly, "It looks like you didn't have enough points for a visit." I said, "I know I had more than enough points. I would not have had them drive 4 ½ hours if I did not have enough points. She had to have double counted my points."

Swanson smirked and said, "It doesn't matter now. I already sent them home."

I said, "This is my daughter's birthday!"

"Cassity," said Swanson. "You'll have to man up! This isn't going to be the first birthday you miss."

It took everything I had not to pin him against the wall. He lived for this kind of stuff to do to inmates. Clearly, twenty-seven years of work at Leavenworth had warped him in a bad way.

Correction Officer Mac was a tall, thin black man with a low, bellowing voice who intimidated most inmates by his mere presence. I definitely tried to avoid any contact with him, but Julie's and my wedding anniversary was the following weekend.

The Counselor slated to be on visiting duty was notorious for doubling inmate's visiting points. It was toward the end of the month, and I wanted to verify that I had enough points for a Monday visit with Julie.

I nervously went up to the bubble to speak to Mac.

He finally looked up and said, "What do you need Cassity?"

I said, "Mac, my anniversary is Monday, and I wanted to make sure I have enough points for a visit."

He swiveled around in his chair to look at the computer screen. This was not a chore that any CO liked to perform for inmates. "Yep," he said. You have four points for a visit on Monday." I told Mac that I really appreciated him taking the time.

Monday rolled around and I came back early from work at the warehouse to shower and get ready. I had a special uniform I saved for visits. I was always nervous before a visit. The general worry patterns we all fall into at times. Would Julie have car trouble? Had one of the girls gotten sick? Did I have enough points? But I had double-checked this with Mac.

From the front of the building, I saw Julie enter. My name was not called over the intercom. My mind immediately began to race. I then thought I saw her leave and walk out. I went down the hallway and out the side door to the double fence where I could see the parking lot. My heart was racing. I could see Julie walking to the car. I yelled at her to get her attention. "Julie, what's wrong?"

"The C.O. lady says we're out of points."

I told Julie that I had double checked the visiting points. I told Julie to hang on. I would get this cleared up. I raced down the hallway to the bubble where Mac was. "There's been a misunderstanding with the visiting points with the C.O.," I pleaded.

He stared at me with irritation in his eyes, got up from his chair, and headed to the visiting building. I waited by the door, but I could barely see through the windows. Five minutes later, he strode back and motioned me to come inside the bubble.

"Cassity," he said. "You're in a heap of shit. The C.O. saw you talking to your wife through the fence. I could give you a level one shot immediately and send you to the hole for having unauthorized contact with the public. I have personally communicated with your wife, and told her to leave the premises immediately because she was trespassing. I have not decided what I am going to do with you. I want you to go sit in the cafeteria, and do not say a word to anyone."

I looked at him in disbelief. Gone was the idea that he was going to stand up for me. I was devastated and scared of what was coming my way. A level one shot in prison was very serious, and a trip to the hole was terrifying. And that wasn't my biggest worry. I had not yet been officially accepted into the RDAP program. I was on the wait list. Did I just add a year to my sentence at this hell hole by asking Julie what had happened to her inside the visiting building?

There was nothing I could do, but sit and run all of these awful scenarios through my mind in different ways with the same awful conclusion. I sat in that cafeteria chair for three hours. What was going through Julie's mind? However you described mind torture, this was the definition of it.

Finally, Mac came to me and said, "Cassity, go call your wife, and tell her you are okay. Then come see me in the bubble."

I called Julie. She was worried sick about what had happened, and how Mac had accused her of trespassing. I told her everything would be okay and went to see Mac in the bubble.

"Cassity," he said. "What should I do with you? I have looked up your file. You were a big man, a CEO, a multimillionaire. I bet you are used to getting your way, and barking orders to the little people. Well, you are not the big man here at Leavenworth. I could send you up the hill for some time in the hole. I could also give you a level 1 shot that would ruin your good time for the rest of your stay, BUT I think these last few hours have been torture enough for you. Am I right?"

I cautiously replied, "Yes sir."

Mac stared at me for a few seconds, and said, "Alright, Cassity I think we are good here. Now go on now."

I honestly can't explain the sigh of relief that left my whole body. I was completely drained. I had spent the last three hours walking through my mind how I would survive the hole, and how I had lost my good time on top of losing my year off by not being able to be accepted to the RDAP program with a shot on my record. I have never experienced that type of terror and wouldn't wish it on anyone.

I called Julie back, and explained the whole ordeal. We couldn't really be open because all phone calls are recorded.

Happy 25th wedding anniversary, dearest Julie, I thought after I hung up.

CHAPTER 57:

Serving in Prison

I liked my warehouse job. I had learned how to do all my clerk duties with the invoices and logging inventory. Building the food pallets was great exercise. I enjoyed learning how and getting certified to drive a fork lift. I felt a sense of freedom driving the warehouse truck down to the camp, and unloading it. If only my friends back home could see me now. I also had the added benefit of having a workout station behind the food racks.

Noll was a great boss to work for and a good family man. Leavenworth had a lot of land and used some of it to grow vegetables. We grew over 100,000 lbs. of vegetables a year. The vegetables were given to community organizers every Tuesday throughout the summer at our food warehouse loading dock. Noll decided that he wanted me to be in charge of weighing the vegetables, loading them, and recording all of this in our log book. This gave me an opportunity to meet and converse with normal people in the community while I loaded their truck with vegetables.

The first week in June 2014, Noll said, "Cassity, I just got a call from down at the camp. They said you're needed immediately."

It didn't sound good. It was a Friday afternoon. One thing about prison is that anything can change in a flash, and you have no control. Things just automatically started racing through my mind. Did I do something wrong?

I went to the case manager's office and waited. He finally called me in. It felt good in there because his office had a window unit AC. He said, "Cassity, we're overcrowded, and have a shortage of beds. I need your bed for a new

228 • *Nightmare Success*

inmate, and there is a bed open in the RDAP dorm. I need you to get your things and move in fifteen minutes."

I asked, "Does this mean I am starting RDAP?"

The case manager said, "How the hell should I know. I just need you moved. Now get out of here."

As bad as A2 was, I had gotten used to it. I would be leaving Jay and Romo. Jay helped me get my stuff from my locker. The RDAP dorm was cleaner and much quieter. I eventually found out I would not start RDAP until November, but it at least it meant I was approved to get into the program. That was a real positive!

We had a new guy who had started at the warehouse, and quit because he said it was too much work. I asked Noll if we could hire Jay. I told him Jay was a good guy, and I could help train him. Noll liked that idea.

Jay came by to meet with Noll, and they immediately hit it off. Jay had owned a sporting goods hunting store back home. They both fell right into everything hunting related. It was a match. I finally had one of my guys up at the warehouse.

Mr. Stanley, Noll's boss, would drop by the warehouse occasionally. He was in charge of the Warden's community dinners held at the Officer Training Center. He told Noll about the dinner, and what he was thinking about for the menu, and added that he needed responsible guys to help cook and serve the desserts.

"How about Cassity and the new guy?" Noll said.

There was going to be close to 100 people from the Leavenworth community. Stanley bought us chef's uniforms and added a few other guys who worked in the kitchen.

We all headed over to the OTC for the day. Jay and I were assigned to cutting strawberries for the strawberry shortcake. I have no idea how many strawberries we cut, but it was more strawberries than I had ever seen before. We were both to wear our white chef coats when we brought the food out to the buffet tables. We then served strawberry shortcake on fancy serving carts to each table.

I craved being around people who were not inmates or CO's. While I was serving food, I could pretend I was no longer an inmate. I was a waiter working at an ordinary restaurant.

Jay and I did such a good job that we were asked to do two more Warden dinners. Politically, it was not a bad idea to make the Warden look good, and he remembered your name instead of your number.

Jay had really picked up on things quickly at the warehouse. It was always good when you stood in for someone, and they performed well. Ralph Jackson, the Black Arkansas Highway Patrolman, seemed to be always snippy with Jay. So many arguments were so ridiculous in prison. Noll liked to play country music all day long. That suited Jay and I just fine. One day when we were building our food pallets Jay turned up a song that he liked. Ralph jabbed Jay with the comment that he must be racist because he listens to country music. Jay just kind of laughed it off, but it really pissed me off. I said, "Ralph you are an educated guy, you know that comment is bullshit. Why are you hassling Jay? That is like me saying you are racist listening to rap music. Ralph gets his hackles up and says, "oh, so Cass wants to stand up for his country boy? Name me one black country singer." I immediately responded, "Charlie Pride and Darius Rucker." Ralph just stared at me, getting madder. I said, "Jackson, can you name a white rapper?" He didn't respond. "I can name you a couple of white rappers…how about Vanilla Ice and Eminem?" Ralph immediately slams the forklift to a stop and jumps off. We are staring at each other nose to nose pissed. Ralph says, "You want me to whip your ass?" I said, "If you are that fucking stupid with two months left on your sentence." We stared at each other a few seconds longer without moving. Ralph turned and got back on his forklift. Not another word was said. He did stop hassling Jay. What a stupid argument saying someone was racist for listening to country music, but that was life at Leavenworth. Things got hot in a hurry over very stupid things.

I guess that is why it felt good to try to do normal things as much as possible like loading up vegetables for the community, and serving at the Warden's dinner. Life inside was clearly outside the norm.

It was just a few months later in September when Jay found out he was getting released earlier than expected. I could not have been happier for Jay and his wife Jamie. He had a great family that frequently visited him. It was the first time that someone I was really close with was being released. Jay and I had come to Leavenworth the exact same day. We leaned on each other as we learned the ropes of prison. When you become close to someone in prison, you see them every day. They become part of your familiar routine. It is an odd time of readapting and setting up different daily routines with other people once they leave. It also just brings it all back home in your mind that I have a long way to go. I am not getting out anytime soon. The flip side of this equation was being happy for your friend, and knowing that people really do make it out of this prison hole.

CHAPTER 58:

Doing Time in RDAP

In November, 2014, after living in the Residential Drug Abuse Dorm, RDAP, since June, I was officially accepted into the program. If I successfully made it through the nine month program, I would get a whole year shaved off my sentence. Alcohol is considered a drug, and this is the only Bureau of Prison program that reduces significant time from an inmate's sentence.

The RDAP program was founded to provide a more solid foundation for inmates to reenter society, helping us recognize specific trigger situations, and providing rational thinking tools to overcome past behaviors. National statistics show that inmates who complete the program have a lower recidivism rate. The recidivism rate for inmates is jaw dropping high, 2/3 return in three years, and ¾ return in five years.

I had admitted in my sentencing report that I was drinking too much the year before I entered prison, a truthful statement. I clearly was using alcohol as a coping mechanism at night to ease my stress level.

There were 100 guys in the program. When the meeting began, one by one, we rose and shouted our number. Together, we would repeat the RDAP creed, then someone would come to the podium to use the 'word of the day' in a sentence. Then there would be a long line of people to use the word of the day in a sentence. You received participation points for this. We would always end with an upbeat ritual. These upbeat rituals varied from activities like musical chairs, pin the tail on the donkey, trivia, or whatever the group had been okayed to do that day. We would then break into our individual groups of 30 or so people to work with our assigned teacher in our current workbook. When you finished that workbook, you moved on to another class that would last another couple of months until you had completed the nine month program. The Promised Land was when you had made it to the black chair graduation ceremony. All the graduates sat in black chairs; thus the name.

Our first meeting took place in a cold, crowded old band room. None of us really knew what to expect, and almost all of us were voluntarily taking this program simply to get the time off. There were some good instructors who really wanted to help, and there were other instructors clearly looking for anything to set someone back in the program. If you were set back, you had to start over and take one of the courses again. This could add additional months.

My group was lucky enough to start with Ms. Matthias. She acted hard, but she really cared for the guys. One of our first big assignments was to write a 'readiness statement,' and truthfully confront the mistakes that you made and who they had hurt in your life. One by one each of us went up to the podium in this jammed in, cold little band room to read our readiness statements.

I was caught off guard at how humble and brutally honest these men were reading their statements. They were admitting tough mistakes, and were wanting to improve themselves with a real second chance with their lives. There were a lot of tears, and you don't cry in prison, at least, not that anyone would ever see. One of the guys completely broke down while he was reading his statement. My new quiet friend, Kimbrick Jones, jumped up from his chair, and began reading his statement for him. It was a very emotional moment for all of us, and bonded our group in a real and unexpected way. I didn't know what to expect with RDAP, but I was inspired by the hope and honesty I felt in that room that day. No one ever spoke of what happened in our group in the general prison population. It was like we were in our own bubble.

As the program moved along, I found that some of my past experiences could be helpful to several of the guys in the program. One day I was assigned to cover the topic of goal setting and plans. This topic used to be one of my favorites to teach with our sales company NPS. If taught properly, planning and goal setting can be inspiring to someone who has not done this before. It opens the door to possibilities in the mind. After I was done speaking, I had guys coming up to me afterwards saying, "Man, Cass, that really made sense to me. That is the most good of anything I have gotten since I have been at Leavenworth. Do you think you could sit down individually with me, and help me with my goals?" I began doing this with some of the guys, and I really got a lot of personal fulfillment out of helping those who wanted my help. This was not manual labor; I was engaging my brain again by teaching things I had learned that had helped me.

When our black chair graduation ceremony date was approaching, our class of 30 guys had to nominate someone who would give our graduation speech. My class decided it should be me to give our speech. It is odd. I was taking this program to just get the year off, but along the way I learned a lot about myself, and I have to say I was very proud to be selected by the guys in my class to represent us.

We had all been through a lot together in those nine months. We had all adapted to this new controlled, and strange environment, and it felt like an accomplishment to be completing it. I closed my speech with a quote from Seattle Seahawks NFL Coach Pete Carroll from an article in Sports Illustrated. The question by the reporter was how do you comeback from what many have said was the worst call in Superbowl History? Coach Carroll replied, "I refuse to be defined by those 11 seconds…I choose to "use it" to improve myself and my team. I will not let a mistake, or a setback distract me from my goals." Good words for us all to live by.

CHAPTER 59:

The Civil Case Nightmare

In addition to the federal indictments, we were also being tried in Civil court on the same charges. The case had been moving along. I was representing myself pro-se because I was flat out broke. There were forty-four other defendants, so I believed I could read and copy most of the motions they were filing. Leavenworth opened up a special closet for all the files that were mailed to me weekly.

In May, 2014, I became the talk of the prison when thirty-five attorneys showed up in a parade of rental cars to take my deposition in the Officer Training Center. "Damn," they said. "What the hell is going on?"

I'd been quiet about this, but word had gotten out. Unusual. Inmates lined our side of the barbed wire fence watching the attorneys arrive. The Hispanic guys began to jokingly call me *El Padrino*, the Godfather. I liked to be known as Cass much better, but there was nowhere to hide with all of the good fun my fellow inmates were having at my expense.

It was very surreal to walk into a cavernous room in my khaki prison uniform to see thirty-five attorneys dressed in suits. I sat down at a long table equipped with a microphone. A court reporter sat next to me. Warden May entered and welcomed everyone to Leavenworth, asked if the accommodations were suitable, got thirty-five nods, and left. Mr. Goodwin sat next to me. None of it seemed real to me on any level, anymore. I was about to be deposed by Larry Pozner, who literally wrote the book on how to cross examine witnesses, along with the other attorneys.

The deposition lasted two days. but, there was one positive outcome. The attorneys bought me a milkshake from Sonic and a sausage pizza from Pizza Hut for lunch.

A few months passed, and I was called into Mr. Goodwin's office for a call with Larry Pozner, who was the lead attorney for the plaintiffs in the case. He told me he was ready to dismiss me from the civil trial and asked to sign an affidavit. We worked out the details, and Larry faxed Mr. Goodwin the document for me to sign, along with my official dismissal from the Civil Case. I could not believe the ordeal was finally over.

With the Civil trial being behind me, I needed to focus on RDAP. Once I completed this program, I would only have a little over a year left in my sentence. That is not to say it was all smooth sailing. I also occasionally threw myself one hell of a pity party. My youngest daughter had just won State in tennis. I would have given anything to be there to experience that celebration. My oldest daughter, Courtney, was graduating Magna Cum Laude in December. I had missed so much and these pity parties sat on me like a dark cloud for days. I would eventually pull myself out of the dark hole by thinking about how lucky I was to have my family waiting to create new memories when I finally got home to them.

As I was walking through one of my dark funks along the prison fence, a white-haired, energetic, wiry guy walked up beside me. He was a new guy who I had seen around. He said, "Hi I am Doug Watson. Are you the NPS funeral guy, Brent Cassity?"

I was thinking, oh no, what could this possibly be about? I looked back at Doug, and said, "That would be me."

Doug continued, "Wow, what a small world. I used your NPS preneed product for years at my funeral home."

Where is this going, I wondered.

Doug said, "I really loved your product. I had the best NPS Advantage Rep. Andrea Cassil. It is too bad what happened to your company."

Needless, to say, I sighed internally with relief. Doug and I ended up in the same RDAP group, and I really enjoyed his company.

Life can play tricks on you when you least expect it. I was thinking I knew what was in front of me. I had been dismissed from the Civil case, and was doing well in the RDAP program. In January, two months into the RDAP program, I heard my name called over the intercom to go and see Mr. Goodwin.

He waved me into his office, and said, "I have some unexpected news for you. We've received a court order that you are being shipped to St. Louis for the civil case the first or second week of February."

"I don't understand, I said. "I've been dismissed from the case."

Goodwin said, "Cassity, I sat through two days of your disposition, I can't even believe you're here. The last thing I could explain is why they want to ship you to St. Louis. It has something to do with your affidavit. You need to give live testimony."

Of the forty-four defendants in the case, one defendant remained, PNC Bank, represented by Williams and Connelly out of Washington DC. The plaintiffs were banking on the notion that PNC Bank would spend money. My only hope was that PNC bank would settle with the plaintiffs before the trial date. I only had two weeks for this settlement to happen, or I was going to go on a nightmare journey.

My bigger concern was that I would be knocked out of the RDAP program. An inmate could only miss ten days of the program. My other concern was traveling as an inmate to a county jail. I had heard horror stories of inmates getting lost in the system. This trial could go on for months while I waited in the county jail to be called as a witness.

I called Julie to tell her about this totally unexpected news. We had no idea which jail I would be shipped to. Julie said she would to try to get a hold of Scott Rosenblum, Dad's attorney, as we had been friends with Scott over the years. Julie and Courtney met with Scott the next day. He had a good relationship with the Judge, and agreed to meet with Judge Webber to see what could be worked out. Scott and his team were able to get a commitment from the judge that I would be the first witness called for the trial.

The plan would be that I would travel on a Wednesday. I would testify on Thursday, and travel back to Leavenworth on Friday. The Judge called

Dr. Wells who ran the RDAP program to make sure that this would not interfere with my position. Dr. Wells assured the Judge that this schedule would work without effecting my position in the program. I still held out hope for the case to settle, but my mind was swimming with all the things that could go wrong.

Strangely enough, one of Pozner's attorneys showed up at Leavenworth prison to prep me for my testimony. My affidavit had only stated that I was at a meeting regarding our NPS Trust where the bank president had made the comment that he would gladly look favorably upon any future loan business that we might have.

The attorney prep session gave me the unique opportunity to see how I could weave in some of our story around the questions they would ask me. No one had heard our side of the story after all of these years.

The day finally came. My name was called over the intercom at 8:30am Wednesday morning. Inmates had told me that if I was traveling with Federal Marshals they would be nice, and even stop at Taco Bell or McDonalds along the way. I was thinking, 'Damn, I am walking into the complete unknown, but I'll be fortified with a burrito and a Big Mac.'

I was met out front of the prison camp with the white van. The van took me back to the exact gate I was standing at to voluntarily surrender over a year ago. I stood there waiting for someone from inside the big house to escort me in. Finally, after about fifteen minutes a prison guard came to the gate. The guard led me into a solitary cell and slammed the door shut. I sat there for four and half hours doing nothing but creating a thousand different awful scenarios. I had the pity party of all pity parties. Why was I the only one in my family having to go through all of this?

The metal cell door slid open. "Let's go!" the prison guard shouted.

Two men dressed in sheriff uniforms that said 'Warren County' walked toward me, carrying shackles. They hooked them around my waist, around my ankles, and around my wrists as if I were a wild animal. They opened the van door, and I awkwardly slid in. I was now in a soundproof cage. Suddenly, the door opened, and another shackled inmate slid in next to me.

"Man," he said. "I've been through hell. I have been telling these damn prison guards for two days that I was not supposed to be at Leavenworth Penitentiary. They say everyone says that. I finally got someone to check my file. They're taking me over to the private prison. Is that where you are going?"

I said, "I think I am going to some county jail in St. Louis."

His story scared the shit out of me. This inmate was put in the wrong prison. About ten minutes later we pulled through the gate of another prison. The door slid open. The sheriff grabbed the inmate, and he was gone. There was a part of me that thought they might mistakenly take us both into this privately run prison. I had heard bad things about how those prisons were run. In my opinion, you never want businessmen trying to save his company money while making a profit to house you while you serve your sentence.

The van made it out to the highway pointed east to St. Louis. It was strange see the world again. All of it moved a lot faster than I remembered. One of the sheriffs opened up the cage window, and threw me a brown paper bag. It contained a bologna and cheese sandwich and warm milk. This was a far cry from Taco Bell or McDonalds. My mind drifted back into the terrified thoughts of how this jail thing was going to work for me as I gazed out on the countryside.

It was getting dark when the van pulled off the Warrenton exit. I was heading to the Warren County jail forty minutes outside of St. Louis. The jail garage door opened and the van went inside the basement.

I arrived at a processing room with holding cells surrounding the room. The sheriffs took me to a bench, and removed the shackles. They then handcuffed me to the bench where I sat for three hours as the shifts changed. I heard people yelling at me from inside their cells, "Hey why you here?"

I looked straight ahead. An officer finally unlocked me from the bench, and led me into a tiny cell where there were two other men who appeared to be drunk. The cell smelled like a rotten sewer. One of the guys stood up and pissed on the mattress on the floor, and then sat back down on the mattress. The cell door opened and they slid in three trays of food. It looked like the food had just been collected from the trash can. My two roommates ate it like it was their last meal.

I offered my tray to the men in an attempt to get on their good side. I had more than lost my appetite. I began to think this cell was going to be my home for the next few days. The man who pissed on the mattress began telling me a story about land he owned not too far from the jail, but now he only owned a few acres on Mars.

Suddenly, the cell door opened and the guard said, "Cassity, let's get you processed." They took me into a small room with a shower. The guard told me to strip down, and bend over. I was then told to take a shower, and they handed me an orange uniform and orange looking crock shoes. When I was through they handed me a rolled up mattress, sheets, and a towel.

I felt a lot better by the time they led me to an elevator and from along a winding hallway, you could see the open pod rooms behind the one way glass windows. The guard led me to my cell where a twenty something white small guy with short hair stood. He was pretty normal looking. I said, "I guess I am your new bunky." He said, "Cool." There were two metal bunks with a stainless steel toilet and sink like you see in the movies. This guy had a lot of stuff strung over the top bunk. He was using the top bunk bed like a shelf. I said, "Hey, I will just throw my mattress on the floor, so it doesn't disturb your stuff." The guy said, "That is really cool man. Thanks! Where are you from?" I told him that I was coming in from Leavenworth for a trial. That seemed good enough that he did not want to ask me anymore questions.

I walked out of our cell onto a metal platform that looked over the two storey room. There was a small TV up in the corner of the room And there were several guys sitting around metal looking picnic tables on the first floor. I saw three phones on the wall. I wanted to call Julie. I knew she had been worried sick. She had no idea what county jail I was in. I could feel that I was being stared at as I was walking towards the phones. I was hoping that there wasn't some unspoken rule about the phones I didn't know about. The population looked like the Leavenworth population but the place definitely had a different feel to it. I felt more like a caged animal.

I figured out how to make a collect call to Julie and she answered on the first ring. It felt so good to hear her voice. My touchstone to the outside world. I told her that I was in Warrenton. She was relieved to know that I had made it, but I could hear in her voice that she was worried. I told her I had become an expert adaptor. I was only going to be here a few days. I told her I could do anything for a couple of days. We were both hoping against hope that everything would go as planned. I would testify tomorrow and be back on the road to Leavenworth by Friday.

I got off the phone and sat down at the end of the metal picnic bench. I looked up to see what was on TV. There was a huge 30 something year old black man sitting next to me and he introduced himself. He told me he was from St. Louis and owned several banks, and was big into real estate. I told him that I was from St. Louis, but I had been at Leavenworth for the last year. He let me know that he was in a heap of trouble. He was supposed to report to Marion prison camp, and showed up two days late. He said, "Did you know that could cost me an additional five years to my sentence? They are trying to decide what to do with me, and that is why I am here waiting for my hearing in St. Louis." I said Darius, "If you ever get back to Marion, my Dad is doing a ten year stint there. You will have to look him up to help you get settled in." I felt like Darius and I were kind of connecting. He seemed like a nice enough guy. There were some skinhead looking guys that looked like they were looking for any trouble they could find. One of the skinheads came up to me and said, "Heard you are one of those federal prisoners? You think you are better than us…huh?" I replied, "I do not." Darius looked at the skinhead and he just slithered away for the moment. I wanted to do anything to avoid getting in any kind of physical altercation. I also knew from being in prison, I could not be pushed around. I had to hold my ground no matter how scared I really was, and this was scary shit.

That night the guards ordered us into our cells. The metal cell doors slammed shut at once, which caused a deafening noise. I was laying on the floor with my mattress when I heard a shout, and then there was yelling and screaming coming from everywhere. My roommate got up from his bed, and started yelling out of the square hole in the metal door. What the hell was going on? I felt like I was at the zoo. I couldn't even decipher what they were saying when they were yelling. This went on for hours. I finally was so tired from the day that I drifted off to sleep with all the ruckus still going on. I had finally hit a bottom I didn't even know existed.

At 6:00 am I was already awake. The loud metal clank of all the cell doors being unlocked made sure everyone was awake. I would soon head to downtown St. Louis to testify in the Federal Courtroom in the Eagleton Building. The last time I entered that building I had been sentenced to five years in prison.

I began to get anxious. I kept thinking that the guards would come and get me at any minute. It had been four long torturous hours, and no one had entered the pod to summon me. My mind began to spiral downward into the abyss. I was going to be stuck in this hell hole for months. They had forgotten about me.

I got on the phone and called Julie to let her know that it did not look like I was going to court today. She again sprang into action to see what she could find out and eventually contacted Scott. He said he would find out what he could about what was going on. A guy sitting at the metal table with me, said, "Man, if you're waiting on the courts, you might as well get settled in. I have been here for five months."

It was now drifting later into the afternoon. I called Julie again to see if she had had any update. She told me that Scott had found out that there were some procedural issues that pushed the start of the trial back a day. It also meant that no matter what, I was going to stay at this county jail, at least through the weekend. I had no control, and I never got used to that feeling.

I was bored stiff with waiting when all of a sudden two rough looking black guys started yelling and pushing each other. Fists started to fly. The guards rushed into the pod dressed in riot gear, knocked both the men to the floor, and handcuffed them. They were hauled away in a matter of minutes. All that was left were pools of blood on the floor.

242 • Nightmare Success

I decided I preferred boring over that episode. A guard entered the pod again, carrying a white bag. He called my name. I approached him and he handed me the bag. He told me that my wife had brought a bag of socks, t-shirts, and underwear. Julie had called the county jail to ask if she could buy me some clothes, and they said it was fine if they were all white. The clothes created a buffer for me with the other jail mates. They began asking if they could have my clothes when I left the jail. Some of the guys were having a get together with their commissary items and invited me to their little party. I now had some leverage with my new socks and shirts thanks to Julie!

The next morning at 6 a.m., I was shackled again and loaded into the van. It was a strange sad feeling to be driven into my hometown in a county jail van. We pulled into the basement of the Federal Court Building. I was led into another solitary holding cell. The federal marshal brought me the court clothes that Julie had dropped off. I stepped into my tailor-made black suit, my shoes, shirt, and tie. I was back to Brent Cassity, except I had lost 35 pounds, so I looked I was starring in a scene out of the movie *BIG* with Tom Hanks. Still, I felt good. I was ready to get this over and done.

Two hours later, a friendly Federal Marshal unlocked my cell door. He put new shackles around my ankles, a very humbling moment. He opened the side door to the courtroom, and led me to the nearby witness chair. I looked over the packed courtroom, but didn't see anyone I recognized.

Mr. Pozner began and opened with all the normal questions: who I was, what position I held, where I now resided etc. I was being polite, but looking for an opening to expand on what this case was about to the jury. It finally happened.

"Mr. Cassity," said Pozner,"Your company sold preneed policies, and also owned the insurance company, correct?"

"Yes," I said. "And I believe that is the crux of this case, deciding how those insurance policies are to be valued in the trust." I went on to say, "In 1993, the Missouri Attorney General believed the insurance policies should be valued at their cash value, and our company believed they should be valued at their face value. If the policies were at cash value our company would have been underfunded. If the policies are valued at face value our company trust would be overfunded by the statute. NPS believed the face amount was the proper valuation because regardless if someone had paid $100 on their policy or paid it in full, we were responsible for the full amount of the preneed policy at the time of their death."

"In 1993, the Attorney General and NPS went to the court to seek a declaratory judgement to have the statute interpreted. When the trial judge indicated he was leaning on the idea of valuing the policies at their face amount, the Attorney General of Missouri sought to seek a Consent Agreement with NPS where our policies would be valued at their face amount. "

Mr. Pozner immediately jumped towards the judge's bench. "Wait, he can't say that. That needs to be stricken from the record."

I could hear all the attorneys speaking to the judge. Judge Webber said, "Do I need to remind you Mr. Pozner that this is your witness?"

I was later able to share facts that our company had been audited every year, and that we had never missed paying a claim with over half a billion paid in thirty years. This case had always been about accountants arguing different theories, not how the clients would be paid. I also shared that we had operated under the Consent Agreement for 14 years until the Federal Government came in with the old argument that the banks should be valuing the insurance policies at cash value. Suddenly, our company was woefully underfunded.

After two hours of questioning, it was Williams and Connelly's turn. Before we began, there was a break. Judge Webber left his bench, and came down and stood in front of me at the witness box. He asked if I was doing okay. He said he was sorry that I had to be transported here for the trial. He wanted to know my opinion about the RDAP program because he had recommended it in several cases. I told him that it is the best program the BOP had to offer an inmate.

He then asked how my Dad was doing. I told him that he was doing fine, and we communicated by the TRULINKS inmate system. When Judge Webber went back to the bench, the Federal Marshal said, "That was something. I have never Judge Webber leave his chair to come down to speak to a witness."

But, Judge Webber had ruled for my family early on in the Civil Case when the plaintiffs were attempting to freeze our assets.

Williams and Connelly and I were on the same team as the defendants. The attorney stood up, and said, "Mr. Cassity, is it your understanding that, in fact, the Texas Department of Insurance ordered a stay of releasing the Hannover Arbitration decision, after the Arbitration panel had already dismissed with prejudice all fourteen claims of fraud and misconduct against your companies? Your company was seeking damages of over $250 million for these false claims."

"Yes," I replied, "That is my understanding."

"In your opinion, it wasn't NPS that caused the company to fail. It was the reckless actions of the Texas Department of Insurance that caused the company to fail."

Again, "Yes that is my opinion."

It was over. PNC Bank lost the jury trail, and appealed the ruling to the 8th Circuit Court of Appeals where the jury judgement was overturned.

Back in my cell, I changed out of my suit and into my orange uniform. I was mentally worn out. When I got back to the pod, I called Julie to let her know how the trial went. I did not want her to be in the courtroom. I was mostly worried that she could get hassled by one of the reporters and cameras that were scattered around everywhere. The next day was Valentine's Day. Julie and I had our Valentine's Day visit behind the glass with the telephone just like you see in the movies. Thirty quick minutes.

The nights in the cell never normalized. The yelling and screaming went on like clockwork. It was Sunday, and I was already well over my stay. My mind was lost in bad thoughts, when suddenly a guard came in the pod and yelled my name to come with him. They led me downstairs to what looked like a hospital room. The guard said the nurse will be with you in a moment. I was thinking, "My god, they have me confused with some other inmate." The nurse came in and said, "They called me in because they forgot to give you a TB shot when you were processed through the other day." I said, "I actually received a TB shot before I left Leavenworth to travel here. Is it the thing that you look to see if it bubbles up on your arm?" The nurse said, "Yes, it is. Let me look at your file." She began punching keys on the computer. She turned back to me and said, "Yep, you sure did have it. What a waste of time for them to call me in on a Sunday. You are free to head back up to your pod. I will call a guard." Just like that I was back inside the pod. I sat down on the metal picnic looking bench. One of the skinhead punks came up to me, and said, "Why did you go downstairs?" I said, "The nurse was going to give me a TB shot, but I already had one. It was just a mess up." The punk moved closer to me and said, "Man, that is bullshit. You lying sack of shit. The nurse doesn't work on the weekends. You were fucking snitching on us about smoking." This punk was speaking louder and more aggressively with each word. Now his young punk posse was starting to surround me. I was thinking that this is how this happens. I am going to get beat up to a bloody pulp in a hurry.

About that time, I feel a big shadow over my shoulder. I hear Darius's low voice begin to speak, "What do we have going on here?" I repeated what happened with the nurse mess up. Big Darius says, "Shit happens, these fuckin' guards don't know what they are doing. There is no upside for Cassity to do any snitchin'. He's just here for a minute anyhow. Now go on and find something else to do boys." And that was it. I came that close to a serious beat down, all but for my new mountain man of a friend Darius. The punks just slithered away. Most of these guys were bored out of their minds. Fighting was just a way to kill time.

That night the guards dropped off razors in the small opening in our metal door, so the inmates could shave in their cell sink. All of sudden there was a banging sound and yelling. I could hear the guards running down the steel platform. The next thing I know they order our cell door to open and they throw this little Hispanic guy in our cell whose nose is bleeding. The little guy had tried to cut Darius with a razor in their cell because he said Darius had been making him wash his underwear and t-shirts in the cell sink. Now we had three guys in a two man cell. This place was everything I had heard it could be. People spend months in these county jails. It could not be more dangerous or inhumane.

That Monday came and went because it was Presidents Day. No one was going to do any transporting on a holiday. Early that Tuesday morning, I learned they would transport me back to Leavenworth. At least, I hoped that was where I was going. I was shackled up again and loaded into the van.

When we pulled up to the Leavenworth gate, I received the full welcome treatment. I had walked past this event many times on my way to the warehouse. Now it was me. The Leavenworth guards surrounded the van with two white pick-up trucks. The guards got out of their trucks with their shotguns loaded and aimed.

Once I was processed back in, I was put in a solitary cell for over four hours. This is when you are allowed to let your mind go crazy until you get to where you are supposed to go. The camp inmate always thinks they will mistakenly be inserted into the medium security prison population.

Finally, the guard who delivered the mail came by and slid the cell door open. He said, "Come on Cassity, you can ride with me back to the camp."

We drove by and picked up the guys from the depot where Jim Clark worked. Clark climbed in the truck, smiled, and gave me a high five. He said, "Welcome back, Cass!". It really felt good to be back at Leavenworth after the county jail nightmare.

I got back to my bunk with my locker. Clark and the guys had put some commissary snacks there for a nice welcome back. I sat there on my plastic chair next to my bunk, and looked around. This was the home I knew for now.

CHAPTER 60:

Golf in Prison

In August, 2015, I had finally made it to my last of nine months in RDAP. I had added a goal to my list the first week I arrived. I wanted to work at the Fort Leavenworth Golf Course. Five inmates were chosen to leave the prison every day for work to maintain the course. I had been at the prison long enough to earn the privilege to leave the prison grounds to work in the community.

I had stayed in close contact with the two inmates who had worked at the golf course the longest. Now, there was an open spot. I worked it out with the two inmates to have Mike, the golf superintendent, call my counselor Goodwin to request me as a potential golf worker. I also worked it out that when the guys were being dropped off back at the camp one day, I came out to the van and introduced myself to Drew, the assistant superintendent. We immediately hit it off.

Goodwin said he would do all he could do to get it approved with Ms. Alexander. He said that Noll at the warehouse would also call her. The next day Goodwin called me into his office, and said, "Ray-- the Ray Romano joke never got old to Goodwin--you finally got what you have been asking for. Ms. Alexander signed off. You start tomorrow."

I could have hugged Goodwin! It was as though I had received a big, corporate promotion. I was going to be able to leave the prison to work seven days a week at the golf course. It felt like it was as big an accomplishment as I had ever achieved, whether behind prison walls, or out in the world.

I knew absolutely nothing about maintaining a golf course, but I hadn't known how to drive a fork lift either when I joined the food warehouse crew. I was eager to learn something new.

I had trouble sleeping the night before my first day on the job. I would be mingling with the general public on the golf course with no prison guards. This was going to be the best way for me to finish out my last year and a half at Leavenworth.

My boss, Drew, picked me up. He was in his 30's with a long beard like the guys in Duck Dynasty, very friendly, with a fun personality. We pulled out of the Leavenworth campus, and onto the main road in front of the prison. When we pulled through the entry gates of Fort Leavenworth, I felt that I had entered a world I dimly remembered. Everything was well kept and orderly. We parked in front of a brand new metal building full of different kinds of Toro mowers.

Drew introduced me to the crew who were sitting in a variety of chairs in the work area. Mike, the Head Superintendent, got up and shook my hand and welcomed me to the crew. His black lab Harley came to work with him every day, and he was very much a part of our crew. Mike introduced me to Frank the heavyset retired Football Coach, young lanky Gavin with some long stuff growing off his chin, and finally the black toothless Sly. It was difficult to know how old Sly was, but he had an opinion about everything.

Mike and Drew showed me over to my locker. They gave me a hat and some gloves, and told me I would get my winter wear stuff when winter rolled around. The golf course guys never treated us as inmates. We were just part of the crew taking care of the golf course.

"Brent," said Mike. "Come with me and I'll show you how to cut the holes for the golf greens. While Mike and I talked, we discovered we both had a love for reading. As time went on we ended up sharing books and discussing our opinions of different authors.

One of the best perks about the golf course was they paid for our lunches. We were able to order off the menu from the bowling alley. This was perfect for me because I have never met a bowling alley menu that I didn't love. They had cheeseburgers, pizzas, calzones, chili, chicken fingers, French fries, and I ordered an ice-cream sandwich every day. On top of all that, we were able to go inside the clubhouse anytime and get a free soda.

Drew really took me under his wing teaching me how to handle all the big equipment. He knew my background, and I think he thought it was fun to see me learn how to get comfortable doing something I had never done. By the time my job was nearing an end, I had learned to cut greens, tee boxes, fairways, and the rough. I even learned how to drive and operate the skid-loader. Our crew also rebuilt five bunkers. That was the hardest work we did. In the winter time we cut down 54 big trees, and replanted 125 new ones.

Drew found a left-handed 7 iron club, and said, "Keep it Cass, and you and I can hit some when we have nothing else to do." That rarely happened, but I just liked the thought of having a 7 iron club ready to hit a few balls at any time.

I finally finished the nine month RDAP program, and was allowed to move out of the D-1 RDAP dorm. Clark had secured a 2- room for us in C-1. It was a cell, but it had a regular door, and a window. This was like moving on up into the high end of town suburbs.

Finally, I would have some privacy away from the fifty man open room. It had been over a year and half living that way. Our room consisted of two lockers, a desk, and a bunk bed. Clark only had two months left before he was going home. He decided to smuggle out some paint from the paint shop and paint everything, the lockers, the walls, the ceiling. I think this was Clark's way of keeping his mind occupied. Our cell was the envy of the C-1 cell block.

CHAPTER 61:

Me, the Veteran Inmate

The final night walk arrived for Clark and me. We had walked hundreds of miles on this sidewalk next to the fence crowned with rolling barbed wire that reflected into our eyes when the late afternoon sun hit it. It would be quite some time before we would see each other again as free men.

Clark and Romo had been my 'go to' guys. Clark and I had been kings of the tennis court playing doubles. Our Friday night basketball games between two old DeSmet alums would be coming to an end. It is hard to explain the emotions you have when someone close to you leaves. You could not be happier for them to have their freedom, but they are part of a daily routine that selfishly moves your prison time forward. I felt the same way when my friend Jay left. It leaves an emptiness that needs to be filled in some other way.

The next morning before I headed off to the golf course, I gave Clark the manly guy hug, and wished him luck. We had been through a lot together. But, it was as if they had been zapped and disappeared. When I returned from work my new roommate Strobbe was moving his stuff into our two-man cell. Strobbe and I had gotten to know each other in RDAP. Strobbe looked like the bald Mr. Clean guy on the commercials. He had owned a successful lawn care business and sold some cocaine in the off season. He received a ten-year sentence for that. I also liked that Strobbe was no dummy. He had more street smarts than anyone I had met at Leavenworth.

Strobbe was a good athlete, so I asked him to be my new doubles partner. We were controlling the afternoon court, when one of the Springfield Missouri guys walked out onto the court. He sat down on the bench with a new guy who looked as pale as anyone I had ever seen, like he had just woken up, and gotten out of his casket.

When we were changing sides on the court, he said, "Hey Cass, you lived in Springfield. Did you ever meet Rick Gregg? He is new to our Leavenworth Country Club."

I said, "No, I haven't," and I introduced myself to Rick.

I liked Rick right from the start. We shared some common people we knew from Springfield, but I was still curious why he was so pale.

As we continued playing tennis, I noticed that Rick had taken his shoes off and was walking barefoot in the grass in the open yard area. It was like he had been brought back from the dead and was rediscovering nature. It was kind of bizarre. I knew there had to be a story behind this behavior. When I finished playing tennis, I went to try and find him. He was sitting on a bench by the baseball field.

I plopped myself down beside Rick, and said, "Man, you look like you have been through an ordeal."

Rick said, "Would you believe this is the first time I have been outside in 16 months? Literally, I have been in the Springfield County jail for 16 torturous months."

I had only been in the county jail for six days, which had felt like six years. I could not get my mind around sixteen months. He had also lost over 130 pounds while he was in the county jail, and he joked that he needed to lose the weight, but he wouldn't recommend his weight loss program.

He explained to me how it all happened. He was a big-time real estate developer in Southwest Missouri. The government was investigating him along with tapping his phone calls. On one of the phone calls he was talking to his sons, and the Assistant U.S. attorney claimed he had made a threat about one of the attorneys. As I got to know Rick, it was just the way he talked when he got worked up, but they arrested him and threw him in the county jail until his trial. In the meantime, Rick was frustrating the government because he was refusing a plea deal. After months, the government decided to send a target letter to his wife. Rick was having none of that, and he called his attorney and

252 • Nightmare Success

told him he was falling on his sword to stop all the craziness. This is an all-too-common tactic of our government. Remember the 97% conviction rate they have of indicted individuals? That number is astronomically high for a very good reason.

I realized while I was talking to him that the pendulum at the prison camp had finally swung for me. I was no longer the new guy. I was now the veteran inmate choosing to take Rick under my wing and show him the ropes as Romo and Clark had done for me. Clark had left behind a ton of his stuff for me, such as, shorts, t-shirts, shower shoes, sweatshirt and sweatpants, along with some Tupperware bowls. I told Rick to follow me to my place. I said, "I have some stuff to help you get set up being here."

When we arrived at my two-man cell, Rick couldn't believe it. He thanked me again and again stop thanking me. I told Rick, "You've come at a good time. Clark just left, and I didn't have enough room for all of this in my locker anyway." I told him about going to the Chapel, so he could get some toiletries to hold him over until he was able to make it to the commissary day. I pulled out a commissary sheet and showed him what and how to use it. I was thinking how strange it is that none of this was new to me anymore.

Rick and I went outside and did our first fence walk. This was our first of many 100's of miles of walks along the yard fence. We always used the time to brainstorm the next big idea for once we got out. I really enjoyed having someone to talk business with. I told Rick that at night he could bring his chair and sit along the white wall to watch TV. The other guys really called it the white-collar wall. I also told him that I had the prime sitting spots for movie nights in the gym. It felt good being the veteran inmate helping Rick the way I had been helped. You can't ever stop being you when you are in prison, otherwise you lose yourself, and you might not ever find your way back.

CHAPTER 62:

The Show American Greed: Featuring the Cassity's

I was only a few months away from my release slated for the end of November. Of the 208,847 Federal Prisoners in the Bureau of Prisons, only 407 were white collar guys like me.. Needless to say, I was in a severe minority. The biggest percentage of Federal inmates are drug offenders.

My main goal from day one was to blend into the prison population. It was not the easiest task because many of the inmates had been watching the local news before I arrived. Unfortunately, the Cassity case was heavily covered by the media. This worried me because I didn't want inmates to have preconceived ideas about me before they ever had a chance to get to know me. When I first arrived, it was important for me to listen twice as much as I spoke. I was fortunate to have made some early friendships with Romo and Clark who helped me be accepted, to adapt, and to blend into the prison population.

As much as I tried, there were still events out of my control that made me different or unique. Now, I received an email from my brother that CNBC was going to air an episode of their popular true-crime series, 'American Greed,' featuring our family. A year ago, CNBC had contacted me about their intentions of featuring our family on an episode, but I really never gave it much thought because I assumed they sent out a lot of those letters. I never heard another word about it until Tyler's email, followed by a phone call in which he told me. Tyler said he didn't know when the episode would air, but CNBC had assured him it would be soon. I called Julie to see if she had seen or heard anything about it. She was blown away and upset by the news. Neither of us had seen this coming. There had never been a positive spin on anyone featured in 'American Greed.'

There were four screen TV's in the chow hall. 'American Greed' aired on Thursday night. I could see all four TV's from where I sat. They were still mostly segregated to Black, Hispanic, and White, and I knew the guys watching the Black TV always watched 'American Greed.'

Every Thursday I watched to see if any promotions popped up. Sure enough, as big as life was the Cassity promo, first was my picture with my brother, and then Dad aired for the next 30 seconds showing our homes, businesses, cars, boats, all bigger than life on the TV screen.

The Black guys start pointing at the TV saying, "Hey look, that's Cass on our show!"

Suddenly a surge of people moved to the Black TV to catch the end of the promo. I became the talk of the prison and had absolutely no idea how bad this show was going to be. This was going to be a built-in movie night for the whole prison starring one of our prisoners…me. My imagination began to run wild with possible scenarios. All bad, but just how bad? My mind was worn out thinking about it.

When I talked to Julie the next day, she explained that the local St. Louis news stations were promoting the show. If that wasn't enough the St. Louis Post Dispatch newspaper's version of Page Six society column ran a story. Just in case this was not a show you normally watched, the media made sure to direct everyone on how to tune in.

My buddy Rick and I were about four miles into one of our long walks. I said, "I don't know if I want to be sitting there watching this show with everyone looking for my every reaction to the show. I would rather just walk the track until it is over, but I know I can't. I don't want to look like I can't handle the heat."

Rick listened, and responded, "I agree. You can't avoid the show. Just watch it and try to keep your cool. The guys will respect that you aren't hiding."

I knew what Rick was saying made sense. "I hear ya," I said. "I just get so tired of all this shit sometimes."

The night of the big show finally arrived. The camp was all abuzz with anticipation. One of their own was going to be on all the screens. The chow hall was packed tight with inmates. We also had the CO's who were on duty standing in doorways to watch the biggest prison event anyone could remember. I sat in my normal spot, my back against the cinderblock wall. I could not have been any more nervous. This was going to be one of the longest hours of my life. Stacy Keach, the voice of the show, could make anything sound ominous and dark.

The show began by focusing on Mom and Dad as high school sweethearts from the small country town of Buffalo. That was really the only sentimental, nostalgic piece of the story. It was clear the producers of the show were focused on making my dad out to be this dark wicked mastermind who went from one business deal to another causing destruction and fraud on innocent people.

I was not a central figure in the story. I was given the credit for creating the all-women salesforce named NPS Advantage. The show degraded these women as being sleazy and compared them to Hooters waitresses. This description could not have been further from the truth. It is so difficult to watch a one sided story and not get defensive. These women who numbered over a hundred strong were incredibly professional, talented, intelligent, and goal driven; and they grew our overall sales numbers to over $125 million annually. They represented 2400 funeral homes in over twenty states. It was very upsetting to see these professionals described this way, but it made for a more sensational story.

The show interviewed three funeral directors from the thousands we represented. Miles Olsen, the local St. Louis reporter who had made his career of bringing down the Cassity's, made his splashy day on National TV. There were no customers interviewed from over 100,000 we contracted.

I believe there was a very good reason why the show was edited this way. All the funeral homes were paid their commissions for writing the business they had contracted with our company. They also received the full contract amount for the funeral contract. The amount they did not receive was the additional commission that was called 'growth' because the company was put into liquidation by the State of Texas. Simply, they did not lose money. They did not make as much money as they had intended. Additionally, every customer received the funeral that they had paid for with NPS, so there were no customers to interview that could say they had not received their funeral. That additional information would not have made for juicy, sensational TV.

I was always so proud of our company training, and how so many people were able to create incredible careers for themselves. The company was a large family of loyal people, many of them were with us for over twenty years. I know I will always have deep sorrow at how many lives were drastically changed at our company as all of them lost their jobs that they had invested so much of their lives into. I tried so desperately to save our company, but in the end, I was not able to save the day. There is no way to erase that responsibility, as one of the owners, for the loss of all those jobs. Time will never change just how devastating and heartbreaking that was. Then to have those same people degraded in a show, and being portrayed as predators or sleazy was beyond a hurt I can properly describe in words.

When the show was over, I looked around the room and wondered what everyone was thinking. One of the guys walked by and said, "Damn Cass, a national pimp, ya gunna havfta find me a woman when I get outta ere."

That was the general consensus the inmate population came away with from the show. What a crazy life I was living at Leavenworth. Strange at it seems, I let out a big sigh of relief as I picked up my plastic chair and headed back to my cell to be counted for nighttime count. As bad as it was for me, it was much worse for Dad. He was made out to be a dark, sleazy, shadowy figure that caused destruction on everything and everyone.

As a son, I hated to see him portrayed that way. No matter what, it was over. It was, once again time to step forward and put this behind me.

When Strobbe and I finally settled into our bunkbed that night, Strobbe said, "Cass, it wasn't that bad. I have to admit it was definitely entertaining for everyone, but you came out okay in the whole story."

It was nice that my bunkmate didn't want me to worry about it. Strobbe was a good guy. Another day down at Leavenworth.

CHAPTER 63:

Oh No... The Piss Test

I have discussed how inmates fall into crazy daily routines to feel like they are in control of something in their lives while they are incarcerated, but there are other routines that an inmate does for a definite reason. There was a reason why I waited to take a piss after the 4 o'clock count every day for three years. Men were selected to participate in the monthly random piss test before the official 4 o'clock daily count. The last thing that I wanted to happen was to be selected after I had already gone to the bathroom before the random test. There were real consequences if you were not able to fill the cup up to the second red line. This would be treated as a fail or refusal for the test, and earned you a trip to the spooky mysterious hole that was located in the 'Big House' that was housed in its own wing at the penitentiary. Inmates would return from the hole looking noticeably different than when they went in.

As we all eventually do, I had become too comfortable. I had finally arrived in the last year of my sentence. I had never been randomly selected for a piss test in my first two years. There were guys who would keep a look out for the overweight, burly 'piss test man'...the only time he was around the camp was piss test time. All of this had completely slipped my mind, as I headed into the urinal after my days' work at the golf course. As I was just finishing zipping up my pants, my bunkmate, Strobbe, sticks his head around the corner and says, "Cass, they just called out your name with the group for the piss test." I said, "Strobbe, are you fucking with me?" He shook his head and said, "No Cass, I am not fucking with you. What are you thinking taking a piss?" I said, "I just fucked up. I wasn't thinking." Well, off I went down the dark hallway to meet up with the others that had been called. All I could think was, "what am I going to do?" I was already negative thinking about this big burly man standing over me in a tight space to take a piss in a cup. I could get stage fright with this situation if I had just drunk a six pack. I was freaking out. This was not going to end good for me.

We all settled into the visiting room. The big burly 'piss test man' was at the podium with a stack of plastic cups. The fluorescent lights were glaring with the bathroom door propped open. At this moment it looked like deaths door to me. He explained how the process worked. We would be given a 4 oz. cup of water. That was all the water we received to spur on this process. He said, "Here's the deal guys. You have two hours to piss up to this redline. If you attempt to piss and do not fill it all the way up to the red line, the cup will be tossed out and you will attempt again. If you fail again, you will earn a trip to the hole. You will be given two hours to piss. If you do not piss in two hours that will count as a fail, and it will earn you a trip to the hole. If the cup reads positive that will earn you a trip to the hole. Now some of these cups are really old, so they could give a false positive. If you feel it has given a false positive, you will be allowed to piss again." Oh my god! Now I am thinking these cups are old and bad. I could go to the hole just because the cup is bad. I was already freaked out that I had just taken a piss minutes ago. I knew 4 oz. of water was not going to cause me a rush of waterfall feeling.

We all drank our 4 oz. of water. My strategy was going to be that I would wait until I had ten minutes left out of the two hours before attempting to take the test. Some guys just stood up, grabbed their cup, and stood with the burly man, and pissed like a lazy Sunday afternoon. They went on their way, and it was over for them. Others failed the test, and were told to sit over in the section to be taken in the van to the dreaded hole. There were others that claimed the cup was giving them a false positive, and they said they wanted to have another go at it. They came over and sat with me. I watched all of this for well over an hour and a half. My time was coming and I still had no urge to take a piss. I was starting to gear up for the real possibility that I was headed to the hole. The clock was ticking. The clock finally arrived at ten minutes before 6:30. I nervously walked up to the burly piss man. I said, "I guess it is my time to go." The burly piss man said, "Step right in here. Here's your cup." There I am in this tiny restroom with the bright lights shining and a 280 lb. man breathing down my neck. I stand there for a few seconds, and it seemed like an hour. Finally, something starts trickling out. I am also conscious that the clock is ticking down to the two hour doomsday hour. The liquid goes to the first red line but does not make it to the second red line. I am standing there like a have a scary grizzly bear standing over me with his fangs out. This is just what was going through my freaked out mind. The burly piss man says, "Boy, we need more piss. That is not going to do it. Come with me." I am thinking... shit. He is leading me to the van to go to the hole. I am following him, and he opens the door to go outside in front of the prison. It is January, and it is 20 degrees outside with the Kansas wind cutting right through me. "Okay," he says, "Now take your shirt off." Now I am thinking things have just gotten weird. Is this turning into some weird sexual thing with the big burly piss man? I set my piss cup down, and take my shirt off. I unzip my pants, and I stand there for a few seconds. Then like magic I start pissing and fill up the cup to the red line. I felt like collapsing. I had one minute left. The big burly piss man said, "Yep, that always does it. That cold air will squeeze the piss out of anything." I put my shirt back on. Now I wasn't even cold. I was completely worn out. As I began to walk in, the four guys who failed the piss test were walking past me being loaded into the van to spend days in the hole. I looked at the van as they drove away, and realized I was one minute away from riding away in the white van to the unknown fear of living in the hole. You learn something new every day. If you have to make yourself piss. Take your shirt off in the freezing windy cold. Things you learn in prison.

CHAPTER 64:

Freedom!

You can drive yourself crazy putting your brain through the mental exercise of counting down time in prison. I would manufacture all kinds of crazy ways to divide up weeks, months, seasons, and years to make it feel like I was knocking down more time than I actually was. Let me give you one of my crazy examples of making numbers small. When spring rolled around my second year at Leavenworth, Julie and I said, "Well, we only have one more spring and I will be home. That sounded a lot better than 18 more months. When I finally got down to within 12 months, each month off the calendar felt monumental stepping closer to my freedom date.

The first meaningful thing that happens when you are getting close to getting out is that your name goes up on the bulletin board outside the secretary's office door. This means your name has officially shown up in the system that you are actually close to being released. You meet with this secretary, and you have papers that need to be signed for the halfway house. You also get a form to send home, so your family can send you clothes to wear out the day you are freed. I would walk by this bulletin board every day hoping to see my name. Finally, there it was Brent Cassity 38-224-044. I had finally made the bulletin board list! I couldn't wait to tell Julie. I was going to be able to mail her the form for my clothes. The only rub with all this excitement was that my release date fell on the day after Thanksgiving. They would not release any inmates until the following Monday. I know it doesn't sound like that big of a deal, but after you have been waiting three years…an extra 3 days seems like a lifetime. The other thing that was starting to cloud my mind about my release was the halfway house. I had heard only bad things about the Dismas Halfway House that was located in the worst part of North St. Louis City. People died on Cote Brilliant Boulevard regularly. I would be housed with over 100 ex-felons that were coming from all levels…Maximum security lock up, down to the camp level. I was told by the secretary that I only had six hours to get there and check-in. If I was late it would be treated as an escape while in custody of the BOP. That kind of caught my attention. We had a four and a half hour drive home. There wouldn't be time for a big dinner or party with friends. The secretary did tell me I could talk to my case manager to see if the halfway house would take me a week early. Witchy woman Alexander had retired, so I thought I might at least have a small chance with my new case manager. The problem was he was just as lazy as every case manager who occupied that position. I made an appointment with him, and told him about my dilemma. He listened and finally said, "Alright Cassity, I will make a call but don't expect anything good." That should have been the slogan for the BOP. A few days went by, and I checked back in with him. He said, "Oh I forgot, I will call today." I checked back in with him the next day, and he said there was no room for me at the halfway house for an earlier date. I knew he probably didn't even make the phone call, but it was worth going through the ridiculous exercise.

It was official, I was going to be spending another Thanksgiving in prison, and extra days at Leavenworth past my official release date. No matter what, I was getting out of this place. It is so odd how your mind starts playing tricks on you. I started believing that I was never going to get out of here. They are going to say there has been a mistake in our system, and you owe us another six months. The other thoughts that start streaming through your mind are what if it will be awkward for me to be home. My wife and daughters had figured out how to live without me being home for a long time. All the things I use to do… they had figured out how to do on their own. Even the little things like paying the bills, Julie had taken on that task not for a week, but for the last three years. These are thoughts I just compartmentalized as I was moving through the months and years in prison, but as the time was drawing near they became real anxiety thoughts I couldn't push away from my mind. I also didn't want to talk to anyone about these thoughts. I perceived these thoughts as appearing weak minded and lacking self-confidence. I began to worry that once I was home that my family would be analyzing me. Had I changed? Was I a different man than I was before prison? This was so crazy, and unexpected for me. I should have been bouncing off the wall with excitement that I was leaving this place, and that I would finally be back with my family. All of those thoughts did excite me, like a young child waiting for Christmas morning to open the presents. I had to make sure that I was patient when I arrived home. I needed to observe what had changed around me, and fit back in accordingly. It was going to be like trying to jump in a moving car to catch up with everyone after missing three years of life moving on without me in it. I knew beyond a doubt that my family loved me. I just wanted to come home and be the same Dad and husband I had always been, after living in such a primitive environment. I just had to figure out how to shake off all that prison residue as I walked out to freedom.

As things got closer, it seemed like the last two months someone had literally stopped the clock. I was able to stay busy with my golf course job. I stayed on my routine of working out four days a week, and walking at least five miles a day with Rick. I was going to be returning home 35lbs lighter than when I arrived. I weighed a lean 175lbs. My senior high school weight. The Baby (Connor my youngest daughter) made me a new family calendar each year. I would use the Calendar like a daily diary. I would write something about the day in each square. As my time was drawing near to my release, I realized how much had happened over the last three years here and on the outside. Three years doesn't necessarily sound like ten years, but it is incredible how much happens in those three years. My youngest daughter graduated from High School. I was returning home to her being a sophomore in college. I had missed her winning the State tennis championship her senior year, and her graduation. I left Carly (my middle daughter) as a freshman in college. Now she was a senior in college. I missed Courtney's (my oldest daughter) college graduation. The girls were left without a dad on their college dad weekends. All of these college moves that I use to be such a big part of…Julie had done all of them on her own. Incredible. There was also a death in the family. My aunt Marilyn had died within those three years. Attending the funeral was not an option. My big white lab Tucker, died the second year I was in prison. I say all of this because this is only how my prison sentence affected me during my three years of Leavenworth. As I type this, it makes me emotional how my time in prison affected my daughters and my wife. Each one of them were affected in their own personal way. I beam with pride at how each of them walked through their own personal struggles in those years to get to the other side as survivors! We did it as a strong tightknit family. My release date was a release date for all of us.

The other unfortunate thing that happened leading up to the days before I was released, was that the Bureau of Prisons turned off your phone and email 24 to 48 hours before you were to be released. My original release date was Friday the day after Thanksgiving. I was returning from the golf course Wednesday, and I found out I had been turned off from the outside world. This would mean that I would go through the next five days without being able to communicate with anyone. Julie and the girls were coming for a final visit on Sunday. We had talked about the possibility of being cut off, so I was hoping that Julie would be able to figure out what had happened. Wow…this was going to be the longest five days of my life waiting for freedom day.

I had begun the inmate ritual of going through all my prison stuff, and giving my stuff away. I gave Strobbe my radio and ear phones. I had given Rick all my t-shirts, shorts, sweats, tennis shoes, and other things that he could keep or give away. As I was cleaning out my locker, I ran across my goals I had written down on a sheet of paper my first night by the light of the bathroom in the A2 Cell dorm. I kept this sheet of paper in my calendar. What had I written down? Well, let's see…1. Get a good job to keep me busy and maybe learn something new. 2. Learn all the inmate rules, so I could quickly adapt and blend into the prison population. 3. Learn how to communicate with the outside world with the Trulinks email system, and the phone system. 4. Get officially accepted and complete the RDAP program to get a year off my sentence. 5. Read as many books as possible to keep my mind active, and use it as a mental escape from my surroundings. 6. Get in the best physical shape of my life. I read each one of these, and realized I had accomplished all of these things while being an inmate. Writing down goals and staying focused with my plan had kept me being me. Even in the strangest environment I had ever lived. What a Nightmare all of this had been, but step by step I was able to walk through it to finally get to the other side. I don't know how I could have done it without the love and support of Julie and my three daughters. We had all stepped through the Nightmare together as a family.

Julie and the girls came for their final Sunday visit. Julie had been a nervous wreck being off our routine of talking and emailing each other every day. The whole Cassity family sat around our little visiting table being just completely giddy that this was all going to be over in the morning. We shared all kinds of stories of what we had all been through the last three years. We relived the first scary visit to Leavenworth, and how it had all become our new weird normal. We admitted that we all felt this strange sense of real accomplishment. We had survived together. When the visit was over, we all hugged each other so tight! The next time I would hug them I would be a free man! It was just so hard to believe, I was going to walk out the door and ride home with my family the next morning.

That night Rick and I probably walked eight miles on the sidewalk next to the barb wire fence. We figured we had probably walked from New York to Los Angeles on this sidewalk together. I felt a real emotional pain that I was leaving Rick to soldier on alone at Leavenworth. We pretty much did everything together. The only analogy that I have thought about when leaving friends behind in prison, is possibly what a soldier feels like when he leaves his comrades on the battlefield to return home. I so desperately wanted to leave the hell hole I was living in, but I felt so bad that I was leaving people I cared about behind. Rick had two more years to serve. All his prison routines would change the minute I walked out the door.

I kidded Strobbe that he probably couldn't wait to move down to the bottom bunk, as soon as I walked out the door. He had been a really good bunkmate. We had lived over a year together in the 8x10 room. We came from totally different backgrounds, but Strobbe was a smart guy, who loved his kids. He had a fun, great dad who always came to visit him. I really hoped the best for him when he returned home to his family the following year.

I laid in my bed after the 10 o'clock standing count. This would be the last count of my prison life. Gosh, how many counts had I been through the last few years? It was all so routine now, as opposed to being scared to death the first night they yelled count and Romo told me what to do. The clock was ticking down to freedom morning. I tried to read my book, but I just couldn't concentrate. I fell asleep my first night in prison, and I was having trouble falling asleep my last night in prison. How ironic is that?

I woke up the next morning early. I said my goodbyes to Strobbe before he headed off to the food warehouse. Everyone at breakfast knew I was leaving. There were a lot of send offs. It is really hard to remember what happened before I walked out to freedom that morning. Everything was one big, nervous, excited blur. I was sitting with Rick in my 2-man room talking, and then my name came over the intercom to come to the bubble (aka officer's station). I came and stood at the door of the bubble. The C.O. said, "Cassity, here's your personal clothes to go change into. I need you to also sign these release papers." I have no idea what I signed because I also knew it didn't matter what it was. If they wanted me to sign something to get out of here, I was signing it.

I went back and broke open my stuff. It was my clothes! A piece of home right here in prison. My own shirt, jeans, socks, and shoes…it felt so weird wearing my own clothes in prison. I was the only inmate with street clothes on. I have to admit the clothes were a little looser being 35lbs lighter, but it didn't take away the awesome feeling. I had to wait thirty more minutes before they would officially release me. It felt like the longest thirty minutes of my life. My family was right there on the other side waiting in the parking lot to take me home.

Rick said he would like to walk me out to the car to say goodbye to everyone. I told him that would be great. All of a sudden, my name was called over the big intercom. It was time. It was really going to happen!

We began to walk out of my two man cell, and Rick began to get emotional. We hugged, and he said, "You go on, I can't go out there like this." He turned and started walking down the long dark hallway back to his cell.

I said, "Hey, Rick…you take care of yourself. I will stay in touch with you!"

I turned and pushed the door open to the main bright, white hallway. It was full of my fellow inmates shouting, "Good luck Cass." "Look at Cass in those Cowboy boots, damn." "See ya' Cass."

As I walked by, we slapped in high fives. I finally made my way to the bubble, and the C.O. said You are free to go, Cassity."

That's it? I thought. I just walk out?

It's that simple. You just walk out, one step in front of the other, and there is your wife, your three beautiful daughter. There is your life.

I hugged Julie who was shaking. Kissed each of the girls. Carly took a picture of all of us, and posted a quote on Facebook with the picture. "You don't know how STRONG you are until being STRONG is the only choice you have. Welcome home Dad! Everything feels right again!"

You walk each moment of every day with gratitude.

And what did I think at that moment? Together, my family and I had just accomplished Nightmare Success!

EPILOGUE

So, what happened after I got in the car with my family, and drove off to freedom? Getting out of prison was like trying to jump into a moving car to catch back up with society, but I am so grateful to no longer be missing out on big family moments.

I was so happy to be able to attend the college graduations of my middle daughter Carly and the baby of the family Connor. My oldest daughter Courtney married Christian, and it was fun for all of us to create a new family memory.

Julie and I love having family dinners with our girls and their guys. Those get togethers even take on more special significance after going through what we have all experienced. We enjoy our simple after dinner walks with our Labrador retrievers, Stanley and Wayne, and catching up on our day.

My Dad was released from prison in March of 2020 and died just two months later in May of 2020 at the age of 74 from a heart attack. I had several unresolved issues with Dad, but I never had that "talk" to try to resolve our issues before he died. Maybe there was not a talk we could have had that would have satisfied what I was hoping for with him. No talk could have ever put our father/son relationship back to where it used to be before the business nightmare saga.

I am enjoying my work life of being the Vice President of Business Development for a real estate company. I like being able to use all the experiences I have had in my business life to help others take the next steps to build their own business. I work for my friend, Jose Ponce, who has been there for me through it all and gave me an opportunity when I really needed it.

As always, I have set goals for the second act of my life. One was to complete this book. I plan to use my experience to speak to others who may believe a second chance is not possible, or they are stuck being fearful to take the next step forward to get to where they want to be. My Podcast Nightmare Success: In and Out, explores the experiences of guest ex-inmates of their time in prison and out.

If all goes as planned someday… I hope to be living in a comfortable lake house on Table Rock Lake with a cool boat riding into the sunset with Julie by my side listening to my favorite Eagles song "Take it Easy"…Nightmare Success!